MW01517140

YOUR CHINESE
HOROSCOPE 2001

ABOUT THE AUTHOR

Neil Somerville is one of the leading writers in the West on Chinese horoscopes. He has been interested in Eastern forms of divination for many years and believes that much can be learnt from the ancient wisdom of the East. His annual book on Chinese horoscopes has built up an international following and he is also the author of *What's Your Chinese Love Sign?* (Thorsons, 2000).

Neil Somerville was born in the year of the Water Snake. His wife was born under the sign of the Monkey, his son is an Ox and daughter a Horse.

YOUR CHINESE HOROSCOPE 2001

NEIL SOMERVILLE

What the Year of the Snake holds in store for you

Thorsons

TO ROS, RICHARD AND EMILY

Thorsons
An Imprint of HarperCollins*Publishers*
77–85 Fulham Palace Road
Hammersmith, London W6 8JB
The Thorsons website address is:
www.thorsons.com

Published by Thorsons 2000
10 9 8 7 6 5 4 3 2 1

© Neil Somerville 2000

Neil Somerville asserts the moral right to
be identified as the author of this work

A catalogue record for this book
is available from the British Library

ISBN 0 7225 3969 X

Printed and bound in Great Britain by
Caledonian International Book Manufacturing Ltd, Glasgow, G64

CONTENTS

———•◆•———

ACKNOWLEDGEMENTS

In writing *Your Chinese Horoscope 2001* I am grateful for the assistance and support that those around me have given.

I wish to acknowledge Theodora Lau's *The Handbook of Chinese Horoscopes* (Harper & Row, 1979; Arrow, 1981), which was particularly useful to me in my research.

In addition to Ms Lau's work, I commend the following books to those who wish to find out more about Chinese horoscopes: Kristyna Arcarti, *Chinese Horoscopes for Beginners* (Headway, 1995); Catherine Aubier, *Chinese Zodiac Signs* (Arrow, 1984), a series of 12 books; Paula Delsol, *Chinese Horoscopes* (Pan, 1973); E. A. Crawford and Teresa Kennedy, *Chinese Elemental Astrology* (Piatkus, 1992); Barry Fantoni, *Barry Fantoni's Chinese Horoscopes* (Warner, 1994); Bridget Giles and the Diagram Group, *Chinese Astrology* (Collins Gem, HarperCollins*Publishers*, 1996); Kwok Man-Ho, *Authentic Chinese Horoscopes* (Arrow, 1987), a series of 12 books; Lori Reid, *The Complete Book of Chinese Horoscopes* (Element Books, 1997); Paul Rigby and Harvey Bean, *Chinese Astrologics* (Publications Division, South China Morning Post Ltd, 1981); Ruth Q. Sun, *The Asian Animal Zodiac* (Charles E. Tuttle Company, Inc., 1996); Derek Walters, *Ming Shu* (Pagoda Books, 1987) and *The Chinese*

ACKNOWLEDGEMENTS

Astrology Workbook (The Aquarian Press, 1988); Suzanne White, *Suzanne White's Book of Chinese Chance* (Fontana/Collins, 1978), *The New Astrology* (Pan, 1987) and *The New Chinese Astrology* (Pan, 1994).

Every year has its opportunities,
if you know where to look.
Neil Somerville

INTRODUCTION

The origins of Chinese horoscopes have been lost in the mists of time. It is known that Oriental astrologers practised their art many thousands of years ago and even today Chinese astrology continues to fascinate and intrigue.

In Chinese astrology there are 12 signs named after 12 different animals. No one quite knows how the signs acquired their names, but there is one legend that offers an explanation.

According to this legend, one Chinese New Year the Buddha invited all the animals in his kingdom to come before him. Unfortunately, for reasons best known to the animals, only 12 turned up. The first to arrive was the Rat, followed by the Ox, Tiger, Rabbit, Dragon, Snake, Horse, Goat, Monkey, Rooster, Dog and finally Pig.

In gratitude, the Buddha decided to name a year after each of the animals and that those born during that year would inherit some of the personality of that animal. Therefore those born in the Year of the Ox would be hardworking, resolute and stubborn, just like the Ox, while those born in the Year of the Dog would be loyal and faithful, just like the Dog. While not everyone can possibly share all the characteristics of a sign, it is incredible what similarities do occur and this is partly where the fascination of Chinese horoscopes lies.

In addition to the 12 signs of the Chinese zodiac there are also five elements and these have a strengthening or moderating influence upon the sign. Details about the effects of the elements are given in each of the chapters on the 12 signs.

To find out which sign you were born under, refer to the tables on pages xii–xv. As the Chinese year is based on the lunar year and does not start until late January or early February, it is particularly important for anyone born in those two months to check carefully the dates of the Chinese year in which they were born.

Also included, in the Appendix, are two charts showing the compatibility between the signs for both personal and business relationships, and details about the signs ruling the different hours of the day. From this it is possible to locate your ascendant and, as in Western astrology, this has a significant influence on your personality.

In writing this book, I have taken the unusual step of combining the intriguing nature of Chinese horoscopes with the Western desire to know what the future holds and have based my interpretations upon various factors relating to each of the signs. I have pleased that over the years in which *Your Chinese Horoscope* has been published so many have found the sections on the forthcoming year of interest, and hope that the horoscope has been constructive and useful. Remember, though, that at all times you are the master of your own destiny. I sincerely hope that *Your Chinese Horoscope 2001* will prove interesting and helpful for the year ahead.

THE CHINESE YEARS

Rat	18 February	1912	to	5 February	1913
Ox	6 February	1913	to	25 January	1914
Tiger	26 January	1914	to	13 February	1915
Rabbit	14 February	1915	to	2 February	1916
Dragon	3 February	1916	to	22 January	1917
Snake	23 January	1917	to	10 February	1918
Horse	11 February	1918	to	31 January	1919
Goat	1 February	1919	to	19 February	1920
Monkey	20 February	1920	to	7 February	1921
Rooster	8 February	1921	to	27 January	1922
Dog	28 January	1922	to	15 February	1923
Pig	16 February	1923	to	4 February	1924
Rat	5 February	1924	to	23 January	1925
Ox	24 January	1925	to	12 February	1926
Tiger	13 February	1926	to	1 February	1927
Rabbit	2 February	1927	to	22 January	1928
Dragon	23 January	1928	to	9 February	1929
Snake	10 February	1929	to	29 January	1930
Horse	30 January	1930	to	16 February	1931
Goat	17 February	1931	to	5 February	1932
Monkey	6 February	1932	to	25 January	1933
Rooster	26 January	1933	to	13 February	1934
Dog	14 February	1934	to	3 February	1935
Pig	4 February	1935	to	23 January	1936

Rat	24 January	1936	to	10 February	1937
Ox	11 February	1937	to	30 January	1938
Tiger	31 January	1938	to	18 February	1939
Rabbit	19 February	1939	to	7 February	1940
Dragon	8 February	1940	to	26 January	1941
Snake	27 January	1941	to	14 February	1942
Horse	15 February	1942	to	4 February	1943
Goat	5 February	1943	to	24 January	1944
Monkey	25 January	1944	to	12 February	1945
Rooster	13 February	1945	to	1 February	1946
Dog	2 February	1946	to	21 January	1947
Pig	22 January	1947	to	9 February	1948
Rat	10 February	1948	to	28 January	1949
Ox	29 January	1949	to	16 February	1950
Tiger	17 February	1950	to	5 February	1951
Rabbit	6 February	1951	to	26 January	1952
Dragon	27 January	1952	to	13 February	1953
Snake	14 February	1953	to	2 February	1954
Horse	3 February	1954	to	23 January	1955
Goat	24 January	1955	to	11 February	1956
Monkey	12 February	1956	to	30 January	1957
Rooster	31 January	1957	to	17 February	1958
Dog	18 February	1958	to	7 February	1959
Pig	8 February	1959	to	27 January	1960
Rat	28 January	1960	to	14 February	1961
Ox	15 February	1961	to	4 February	1962
Tiger	5 February	1962	to	24 January	1963
Rabbit	25 January	1963	to	12 February	1964
Dragon	13 February	1964	to	1 February	1965
Snake	2 February	1965	to	20 January	1966
Horse	21 January	1966	to	8 February	1967

Goat	9 February	1967	to	29 January	1968
Monkey	30 January	1968	to	16 February	1969
Rooster	17 February	1969	to	5 February	1970
Dog	6 February	1970	to	26 January	1971
Pig	27 January	1971	to	14 February	1972
Rat	15 February	1972	to	2 February	1973
Ox	3 February	1973	to	22 January	1974
Tiger	23 January	1974	to	10 February	1975
Rabbit	11 February	1975	to	30 January	1976
Dragon	31 January	1976	to	17 February	1977
Snake	18 February	1977	to	6 February	1978
Horse	7 February	1978	to	27 January	1979
Goat	28 January	1979	to	15 February	1980
Monkey	16 February	1980	to	4 February	1981
Rooster	5 February	1981	to	24 January	1982
Dog	25 January	1982	to	12 February	1983
Pig	13 February	1983	to	1 February	1984
Rat	2 February	1984	to	19 February	1985
Ox	20 February	1985	to	8 February	1986
Tiger	9 February	1986	to	28 January	1987
Rabbit	29 January	1987	to	16 February	1988
Dragon	17 February	1988	to	5 February	1989
Snake	6 February	1989	to	26 January	1990
Horse	27 January	1990	to	14 February	1991
Goat	15 February	1991	to	3 February	1992
Monkey	4 February	1992	to	22 January	1993
Rooster	23 January	1993	to	9 February	1994
Dog	10 February	1994	to	30 January	1995
Pig	31 January	1995	to	18 February	1996
Rat	19 February	1996	to	6 February	1997
Ox	7 February	1997	to	27 January	1998

Tiger	28 January	1998	to	15 February	1999
Rabbit	16 February	1999	to	4 February	2000
Dragon	5 February	2000	to	23 January	2001
Snake	24 January	2001	to	11 February	2002

Note: The names of the signs in the Chinese zodiac occasionally differ in the various books on Chinese astrology, although the characteristics of the signs remain the same. In some books the Ox is referred to as the Buffalo or Bull, the Rabbit as the Hare or Cat, the Goat as the Sheep and the Pig as the Boar.

For the sake of convenience, the male gender is used throughout this book. Unless otherwise stated, the characteristics of the signs apply to both sexes.

WELCOME TO THE
YEAR OF THE SNAKE

One moment still and silent, basking under rocks or in long grass, the next deadly and venomous, surprising unsuspecting prey – never underestimate the snake.

Nor its year.

The Snake year is a time of dramatic and historic developments and 2001 will be no exception. This will be a very active year politically with many significant events taking place. These will include some sweeping changes, with certain governments and well-established regimes losing power, either through the ballot box, public pressure or military intervention. Among the areas most likely to be affected are Eastern Europe, the Middle East and Africa, although any country holding an election could see a major swing in public opinion resulting in a transfer of power. The political volatility that the Snake year so often brings was particularly demonstrated in 1989 with the sudden collapse of so many Communist regimes in Eastern Europe, and significant transfers of power will again take place in 2001.

However, despite the upheavals that occur, the year will also bring some historic meetings between world leaders. These will aim to encourage a greater understanding between nations as well as bring about a reconciliation in areas of dispute. Some far-reaching results are likely to ensue and again the ability of the Snake year to set in motion epoch-making events cannot be underestimated. It was, for instance, in the last Snake year that Presidents Bush and Gorbachev held their first summit and declared the ending of the Cold War. In the same year Nelson Mandela met President Botha and so started a chain of events which was to mark the ending of white rule in South Africa. Events in 2001, too, will have profound consequences which will shape the decade ahead.

One area which will be the focus of much attention will be the environment, and disturbing new findings on global warming are likely to prompt a greater international effort to protect the planet and its natural resources. Many governments will introduce legislation to promote conservation, recycling and the more efficient use of resources. Environmental issues do figure strongly in Snake years and it was in the last one that the European Community set a time limit on the banning of all CFCs, while in the United States President Bush introduced several important proposals to reduce the growing menace of air pollution.

Some of the environmental measures taken in 2001 will, over time, have some impact, but unfortunately the year could also be marked by some quite serious accidents which will have damaging consequences. These could include oil spills, chemical leakages and also wide-scale burning, caused either by man or by volcanic eruption. Some of what happens may, rightly or wrongly, be considered responsible for some of the freak weather conditions that will be experienced during the year. Weather-wise, many statistics will be broken in 2001, with some notably severe winter conditions and damaging gales and hurricanes.

A more positive feature of the Snake year will be the emphasis placed on learning and self-development. As a consequence, many people will take it upon themselves to learn new skills or study subjects that they feel could be of personal value. To assist with this, government funding will be given to adult learning centres and to projects which encourage people to further themselves and their education. Similarly, many people will aim to take better care of themselves and this will lead to more health awareness, a growing demand for fitness facilities and renewed interest in aerobics, yoga, *tai chi* and other forms of exercise that promote physical (and sometimes also mental) well-being.

In addition, the arts will be the focus of much attention, with some exciting new trends and styles emerging over the year. This is especially true of some of the fashions that will make their first appearance in 2001. In some cases these will mark the start of a craze and a 'new look'. The world of music, too, will introduce some major new artists who will not only attract a large following but also be an important influence for years to come. Snake years are all for originality.

The Snake year is also generally favourable for business and enterprise. Some major international mergers will take place and notable successes will be enjoyed by those prepared to adapt and seize the opportunities offered by global marketing. E-commerce and the Internet really will start to have a marked effect on consumerism and provide yet further opportunities for the innovative and forward-thinking. In addition, further services are likely to be available through interactive television and this too could begin to develop in a big way over the year. The technology of the twenty-first century will certainly start to be felt – and this is only the beginning.

However, while the Snake year can be a positive one for enterprise, it is a time for investors to be wary. In the past Snake years have certainly seen much volatility in the stock market including, in 1929, the Wall Street Crash. This year major fluctuations will also occur in stock markets around the world and sometimes falls could be triggered by the speed with which stocks can be traded and the way in which sell orders can result when a price falls below a certain point. A wave of sales could quickly become a flood and these falls should serve as a salutary warning to investors. Keep your wits about you and rather than risk all in a volatile market, consider bonds and other safe securities.

Overall, this will certainly be an eventful and historic year. It will also be an important one for the individual, with many people deciding to take more responsibility for their well-being and searching for greater fulfilment in what they do. Throughout the year the emphasis is on self-development, learning and cultural activities.

I sincerely hope that this will be a good year for you and that you will benefit from the more positive aspects that prevail. Develop your skills and pursue your goals. The Snake year favours those keen to have a go and nurture the talents that lie within.

Good luck.

31 JANUARY 1900 ～ 18 FEBRUARY 1901   *Metal Rat*

18 FEBRUARY 1912 ～ 5 FEBRUARY 1913   *Water Rat*

5 FEBRUARY 1924 ～ 23 JANUARY 1925   *Wood Rat*

24 JANUARY 1936 ～ 10 FEBRUARY 1937   *Fire Rat*

10 FEBRUARY 1948 ～ 28 JANUARY 1949   *Earth Rat*

28 JANUARY 1960 ～ 14 FEBRUARY 1961   *Metal Rat*

15 FEBRUARY 1972 ～ 2 FEBRUARY 1973   *Water Rat*

2 FEBRUARY 1984 ～ 19 FEBRUARY 1985   *Wood Rat*

19 FEBRUARY 1996 ～ 6 FEBRUARY 1997   *Fire Rat*

THE
RAT

THE PERSONALITY OF THE RAT

I want to be all that I am capable of becoming.
Katherine Mansfield: a Rat

The Rat is born under the sign of charm. He is intelligent, popular and loves attending parties and large social gatherings. He is able to establish friendships with remarkable ease and people generally feel relaxed in his company. He is a very social creature and is genuinely interested in the welfare and activities of others. He has a good understanding of human nature and his advice and opinions are often sought.

The Rat is a hard and diligent worker. He is also very imaginative and is never short of ideas. However, he does sometimes lack the confidence to promote his ideas as much as he should and this can often prevent him from securing the recognition and credit he so often deserves.

The Rat is very observant and many Rats have made excellent writers and journalists. The Rat also excels at personnel and PR work and any job which brings him into contact with people and the media. His skills are particularly appreciated in times of crisis, for he has an incredibly strong sense of self-preservation. When it comes to finding a way out of an awkward situation, the Rat is certain to be the one who comes up with a solution.

The Rat loves to be where there is a lot of action, but should he ever find himself in a very bureaucratic or restrictive environment he can become a stickler for discipline and routine.

He is also something of an opportunist and is constantly on the look-out for ways in which he can improve his wealth and lifestyle. He rarely lets an opportunity go by and can become involved in so many plans and schemes that he sometimes squanders his energies and achieves very little as a result. He is also rather gullible and can be taken in by those less scrupulous than himself.

Another characteristic of the Rat is his attitude to money. He is very thrifty and to some he may appear a little mean. The reason for this is purely that he likes to keep his money within his family. He can be most generous to his partner, his children and close friends and relatives. He can also be generous to himself, for he often finds it impossible to deprive himself of any luxury or object he fancies. The Rat is also very acquisitive and can be a notorious hoarder. He hates waste and is rarely prepared to throw anything away. He can also be rather greedy and will rarely refuse an invitation for a free meal or a complimentary ticket to some lavish function.

The Rat is a good conversationalist, although he can occasionally be a little indiscreet. He can be highly critical of others – for an honest and unbiased opinion, the Rat is a superb critic – and sometimes will use confidential information to his own advantage. However, as the Rat has such a bright and irresistible nature, most are prepared to forgive him for his slight indiscretions.

Throughout his long and eventful life, the Rat will make many friends and will find that he is especially well suited to those born under his own sign and those of the Ox, Dragon and Monkey. He can also get on well with those born under the signs of the Tiger, Snake, Rooster, Dog and

Pig, but the rather sensitive Rabbit and Goat will find the Rat a little too critical and blunt for their liking. The Horse and Rat will also find it difficult to get on with each other – the Rat craves security and will find the Horse's changeable moods and rather independent nature a little unsettling.

The Rat is very family orientated and will do anything to please his nearest and dearest. He is exceptionally loyal to his parents and can himself be a very caring and loving parent. He will take an interest in all his children's activities and will see that they want for nothing. The Rat usually has a large family.

The female Rat has a kindly, outgoing nature and involves herself in a multitude of different activities. She has a wide circle of friends, enjoys entertaining and is an attentive hostess. She is also conscientious about the upkeep of her home and has superb taste in home furnishings. She is most supportive to the other members of her family and, due to her resourceful, friendly and persevering nature, can do well in practically any career she enters.

Although the Rat is essentially outgoing and something of an extrovert, he is also a very private individual. He tends to keep his feelings to himself and while he is not averse to learning what other people are doing, he resents anyone prying too closely into his own affairs. He also does not like solitude and if he is alone for any length of time he can easily get depressed.

The Rat is undoubtedly very talented, but he does sometimes fail to capitalize on his many abilities. He has a tendency to become involved in too many schemes and chase after too many opportunities all at one time. If he were to slow down and concentrate on one thing at a time he could become very successful. If not, success and wealth could elude him. But the Rat, with his tremendous ability to charm, will rarely, if ever, be without friends.

THE FIVE DIFFERENT TYPES OF RAT

In addition to the 12 signs of the Chinese zodiac, there are five elements and these have a strengthening or moderating influence on the sign. The effects of the five elements on the Rat are described below, together with the years in which the elements were exercising their influence. Therefore all Rats born in 1900 and 1960 are Metal Rats, those born in 1912 and 1972 are Water Rats, and so on.

Metal Rat: 1900, 1960
This Rat has excellent taste and certainly knows how to appreciate the finer things in life. His home is comfortable and nicely decorated and he is forever entertaining or mixing in fashionable circles. He has considerable financial acumen and invests his money well. On the surface the Metal Rat appears cheerful and confident, but deep down he can be troubled by worries that are quite often of his own making. He is exceptionally loyal to his family and friends.

Water Rat: 1912, 1972
The Water Rat is intelligent and very astute. He is a deep thinker and can express his thoughts clearly and persuasively.

He is always eager to learn and is talented in many different areas. He is usually very popular, but his fear of loneliness can sometimes lead him into mixing with the wrong sort of company. He is a particularly skilful writer, but he can get side-tracked very easily and should try to concentrate on just one thing at a time.

Wood Rat: 1924, 1984

The Wood Rat has a friendly, outgoing personality and is most popular with his colleagues and friends. He has a quick agile brain and likes to turn his hand to anything he thinks may be useful. His one fear is insecurity, but given his intelligence and capabilities, this fear is usually unfounded. He has a good sense of humour, enjoys travel and, due to his highly imaginative nature, can be a gifted writer or artist.

Fire Rat: 1936, 1996

The Fire Rat is rarely still and seems to have a never-ending supply of energy and enthusiasm. He loves being involved in the action – be it travel, following up new ideas or campaigning for a cause in which he fervently believes. He is an original thinker and hates being bound by petty restrictions or the dictates of others. He can be forthright in his views, but can sometimes get carried away in the excitement of the moment and commit himself to various undertakings without checking what all the implications might be. Yet he has a resilient nature and with the right support can often go far in life.

Earth Rat: 1948

This Rat is astute and very level-headed. He rarely takes unnecessary chances and while he is constantly trying to improve his financial status, he is prepared to proceed slowly and leave nothing to chance. The Earth Rat is probably not as adventurous as the other types of Rat and prefers to remain in familiar areas rather than rush headlong into something he knows little about. He is talented, conscientious and caring towards his loved ones, but at the same time can be self-conscious and worry a little too much about the image he is trying to project.

PROSPECTS FOR THE RAT IN 2001

The Chinese New Year starts on 24 January 2001. Until then, the old year, the Year of the Dragon, is still making its presence felt.

The Year of the Dragon (5 February 2000 to 23 January 2001) will have been a generally positive one for the Rat and in what remains of it he can still achieve a great deal.

Particularly well aspected are work matters and many Rats will have been able to advance their position over the year, either by taking on different responsibilities or by moving to a new post. For Rats who are seeking work or who would like to make a career move, the closing months of the Dragon year will offer some interesting openings and, by making enquiries and actively following up suitable vacancies, the Rat's patience and persistence will be rewarded. For career developments, late September, October and December could produce some interesting opportunities. In addition, the Rat should promote any ideas he has, as he could find these well received.

The Dragon year is a positive one for financial matters, although the Rat should keep watch over his level of spending and, if possible, aim to make some savings. Without some restraint, he could find himself succumbing to too many temptations and not always putting his money to best use.

On a personal level the Rat will be on fine form at the end of the Dragon year. He will greatly appreciate the support he receives from those around him and if he has any concerns, feels under pressure or would like help over any matter, he should not hesitate to ask. Late in 2000 he will have every reason to be grateful for the assistance others are able to give. Also, as the year draws to an end, there could be a family event or some personal news which will bring the Rat much happiness. December, in particular, will be an active and pleasurable month.

For any Rat who may feel alone or would like new friends, the last quarter of the year will bring excellent chances to meet others and a friendship made in the Dragon year could develop well in the future.

In most respects the Rat will fare well in the Dragon year and by going after his objectives, whether vocational or personal, he can obtain some truly pleasing results.

The Year of the Snake starts on 24 January and will be a variable one for the Rat. In many of his activities he will need to exercise care and he could also have some problems to overcome. However, despite this, the year will certainly not be without its pleasures.

In his work the Rat could find his progress not always matching his expectations. Some of the tasks he has to carry out may be both time-consuming and challenging, and he may also have to contend with a few problems. However, while the Snake year may sometimes be taxing, the Rat is blessed with a resourceful nature and this will often help him to triumph where others might flounder. It is important that throughout the year the Rat keeps faith with himself and his abilities. The year may bring its trying moments, but the Rat should remember that so often periods of growth have their origins in more difficult times and the experience he obtains in the Snake year will lead to more substantial progress in the future.

If the Rat has recently taken on new duties or is given some over the year he should aim to familiarize himself with these. In addition, he should take advantage of any training opportunities he may be offered. These will not only do much to enhance his prospects but could also allow him to discover new strengths which will be of benefit later.

Those Rats seeking work will need to remain persistent in their quest. In addition to following up suitable vacancies, they should consider different ways in which they can put their skills and experience to good use. Some imaginative thinking could widen the scope of positions they could try for and lead to an opening which could develop in an encouraging manner over the next few years.

For work matters the second half of the year will generally be better than the first, but throughout 2001 the Rat does need to be mindful of the events around him and the views of his colleagues. This is not a year for distancing himself too much from what is going on, for taking risks or being too independent. Rather, it is a time for care, tact and learning.

An area which calls for especial care is finance. In 2001 the Rat could face several large expenses, particularly related to accommodation and transport, which will draw on his resources. To prevent problems from arising, he should make full allowance for these in his budget, especially if he knows about them in advance. He would also find it helpful to take greater control over his general level of spending. Although the Rat can be thrifty, he can also yield to temptation very easily and this could stretch his resources and lead to problems. Greater control of his purse strings would certainly not go amiss.

In addition, the Rat should be wary of taking undue risks. Although he may be keen to improve his lot, he should thoroughly investigate any new scheme or investment he is tempted by. Similarly, with new transactions, the Rat should check the terms and any obligations he may be placed under. Again, care and vigilance could prevent difficulties or misunderstandings from arising at a later stage.

As far as his personal life is concerned, this will be a busy year for the Rat. There will be much activity in his home life, with many demands on his time. Others will look to him for support and, as always, he will be glad to give it. However, there could also be a few domestic problems for him to deal with. Here the Rat's skills in handling personal relations will be of great value. Whenever differences of opinion emerge, the Rat should aim to defuse the situation as far as he can by encouraging open discussion and seeing whether a compromise can be found. Positive effort on his part can do much to prevent difficulties from escalating and possibly spoiling parts of the year. There could, though, be occasions when the Rat is himself partly responsible for some of the differences that arise, perhaps because others do not quite share his views or are not willing to fall in with his plans. If he senses this, the Rat could find that a more accommodating attitude would not go amiss.

However, while family relations will need careful handling, the Rat will gain special pleasure from time spent following the progress and success of loved ones, as well as any interests, activities and projects which he can share. At some of the more demanding moments of the year, he could find it helpful to suggest activities that would give everyone the chance to unwind and enjoy themselves. A local outing, a visit to a place of interest or a get together with friends could be an ideal tonic! The Snake year may contain its testing moments, but it will also have some happy ones and the Rat himself can do much to help bring these about.

The Rat will also enjoy his social life over the year, including meetings with friends and some interesting social occasions. Life for the unattached Rat will be particularly active, with many opportunities to meet others and make new friends. However, where romance is concerned, Rats would do well to let any new friendship develop gradually rather than rush into a hasty commitment.

In view of the active nature of the year, the Rat needs to take good care of himself and make sure that he eats well and exercises regularly. Driving himself too hard, without giving thought to his well-being, could leave him tired, under par and prone to minor ailments. In addition, he should make sure he sets sufficient time aside for his own personal interests, especially those that are in complete contrast to his everyday concerns. If he does not currently have a hobby which he can turn to in his spare time, he really should aim to take one up, as it would be most beneficial for him.

Though this may not be the smoothest of years for the Rat, he does possess some admirable qualities which will help him through some of its more difficult moments and enable him to emerge from the year wiser, more experienced and with some gains to his credit. The Rat is, after all, a survivor and has a happy knack of turning events to his advantage. This year may test this ability more than usual! However, what the Rat does achieve and learn now will do much to help with his personal growth as well as sow the seeds for his future success.

As far as the different types of Rat are concerned, this will be a challenging year for the *Metal Rat*. Over the last 12 months he is likely to have made good progress in many of his activities as well as have greatly impressed others with his diligent and determined nature. In 2001 he will be able to build on this and make additional progress, although it may not always be as easy to achieve as in other years. He will find his best gains will come from concentrating on areas in which he has most experience and building on his existing successes rather than venturing into less familiar territory. If he has recently taken on different duties or is given new responsibilities over the year he should concentrate on these and rise to the challenges given him. Applied and persistent effort will pay off and ultimately be rewarded, even though some of the tasks could be exacting to carry out. In addition to his own duties, the Metal Rat should also take note of all that is going on around him and remain mindful of the views of colleagues. This will not only allow him to play a more informed role in all he does but will also alert him to possible changes as well as emerging opportunities, something a resourceful Metal Rat never likes to miss! Any Metal Rat who does decide to move from his present position or is seeking work would do well to consider what type of work he now wishes to try. By having a clear idea of what he wants and laying emphasis on his experience and specialist knowledge, he will find himself faring much better. Also, when applying to a different company for employment, any background research he can undertake before completing an application form or attending an interview would be well worth the trouble and could make a considerable difference to the outcome. The Metal Rat should also keep a watchful eye over his finances in 2001 and regularly monitor his out-goings. All too often he could find these will creep up and be greater than he has allowed for. Also, if he intends to buy any expensive equipment or make a major purchase in the Snake year, he could find himself saving a considerable amount by waiting for special offers and sales, rather than proceeding too hastily. Again, care and patience could be to his advantage. The Metal Rat's domestic life will be active over the year with many demands upon his time. These will include helping others with their various activities as well as assisting with some problems. Again the Metal Rat's sound judgement and ability to relate well with others will be truly appreciated. Any Metal Rat with a relation in education will find that any additional assistance, support and instruction he feels able to give will turn out to be of great benefit. While the Metal Rat's domestic life will sometimes be demanding, there will still be much for him to enjoy, including mutual interests and joint projects as well as any holidays and outings he is able to arrange. Although he will have much to occupy his time over the year, it is important that the Metal Rat does not neglect his own personal interests or social life. Both can do much to help him unwind as well as bring him considerable pleasure over the year. In 2001 it is important for the Metal Rat to maintain some sort of balance to his life. Although the Snake year may not be an easy one for him, by rising to the challenges it will bring and giving of his best he can still emerge from the year with much to his credit and the experience he gains now will be to his longer term benefit.

Although the Snake year may not be entirely problem-free for the *Water Rat*, it can still prove a constructive one, with certain aspects bringing him much pleasure, especially those connected with his own personal development. With his enquiring mind and wide interests, the Water Rat will be able to extend his knowledge and skills and so prepare himself for future advancement. He should not only take full advantage of any training opportunities he may be offered but also learn more about any skills he has been wanting to acquire. In his heart he knows he is capable of accomplishing much in the future and this will be the time when he will be preparing himself for the greater tasks that lie ahead. Another of the Water Rat's abilities which will prove useful is his effectiveness as a communicator, particularly with the written word. Any Water Rats with literary, journalistic or media aspirations should make every effort to promote themselves and, as a result, could enjoy some worthy successes and encouraging feedback. However, while there will be positive sides to the Water Rat's professional life, this is still a year in which he will need to proceed with care and remain alert to all that is going on around him. He also needs to show some flexibility in his approach, particularly if he is asked to take on new duties or responsibilities. Some of these may not be of his own choosing and they may sometimes place him under pressure, but if he shows himself to be accommodating and resourceful, he will greatly impress as well as add to his experience. Water Rats seeking work or deciding to change their position over the year would do well to give some thought to how they would like to see their career develop over the longer term and then actively pursue any appropriate vacancies. Although their quest for a position may not always be easy, their interest, knowledge and enthusiasm will invariably show through and enable them to ultimately get what they want. Career prospects will brighten noticeably in the second half of the year, especially during the months of September and October. As far as financial matters are concerned, however, the year does call for care. With family, accommodation and transport expenses, there will be many demands on the Water Rat's resources and throughout 2001 he will need to watch his outgoings. He could find it especially helpful to maintain a set of personal and household accounts. The Water Rat's home life will be busy and a lot will be expected of him. As far as possible, he should

prioritize what he has to do, be sensible in the commitments he does take on and not hesitate to ask for assistance
from others. With good organization and management of
his time, he will be surprised at just how much he can actually get done and at how some of the household tasks and
pressures can be eased. Admittedly, though, there will be
times when the Water Rat will feel tired and maybe on
edge. To preserve domestic harmony, he should tell others
how he feels (which might result in more offers of help)
rather than become snappy or irritable. Also, he should not
neglect his own well-being and should ensure he eats a
balanced diet and gives himself sufficient time to rest and
unwind. If he pushes himself too hard, he could find
himself becoming prone to minor ailments and not able to
give of his best. But while the Water Rat's personal life
may be busy and sometimes demanding, it will also
contain many happy times. These will include time spent
on mutual interests, meeting and chatting with friends and
any travel and visits to places of interest the Water Rat can
arrange. There will also be many Water Rats who choose to
spend some of their free time out of doors, with gardening
high on the agenda. Although the Snake year will contain
its demanding moments, the Water Rat can still get much
of long-term value from it, particularly by adding to his
skills and experience. He has a great and exciting future
ahead of him and in 2001 he will be doing much to prepare
himself for it.

The *Wood Rat* is blessed with an amiable and enterprising nature. He strives hard to achieve what he wants
and is always keen to make the most of himself and his
abilities. However, despite his good intentions, not all that

he attempts in 2001 will work as he envisaged and he could have to rethink some of his plans. At the time this may cause him some anguish, but in some cases the events of the year could prove to be 'blessings in disguise' and lead the Wood Rat to come up with stronger and often more appropriate plans. In addition, he will learn from any mistakes or misjudgments he may make and be considerably wiser as a result. In view of some of the decisions the young Wood Rat will need to take in 2001, he should not hesitate to talk matters over with family, friends and those in a position to advise. If he is forthcoming, he will not only benefit from the help he is given, but will also feel reassured to know that he has support behind him and that so many have such strong faith in him. As well as valuing the assistance of his family and friends, he can look forward to many meaningful occasions in their company. He will play a full and lively part in home activities, including various household projects and tasks, and his willingness to help out, especially at busy times, will be much appreciated. Those Wood Rats born in 1924 will also carry out some creative home projects over the year, with what they do winning warm approval. All Wood Rats can look forward to an interesting social life over the year, with times spent enjoying the company of friends and, especially for the younger Wood Rat, in partying and generally going out. The summer months will be particularly active for social matters. However, should the Wood Rat become involved in a difference of opinion with someone at any time over the year, he should aim to sort it out as soon as he can, ideally coming to an understanding rather than letting the matter linger in the background and cause more anguish than is necessary. As with all Rats, the Wood Rat should take extra care with personal relations during the year. For those Wood Rats in education, this will be an important time, with their studies and exams often having considerable bearing on the next few years. In view of this, these Wood Rats should aim to set about any revision and course work they have in a thorough and systematic way and not leave exam preparation to the last moment! Their diligence will be well rewarded. As far as financial matters are concerned, this is a year that calls for care. Those Wood Rats born in 1924 will need to remain especially vigilant when entering into any new transaction and should avoid taking unnecessary risks. If in any doubt, they should seek further advice. Wood Rats born in 1984 will sometimes find their finances sorely stretched and will need to budget carefully. They too should avoid taking undue risks, otherwise they could find money they need either lost or gone. Wood Rats, take note! Generally, although this is a year which requires care, it does have its positive side, not only in the support shown for the Wood Rat but also in the long-term value of what he learns and accomplishes.

Although the Snake year will not be without its awkward moments, there is still much that the *Fire Rat* will enjoy. Particularly well aspected are activities related to self-development and furthering hobbies and interests. Indeed, with the Snake year's emphasis on cultural pursuits, this will be an excellent time for the Fire Rat to further his interests and take up some new ones. Also, some of the more recently retired Fire Rats who find they have more free time at their disposal would do well to consider starting an activity they have long wished to try.

Similarly, if there are any courses run by local authorities or educational establishments that appeal, the Fire Rat should follow these up. By doing so, he can make the year that much more fulfilling. The Fire Rat should also give some thought to his well-being over the year and if he is sedentary for long periods of the day, he would do well to consider taking some suitable exercise, perhaps walking, cycling or swimming. However, before starting on any fitness campaign, he would do well to seek advice on the best way to proceed. Also, if he is overweight or reliant on convenience food, he could find modification of his eating habits and diet of benefit. Any attention that the Fire Rat can give to his health and fitness over the year would certainly be to his advantage. He will also take much pleasure from outdoor activities and those Fire Rats who particularly enjoy gardening will be tempted to redesign certain areas and carry out some projects they have long been considering. Travel, too, is well aspected and the Fire Rat will not only enjoy any breaks or holidays but also some more local outings. These could be made all the more meaningful by following through a certain theme, for instance, looking at sites of historic interest or places that have some other common link. Again, by actively carrying out his plans and making good use of his time, the Fire Rat can make this a satisfying and rewarding year. Financial matters, though, are more awkwardly aspected and the Fire Rat does need to keep a watchful eye over his level of spending and particularly make sure he checks the terms of any new agreement or obligation he enters into. Paperwork, especially any that is tax or finance related, needs careful attention over the year. If the Fire Rat has any doubts over what is being asked of him, he should seek clarification. By being vigilant early on he can do much to avoid problems from arising later. Another area which calls for care is the Fire Rat's relations with others. Although in the main these will go well, he could find himself at variance with someone over the year. If so, he should make every effort to reconcile the matter before it escalates out of all proportion. Similarly, if he feels that support for some of his ideas is lacking or becomes stubborn over a certain issue – and the Fire Rat can be stubborn at times! – he can expect some tricky moments. Fire Rats, take note! This warning apart, the Fire Rat can look forward to a generally active domestic and social life in which he will play a full part. He will be able to encourage the activities of those around him as well as take much pride in the success and personal news enjoyed by a younger relation. He should also make a point of involving others in his own activities, especially any new interests he takes up or projects he starts. For any Fire Rat who would like to extend his social life and add to his circle of friends, there will be several excellent opportunities, especially if he makes the effort to go out more or perhaps joins a local group. Generally, there is much in the Fire Rat's favour over the year, but he does need to be careful in his financial activities and mindful of the opinions of others. If he bears this in mind, then the year can bring him much satisfaction, particularly in his personal interests.

This will be a year of consolidation, reflection and planning for the *Earth Rat*. Many Earth Rats will have seen significant changes over the last 12 months involving either their work, their accommodation or their family.

During the Snake year the Earth Rat will be able to take stock and adjust to these changes as well as give thought to his future. The Earth Rat prefers to move at a steady and organized pace and, for the most part, this is what he will be able to do during 2001. In his work he will aim to make the most of any changes that have taken place and if he has recently taken on new duties, he will concentrate on these and rise, in his own inimitable way, to the challenges given him. Admittedly, sometimes he may find it difficult to make the headway he desires, but his steadfastness and commitment will be both noticed and appreciated. Also, while the Earth Rat may wish to concentrate specifically on his own duties, this should not prevent him from taking an informed interest in all that is going on around him, including any new proposals. Sometimes these could affect his position and the more fully informed he is, the better he will be able to gauge what to do and to follow up any openings that fall available. The year may contain its pressures and uncertainties, but the Earth Rat is both experienced and resourceful and can emerge with some interesting gains to his credit. All Earth Rats should take advantage of any training courses they might be offered or any chances to add to their skills. These could be especially helpful for those Earth Rats seeking work, particularly as it could increase the range of positions open to them. As far as financial matters are concerned, the Earth Rat will need to take care, watch his level of spending and ensure that he makes adequate allowance for any new financial obligations. Extra vigilance on his part can do much to avert possible problems and, if he is uncertain over any financial matter, it would be very much to his advantage to seek clarification. This need for care also applies to any important paperwork he receives, especially anything finance and tax related. Even if the Earth Rat feels that some of what he is being asked is unnecessary, to delay responding or not give all the information required could result in additional correspondence and even extra expense. Earth Rats, take note! As far as the Earth Rat's domestic life is concerned, this will be a busy year and at times he may despair of all that is being expected of him. Whenever he feels under pressure, he should ask those around for additional assistance as well as prioritize various household tasks and activities. This may mean some home projects have to be delayed, but this would be better than putting himself under too much strain. However, despite the activity that will mark his home life, the year will still contain many pleasurable occasions for the Earth Rat, including the times spent sharing joint interests and pursuits with loved ones. A younger relation will be a source of much joy as well as the focus of some well-deserved family celebration over the year. The Earth Rat will also appreciate the companionship of his friends during the year, especially enjoying the opportunity his social life gives him to unwind, and he will have the chance to attend some interesting functions. For those Earth Rats who want to add to their social circle, there will be opportunities to strike up new friendships, especially during the second half of the year. Although the Earth Rat will have much to occupy him in 2001, it is important that he allows sufficient time for his own interests, as well as taking care of his general well-being. This includes making sure he has sufficient exercise as well as eating a healthy and balanced diet. Generally, provided the

Earth Rat remains his usual careful self and adapts to the events the year will bring, he will be content with what he manages to accomplish as well as with what he sets in motion for the future.

FAMOUS RATS

Alan Alda, Dave Allen, Ursula Andress, Louis Armstrong, Charles Aznavour, Lauren Bacall, Shirley Bassey, Jeremy Beadle, Irving Berlin, Kenneth Branagh, Marlon Brando, Charlotte Brontë, Chris de Burgh, George Bush, Lord Callaghan, Glen Campbell, David Carradine, Jimmy Carter, Maurice Chevalier, Barbara Dickson, Benjamin Disraeli, David Duchovny, Noël Edmonds, T. S. Eliot, Albert Finney, Clark Gable, Liam Gallagher, Al Gore, Hugh Grant, Geri Halliwell, Thomas Hardy, Prince Harry, Vaclav Havel, Haydn, Charlton Heston, Damon Hill, Buddy Holly, Mick Hucknall, Englebert Humperdinck, Henrik Ibsen, Jeremy Irons, Glenda Jackson, Jean-Michel Jarre, Gene Kelly, Kris Kristofferson, Lawrence of Arabia, Gary Lineker, Sir Andrew Lloyd Webber, Claude Monet, Richard Nixon, Sean Penn, Terry Pratchett, the Queen Mother, Patrick Rafter, Vanessa Redgrave, Burt Reynolds, Rossini, William Shakespeare, Yves St Laurent, Tommy Steele, Donna Summer, James Taylor, Leo Tolstoy, Henri Toulouse-Lautrec, Spencer Tracy, Anthea Turner, the Prince of Wales, George Washington, Dennis Weaver, Roger Whittaker, Richard Wilson, the Duke of York, Emile Zola.

19 FEBRUARY 1901 ~ 7 FEBRUARY 1902   *Metal Ox*

6 FEBRUARY 1913 ~ 25 JANUARY 1914   *Water Ox*

24 JANUARY 1925 ~ 12 FEBRUARY 1926   *Wood Ox*

11 FEBRUARY 1937 ~ 30 JANUARY 1938   *Fire Ox*

29 JANUARY 1949 ~ 16 FEBRUARY 1950   *Earth Ox*

15 FEBRUARY 1961 ~ 4 FEBRUARY 1962   *Metal Ox*

3 FEBRUARY 1973 ~ 22 JANUARY 1974   *Water Ox*

20 FEBRUARY 1985 ~ 8 FEBRUARY 1986   *Wood Ox*

7 FEBRUARY 1997 ~ 27 JANUARY 1998   *Fire Ox*

THE
O X

THE PERSONALITY OF THE OX

I do not know anyone who has got to the top without hard work. That is the recipe. It will not always get you to the top, but it should get you pretty near.

Margaret Thatcher: an Ox

The Ox is born under the signs of equilibrium and tenacity. He is a hard and conscientious worker and sets about everything he does in a resolute, methodical and determined manner. He has considerable leadership qualities and is often admired for his tough and uncompromising nature. He knows what he wants to achieve in life and, as far as possible, will not be deflected from his ultimate objective.

The Ox takes his responsibilities and duties very seriously. He is decisive and quick to take advantage of any opportunity that comes his way. He is also sincere and places a great deal of trust in his friends and colleagues. He is, nevertheless, something of a loner. He is a quiet and private individual and often keeps his thoughts to himself. He also cherishes his independence and prefers to set about things in his own way rather than be bound by the dictates of others or be influenced by outside pressures.

The Ox tends to have a calm and tranquil nature, but if something angers him or he feels that someone has let him down, he can have a fearsome temper. He can also be stubborn and obstinate and this can lead him into conflict with others. Usually the Ox will succeed in getting his own way, but should things go against him, he is a poor loser and will take any defeat or setback extremely badly.

The Ox is often a deep thinker and rather studious. He is not particularly renowned for his sense of humour and does not take kindly to new gimmicks or anything too innovative. The Ox is too solid and traditional for that and he prefers to stick to the more conventional norm.

His home is very important to him and in some respects he treats it as a private sanctuary. His family tends to be closely knit and the Ox will make sure that each member does their fair share around the house. The Ox tends to be a hoarder, but he is always well organized and neat. He also places great importance on punctuality and there is nothing that infuriates him more than to be kept waiting – particularly if it is due to someone's inefficiency. The Ox can be a hard taskmaster!

Once settled in a job or house the Ox will quite happily remain there for many years. He does not like change and he is also not particularly keen on travel. He does, however, enjoy gardening and other outdoor pursuits and he will often spend much of his spare time out of doors. The Ox is usually an excellent gardener and whenever possible he will always make sure he has a large area of ground to maintain. He usually prefers to live in the country rather than the town.

Due to his dedicated and dependable nature, the Ox will usually do well in his chosen career, providing he is given enough freedom to act on his own initiative. He invariably does well in politics, agriculture and in careers which need specialized training. The Ox is also very gifted in the arts and many Oxen have enjoyed considerable success as musicians or composers.

The Ox is not as outgoing as some and it often takes him a long time to establish friendships and feel relaxed in another person's company. His courtships are likely to be long, but once he is settled he will remain devoted and loyal to his partner. The Ox is particularly well suited to those born under the signs of the Rat, Rabbit, Snake and Rooster. He can also establish a good relationship with the Monkey, Dog, Pig and another Ox, but he will find that he has little in common with the whimsical and sensitive Goat. He will also find it difficult to get on with the Horse, Dragon and Tiger – the Ox prefers a quiet and peaceful existence and those born under these three signs tend to be a little too lively and impulsive for his liking.

The female Ox has a kind and caring nature, and her home and family are very much her pride and joy. She always tries to do her best for her partner and can be a most conscientious and loving parent. She is an excellent organizer and also a very determined person who will often succeed in getting what she wants in life. She usually has a deep interest in the arts and is often a talented artist or musician.

The Ox is a very down-to-earth character. He is sincere, loyal and unpretentious. He can, however, be rather reserved and to some he may appear distant and aloof. He has a quiet nature, but underneath he is very strong-willed and ambitious. He has the courage of his convictions and is often prepared to stand up for what he believes is right, regardless of the consequences. He inspires confidence and trust and throughout his life he will rarely be short of people who are ready to support him or who admire his strong and resolute manner.

THE FIVE DIFFERENT TYPES OF OX

In addition to the 12 signs of the Chinese zodiac, there are five elements and these have a strengthening or moderating influence on the sign. The effects of the five elements on the Ox are described below, together with the years in which the elements were exercising their influence. Therefore all Oxen born in 1961 are Metal Oxen, those born in 1913 and 1973 are Water Oxen, and so on.

Metal Ox: 1961

This Ox is confident and very strong-willed. He can be blunt and forthright in his views and is not afraid of speaking his mind. He sets about his objectives with a dogged determination, but he can become so involved in his various activities that he is oblivious to the thoughts and feelings of those around him, and this can sometimes be to his detriment. He is honest and dependable and will never promise more than he can deliver. He has a good appreciation of the arts and usually has a small circle of very good and loyal friends.

Water Ox: 1913, 1973

This Ox has a sharp and penetrating mind. He is a good organizer and sets about his work in a methodical manner. He is not as narrow-minded as some of the other types of Oxen and is more willing to involve others in his plans and aspirations. He usually has very high moral standards and is often attracted to careers in public service. He is a good judge of character and has such a friendly and persuasive manner that he usually experiences little difficulty in securing his objectives. He is popular and has an excellent way with children.

Wood Ox: 1925, 1985

The Wood Ox conducts himself with an air of dignity and authority and will often take a leading role in any enterprise in which he gets involved. He is very self-confident and is direct in his dealings with others. He does, however, have a quick temper and has no hesitation in speaking his mind. He has tremendous drive and will-power and has an extremely good memory. The Wood Ox is particularly loyal and devoted to the members of his family and has a most caring nature.

Fire Ox: 1937, 1997

The Fire Ox has a powerful and assertive personality and is a hard and conscientious worker. He holds strong views and has very little patience when things do not go his own way. He can also get carried away in the excitement of the moment and does not always take into account the views of those around him. He nevertheless has many leadership qualities and will often reach positions of power, eminence and wealth. He usually has a small group of loyal and close friends and is very devoted to his family.

Earth Ox: 1949

This Ox sets about everything he does in a sensible and level-headed manner. He is ambitious, but also realistic in his aims and is often prepared to work long hours in order to secure his objectives. He is shrewd in financial and business matters and is a very good judge of character. He has a quiet nature and is greatly admired for his sincerity and integrity. He is also very loyal to his family and friends and his views and opinions are often sought by others.

PROSPECTS FOR THE OX IN 2001

The Chinese New Year starts on 24 January 2001. Until then, the old year, the Year of the Dragon, is still making its presence felt.

The Year of the Dragon (5 February 2000 to 23 January 2001) will have been a variable one for the Ox. Dragon years are often characterized by considerable change and activity, and the Ox, who so likes to proceed in an ordered manner, will have felt ill at ease with some of the developments that have taken place. However, he can now take heart. As the next Chinese year approaches the aspects will start to move in his favour and the new year will bring a significant upturn in his fortunes.

To benefit from the improved prospects that await him, at the end of the Dragon year the Ox could find it helpful to make a concerted effort to get as up to date as possible with his various activities. This includes tackling tasks he might have been putting off as well as answering any outstanding correspondence. By dealing with these matters the Ox will not only feel relieved that they are no longer hanging over him but will also find himself freer to enjoy the festivities at the year's end.

The Ox should also give some thought as to what he would like to do over the forthcoming year. By deciding upon his objectives he will find himself channelling his energies in a more purposeful way as well as coming up with some ideas which would be worth developing. He would also find it helpful to discuss his thoughts with those around him and can greatly benefit from their advice as well as be heartened by the considerable affection shown him.

In addition to the encouragement he receives, the Ox will greatly enjoy the company of his family and close friends as the year draws to a close. His social life will become busier and he can look forward to attending some interesting gatherings in both November and December. At this time the Ox will sense the tide is at last turning in his favour and will become more optimistic and positive in his outlook.

Christmas 2000 is likely to be especially pleasant and, come January, the Ox will start the year with renewed confidence, more determined than ever to make something of the next 12 months.

The Year of the Snake starts on 24 January and will be a successful and satisfying one for the Ox. In keeping with the Snake sign, the Ox conducts his activities in a careful and methodical manner and his approach will find favour during the year. This will be a much more stable time for him, giving him the chance to develop his own plans and ideas, often with good results.

Many Oxen will have seen significant changes in their work over the last 12 months and these will have led to uncertainty and sometimes disappointing progress. However, events will now move in the Ox's favour, allowing him to build on his often considerable experience and make better headway. If he is eager to take on fresh challenges, has ideas he wishes to develop or feels the time is now right to pursue a different position, he should set about his aim in his usual determined way. As he will find, purposeful action towards specific goals will be well rewarded.

When openings do arise in the Ox's present line of work, he should actively follow them up and will find his reputation and experience will make him a strong and often successful candidate. Similarly, if he has any ideas or suggestions that could benefit his place of work or advance his position, he should promote them. Again, he will find some of his proposals bringing a pleasing response.

Those Oxen seeking work will also make excellent headway, with many finding their persistence at last being rewarded. To help strengthen any application they make, if they are able to find out any background information about the company or position they are applying for, they could well find this will tip the balance in their favour. In addition to responding to advertisements that interest them, some Oxen could be successful in obtaining a position through a chance remark or someone's recommendation. It has been said that luck is when opportunity meets preparedness, and by being prepared and making the most of the opportunities that occur, the Ox can certainly benefit from several strokes of good fortune over the year.

As he will find, this really is a year for progress and for some long overdue rewards.

Quite a number of Oxen are in positions which draw on their creative abilities and these Oxen would do well to extend their skills as well as actively promote their work. Oxen can be some of the chief beneficiaries of the creative and cultural leanings of the Snake year, and many will thrive in the conducive atmosphere that prevails.

As far as financial matters are concerned, again this will be a positive year for the Ox. Almost all will enjoy an improvement in their income over the year and end 2001 in a stronger financial position. This upturn will tempt many to make some acquisitions for their home or carry out some alterations which will improve both its look and comfort. The Ox will particularly enjoy examining the possibilities available and then seeing his ideas take shape. His home improvements will bring him, and those around him, great satisfaction over the year. However, should the Ox have any funds which he does not immediately need, he would do well to consider setting some aside for his long-term future. Savings made now could grow into a useful asset that the Ox will be grateful for in future years.

The Ox will also obtain much contentment from both his domestic and social life in 2001. His home life means much to him and he will, as usual, play an active role in family matters, both supporting those around him and immersing himself in various household projects. His home life will mostly go smoothly, but if any differences of opinion do arise, the Ox would do well to discuss them and see whether a solution can be found rather than letting them cast too great a shadow over home life. If he is not careful, a contretemps over a comparatively small matter could escalate and cause considerable ill feeling. Also, the Ox should aim to keep his temper in check, otherwise he could regret some things said in a heated exchange. Oxen, do take note of this. Home life and relations with others can provide much happiness over the year but there will be moments when the Ox will need to tread carefully and watch his tongue!

On a social level the Ox can look forward to a pleasing year. Those who may desire more companionship or new friendships or have had some recent sadness to bear really should aim to go out more, especially to places where they are likely to meet others. For some, local societies and groups could be the ideal venue, allowing them to meet others of similar age and interests. For the unattached Ox, romance is splendidly aspected, with a chance meeting developing well and bringing much happiness. The spring and late summer months will be an especially happy and active time for social matters.

The Ox is usually blessed with a robust constitution but in 2001 he should take care of himself and if he feels below par for any length of time seek medical advice. Although he may want to get a lot of things done, he should not jeopardize his own well-being. He should also make sure he gives himself the opportunity to unwind, take exercise and, if circumstances permit, take a proper holiday over the year. He will feel considerably better for having a change of scene and the chance to visit some interesting and, in some cases, unusual destinations.

Overall there is much in the Ox's favour in the Snake year and, by going after his goals in his usual steadfast way, he can achieve a great deal. This is very much a year in which his efforts, patience and hard work will be well rewarded. His home life will bring him pleasure and there are good prospects of making new friends and, for the unattached, starting a meaningful romance.

As far as the different types of Ox are concerned, this is a year which holds considerable promise for the *Metal Ox*. With his determined and methodical approach he can look forward to making substantial progress over the year as well as securing some of his longer term goals. Indeed, over recent years he will have learnt and accomplished a great deal, and the Snake year will give him the chance to build on this experience and put his skills to excellent use. Throughout the year, whether in work or seeking work, the Metal Ox should remain alert for opportunities to pursue and should follow up any openings for which he thinks he might be suited. The early months of the year and late summer could see some particularly exciting developments, with many Metal Oxen obtaining a position which will not only allow them to make more effective use of their skills but also offer excellent chances of future development. In addition to the progress he makes over the year, the Metal Ox would also find it useful to extend his skills, particularly any that help him carry out his duties, as these will be of long-term benefit. In some cases, new computer skills could be of great help. This is also an excellent year for the Metal Ox to advance any work-related ideas. Some of his proposals are likely to develop in a most encouraging manner. The progress that he will make in his work will also lead to an improvement in his financial situation. However, while he will welcome this, often buying himself and his loved ones some treats as well as making useful acquisitions for his home, the Metal Ox would do well to carry out a review of his general financial situation. This includes looking at any savings policies he has and seeing if they can be improved or increased, checking that his levels of insurance are adequate and examining his regular outgoings. This will almost certainly help him make more effective use of his money and could also give him an additional level of security both for now and the future. The Metal Ox will also be encouraged by the support he receives from his loved ones over the year. However, in order for others to help him, he does need to overcome his reticence and discuss his plans more freely with them. He himself can also do much to help those close to him. Others, especially those of a younger age, set much store by his advice and greatly value his help. Generally, the Metal Ox's home life will bring him much satisfaction, but if any matter gives rise to disagreement or dissension, he must work in a conciliatory manner to sort it out before it starts to sour relations. This may mean being more flexible than usual over a certain point, but this could be better than temporarily jeopardizing the fine rapport the Metal Ox so enjoys with his loved ones. Metal Oxen, do take note of this and avoid being unnecessarily intransigent over issues that may not always be that important. The Metal Ox will appreciate meeting up with his close friends over the year and will enjoy some of the parties and functions that he attends. For the lonely or unattached Metal Ox, a new friendship, maybe made following a chance encounter, could really blossom and bring a great deal of happiness. Although the Metal Ox will have a lot to keep him occupied in 2001, he should make sure he sets time aside for his own personal interests and recreational pursuits. These will not only bring him pleasure but also be beneficial in that they will help him to relax and provide a diversion from his usual concerns. In addition, the Metal Ox should make sure that he takes good care of himself, eating a healthy and balanced diet as well as taking exercise. With so many positive developments over the year and so much that he wants to do, it is important that he tries to keep himself on peak form. Overall this will be a splendid year for the Metal Ox and by making the most of his considerable experience and going after the opportunities the year will bring, he will make excellent progress and feel more inspired and fulfilled. The Metal Ox knows he is capable of achieving a great deal and in the Snake year he will be given the chance to prove himself. He will do so with notable success.

Although the *Water Ox* will have some worthy accomplishments to his credit over the last few years, these may still have fallen short of what he would really like to achieve. As a result, as the Snake year begins, the Water Ox will feel more determined than ever to make more effective use of his ideas and experience. His resolve will bring some interesting developments, some occurring quite early on in the year. Water Oxen who are seeking work, who feel the time has come to move from their present position or who wish to take on new challenges should actively follow up any opportunities that arise as well as make approaches to companies and organizations. By taking the initiative and laying stress on their experience and possible contribution, they will be able to open doors that were hitherto closed. As the Water Ox himself recognizes, realizing his ambitions does call for that extra effort and in the Snake year such is his commitment and resolve that he will find that each step forward can give rise to further opportunities, often within a comparatively short space of time. The early months of the year, July and late September are splendidly aspected for work opportunities. The Water Ox will also enjoy an improvement in his level of income in 2001. While this may ease some of the pressure he has been under, he still needs to handle his finances with care. His outgoings are often quite considerable and he would find it helpful to watch his financial position quite closely, ideally maintaining a set of personal and household accounts. The Water Ox will also decide to spend a great deal on his accommodation over the year, especially on new furnishings and equipment. By waiting for sales and other favourable opportunities rather than proceeding too hastily, he could find himself saving a considerable amount. Where his acquisitions relate to the look and décor of his home, his taste and eye for detail will be much admired by others. His home life throughout the Snake year will be active, with many calls upon his time from relations both younger and considerably older than himself. However, the assistance he is able to give will be truly appreciated. The Water Ox will also delight in the progress made by those around him as well as play a full part in family activities, including encouraging mutual interests and arranging some pleasurable events. As far as his social life is concerned, the Water Ox is always one to choose his friends with care and over the year he will strike up some useful acquaintances. Some of those he meets will be especially taken with his sincere and earnest approach and will, in time, prove of great help to him, giving him advice and sometimes assistance in a rather unusual but practical way. For those Water Oxen desiring companionship, romance or a more active social life, the year will also go well, with a new friendship bringing excitement and happiness. In so many respects this is a truly favourable and progressive year for the Water Ox. However, to make the most of it, he should make a determined effort to realize his goals. If he does so, he will achieve some excellent and often far-reaching results. The Snake year is very much a time when the Water Ox will come into his own and show others his considerable potential as well as the many other fine qualities of his character.

This will be a positive and agreeable year for the *Wood Ox* with many aspects of his life going well. For those born in 1985 this will prove an important year as far as education is concerned, with many taking exams and selecting subjects for more specialist study. Although there will be times when the young Wood Ox will feel under pressure and will, in his sometimes forthright way, give vent to his feelings, this will still be a constructive time for him. By working consistently and methodically, and not leaving revision to the last moment, he will obtain pleasing results in much of what he does. He will also become particularly interested in certain subjects and this will do much to influence what he specializes in later and may also have a possible bearing on his future vocation. The Wood Ox has an exciting future ahead of him and what he learns and accomplishes in 2001 will build a base for that future.

However, if there are any topics or subjects which he finds particularly difficult or worrying, he should ask rather than continue unaided. As he will find, those around him can, when asked, offer much constructive guidance. Also, sometimes the Wood Ox does have preconceived ideas about not liking or being able to do something and so closes his mind to making an effort or really trying. If he were prepared to be more open minded and at least make an attempt, he could find certain subject areas more interesting than he originally thought as well as an interesting challenge for him. Sometimes he may not quite realize just how versatile he is until he tries! The Wood Ox's social life is well aspected and in addition to enjoying the company of his band of close friends, he will have a good time at parties and the many other social occasions that he attends. Socially he will find himself much in demand throughout 2001, with the summer months being particularly active. He will also get much pleasure from his hobbies and interests, and for the sporting and outdoor enthusiast, the year will contain some memorable occasions. Many Wood Oxen have a deep interest in music and this, too, would be worth developing over the year. For any Wood Oxen who are thinking of taking up a musical career or one connected with the creative arts, any experience or skills they are able to acquire could prove helpful. The Wood Ox's home life will contain enjoyable elements and he will be grateful for the interest shown in his progress and activities. However, there could be times when his views run counter to those around him and this could lead to heated exchanges. Although it may not always be easy, the Wood Ox should show some willingness to discuss any matter over which there may be disagreement and see whether a compromise can be reached. Often an amicable solution can be found, but the Wood Ox must not let a too inflexible attitude risk souring his home life. He should also remember that those close to him do have his best interests at heart – something which he may not always appreciate! For those Wood Oxen born in 1925, the year will also contain some interesting and rewarding moments. The older Wood Ox will take much joy in following the progress of family members and can also look forward to a celebration over the year, possibly the marriage of a dear relation or the birth of a grandchild or great grandchild. He will be grateful for assistance family members are able to give and if he does have any matters which he feels he needs help with, he should not hesitate to ask. Similarly, with any more strenuous tasks he might have, he should seek assistance rather than take risks with his well-being. Throughout 2001 these Wood Oxen should remember that help and advice are available and should be called upon when needed. Generally, the Year of the Snake holds great promise for the Wood Ox and will give him the chance to develop and use his talents as well as bring him pleasure in many areas of his life.

The Year of the Snake holds considerable potential for the *Fire Ox*, although to get the best from it he would do well to consider just what he wants to accomplish over the next 12 months. This is particularly true for those Fire Oxen who have recently retired or who chose to do so in the Snake year. They may now be able to take up some of the ideas and projects they have had in mind for some time. By setting goals and using their time in a purposeful manner, all Fire Oxen will find this a fulfilling year. Accommodation matters will feature prominently on the agenda for many, with some choosing to move while others will spend time making improvements to their home and in particular altering the décor of certain rooms. For those who do move, the process will take up much of the year, both in finding suitable accommodation and completing the transaction. However, while this may prove trying at times, once installed in his new home the Fire Ox will delight in settling in and discovering the amenities and attractions of his new area. These Fire Oxen will view 2001 as a new chapter in their life, one they are determined to enjoy. However, whether they move or not, almost all Fire Oxen will decide to have a major sort out in their home, both of paperwork that has accumulated over the years and items that have outlived their usefulness. This process will bring the Fire Ox much satisfaction, particularly as it will help to make his home neater and more efficient to run. However, if the Fire Ox tackles any practical project which is in any way hazardous, it is essential he seeks guidance. This is just not a year in which he can compromise his personal safety. The Fire Ox's hobbies and interests will lead to some rewarding times, especially any that take him out of doors, allow him to meet fellow enthusiasts or draw on his creative talents. Also, if he is able to add to his interests over the year, he will find this a stimulating challenge. As always, he will take a keen interest in the activities of family members and will do much to help those dear to him. Those around him will set much store by what he says and does and, in return, the Fire Ox will be heartened by the love and esteem shown him. Encouraging family members to share some of his own activities will lead to some meaningful occasions as well as help preserve the spirit of closeness the Fire Ox so values. He will also enjoy his social life over the year, especially meeting and chatting with friends. In addition, by seeking out those who have similar interests to his own, perhaps through a local society or if he is able, the Internet, he will strike up some new friendships. Any Fire Ox who may have been feeling lonely or had some recent adversity to bear really should make an effort to lead a fuller social life in the Snake year. Admittedly, this may sometimes require effort, but, as the Fire Ox has so often found in life, positive and determined action *does* get results, and so it will be in 2001. Generally the Snake year is a positive and favourable one for the Fire Ox, but there is one potentially troublesome area. Any important correspondence, especially if it relates to accommodation or financial matters, should be dealt with promptly and if there are any aspects which the Fire Ox feels require clarification, he should obtain this rather than take risks or jump to conclusions. This warning apart, the Fire Ox will enjoy himself over the year and, by setting himself specific aims and using his time well, will be pleased with all he is able to accomplish.

This will be a significant year for the *Earth Ox* and one which will herald some interesting possibilities. These will be particularly welcome as many Earth Oxen will have been concerned about some of the more recent developments that have taken place and will feel that they are not making the most of themselves or their ideas. However, the times of frustration are over and the Earth Ox will now be able to move ahead. Almost as soon as the Snake year starts he will resolve to make this a more successful time. He knows that if he wants to achieve certain objectives, the onus is on him, and his determination will now win through. Early in the year the Earth Ox should decide on specific objectives and then work towards them. As Napoleon Bonaparte, himself an Ox, declared, 'Victory belongs to the persevering,' and this certainly holds true for the Earth Ox in 2001. As far as his work is concerned, significant progress is possible. He should not only remain alert for any openings and possibilities arising from his current position but should also look elsewhere. In this, he should bear in mind both his considerable experience and what it is that he now wants to do. By having clear ideas, the Earth Ox will be able to make considerable advances. The early months of the year and late summer will be auspicious for career matters. This will also be a favourable year for the Earth Ox to put forward any ideas he might have, especially any that are work and business related. He could find these developing in an interesting manner. Those Earth Oxen who are seeking work should also remain dedicated to their quest. They could be helped by looking at different aspects of their experience and considering ways in which this could be put to good use. Some enterprising thinking could widen the scope of positions available and reveal some exciting possibilities. The year will also bring an improvement in the Earth Ox's financial situation. While he will enjoy buying himself and loved ones some treats as well as adding to his home and wardrobe, he would do well to invest some of the money he does not immediately need in a saving scheme for his longer term future. This could become a useful asset in years to come. The Earth Ox's home life will also contain some memorable events, including a family celebration. As always, the Earth Ox will play a caring and supportive role and will watch over the progress of those around him with much interest. However, while his home life will contain moments of joy and pride, he should still pay close regard to the feelings and opinions of others in order to preserve domestic harmony. The Earth Ox does tend to be firm in his views and he cannot expect others always to fall in with his plans or accept his ideas without demur. Sometimes open discussion and a more accommodating attitude on his part would not go amiss and would help prevent differences from arising. Earth Oxen, do take note of this. Although the Earth Ox will have much to occupy him over the year he should still ensure he leaves ample time for his social life and recreational pursuits. These not only help him to relax but could also provide some very enjoyable occasions, especially when meeting up with friends both old and new. For those Earth Oxen who wish to add to their circle of friends, there will be excellent opportunities to do so, with one new friendship becoming particularly important over the next few years. Also, if the Earth Ox does not tend to get much regular exercise he would do well to consider starting an activity that would help him to get in better shape. However, before setting out on any new fitness campaign he should seek medical advice concerning the activities most appropriate for him. Overall, the Snake year holds considerable promise and good fortune for the Earth Ox, and by deciding upon his objectives for the year and then going after them, he can achieve some excellent results.

FAMOUS OXEN

Madeleine Albright, Martin Amis, Hans Christian Andersen, Johann Sebastian Bach, Warren Beatty, Tony Benn, Napoleon Bonaparte, Rory Bremner, Benjamin Britten, Frank Bruno, Albert Camus, Jim Carrey, Johnny Carson, Barbara Cartland, Charlie Chaplin, Melanie Chisholm (Sporty Spice), George Clooney, Martin Clunes, Jean Cocteau, Natalie Cole, Bill Cosby, Tom Courtenay, Tony Curtis, Donald Dewar, Diana, Princess of Wales, Marlene Dietrich, Walt Disney, Patrick Duffy, Harry Enfield, Jane Fonda, Gerald Ford, Edward Fox, Michael J. Fox, Peter Gabriel, Richard Gere, Maurice Gibb, Robin Gibb, William Hague, Handel, King Harald V of Norway, Robert Hardy, Nigel Havers, Adolf Hitler, Dustin Hoffman, Anthony Hopkins, Saddam Hussein, Billy Joel, Don Johnson, Lionel Jospin, King Juan Carlos of Spain, B. B. King, Mark Knopfler, Burt Lancaster, k. d. Lang, Jessica Lange, Jack Lemmon, Nicholas Lyndhurst, Mary Tyler Moore, Kate Moss, Mo Mowlam, Alison Moyet, Eddie Murphy, Paul Newman, Jack Nicholson, Leslie Nielsen, Billy Ocean, Gwyneth Paltrow, Oscar Peterson, Colin Powell, Robert Redford, Lionel Richie, Rubens, Greg Rusedski, Meg Ryan, Monica Seles, Jean Sibelius, Sissy Spacek, Bruce Springsteen, Rod Steiger, Meryl Streep, Lady Thatcher, Scott F. Turow, Dick van Dyke, Vincent van Gogh, Zoë Wanamaker, the Duke of Wellington, Barbara Windsor, Ernie Wise, W. B. Yeats.

8 FEBRUARY 1902 ∼ 28 JANUARY 1903   *Water Tiger*

26 JANUARY 1914 ∼ 13 FEBRUARY 1915   *Wood Tiger*

13 FEBRUARY 1926 ∼ 1 FEBRUARY 1927   *Fire Tiger*

31 JANUARY 1938 ∼ 18 FEBRUARY 1939   *Earth Tiger*

17 FEBRUARY 1950 ∼ 5 FEBRUARY 1951   *Metal Tiger*

5 FEBRUARY 1962 ∼ 24 JANUARY 1963   *Water Tiger*

23 JANUARY 1974 ∼ 10 FEBRUARY 1975   *Wood Tiger*

9 FEBRUARY 1986 ∼ 28 JANUARY 1987   *Fire Tiger*

28 JANUARY 1998 ∼ 15 FEBRUARY 1999   *Earth Tiger*

THE
TIGER

THE PERSONALITY OF THE TIGER

The true perfection of man lies not in what man has, but in what man is.

Oscar Wilde: a Tiger

The Tiger is born under the sign of courage. He is a charismatic figure and usually holds very firm views. He is strong-willed and determined, and sets about most of the things he does with tremendous energy and enthusiasm. He is very alert and quick-witted and his mind is forever active. He is a highly original thinker and is nearly always brimming with new ideas or full of enthusiasm for some new project or scheme.

The Tiger adores challenges and loves to get involved in anything which he thinks has an exciting future or which catches his imagination. He is prepared to take risks and does not like to be bound either by convention or the dictates of others. The Tiger likes to be free to act as he chooses and at least once during his life he will throw caution to the wind and go off and do the things he wants to do.

The Tiger does, however, have a somewhat restless nature. Even though he is often prepared to throw himself wholeheartedly into a project, his initial enthusiasm can soon wane if he sees something more appealing. He can also be rather impulsive and there will be occasions in his life when he acts in a manner which he later regrets. If the Tiger were to think things through or to persevere in his various activities, he would almost certainly enjoy a greater degree of success than he would otherwise obtain.

Fortunately, the Tiger is lucky in most of his enterprises, but should things not work out as he had hoped, he is liable to suffer from severe bouts of depression and it will often take him a long time to recover. His life often consists of a series of ups and downs.

The Tiger is, however, very adaptable. He has an adventurous spirit and rarely stays in the same place for long. In the early stages of his life he is likely to try his hand at several different jobs and he will also change his residence fairly frequently.

The Tiger is very honest and open in his dealings with others. He hates any sort of hypocrisy or falsehood. He is also well known for being blunt and forthright and has no hesitation in speaking his mind. He can be most rebellious at times, particularly against any form of petty authority, and while this can lead him into conflict with others, he is never one to shrink from an argument or avoid standing up for what he believes is right.

The Tiger is a natural leader and can invariably rise to the top of his chosen profession. He does not, however, care for anything too bureaucratic or detailed and he also does not like to obey orders. He can be stubborn and obstinate, and throughout his life he likes to retain a certain amount of independence in his actions and be responsible to no one but himself. He likes to consider that all his achievements are due to his own efforts and unless he cannot avoid it, he will rarely ask for support from others.

Ironically, despite his self-confidence and leadership qualities, the Tiger can be indecisive and will often delay making a major decision until the very last moment. He can also be sensitive to criticism.

Although the Tiger is capable of earning large sums of money, he is rather a spendthrift and does not always put his money to its best use. He can also be most generous and will often shower lavish gifts on friends and relations.

The Tiger cares very much for his reputation and the image that he tries to project. He carries himself with an air of dignity and authority and enjoys being the centre of attention. He is very adept at attracting publicity, both for himself and for the causes he supports.

The Tiger often marries young and he will find himself best suited to those born under the signs of the Pig, Dog, Horse and Goat. He can also get on well with the Rat, Rabbit and Rooster, but will find the Ox and Snake a bit too quiet and too serious for his liking, and he will also be highly irritated by the Monkey's rather mischievous and inquisitive ways. The Tiger will also find it difficult to get on with another Tiger or a Dragon – both partners will want to dominate the relationship and could find it difficult to compromise on even the smallest of matters.

The Tigress is lively, witty and a marvellous hostess at parties. She is usually most attractive and takes great care over her appearance. She can also be a very doting mother and while she believes in letting her children have their freedom, she makes an excellent teacher and will ensure that her children are brought up well and want for nothing. Like her male counterpart, she has numerous interests and likes to have sufficient independence and freedom to go off and do the things that she wants to do. She also has a most caring and generous nature.

The Tiger has many commendable qualities. He is honest, courageous and often a source of inspiration for others. Providing he can curb the wilder excesses of his restless nature, he is almost certain to lead a most fulfilling and satisfying life.

THE FIVE DIFFERENT TYPES OF TIGER

In addition to the 12 signs of the Chinese zodiac, there are five elements and these have a strengthening or moderating influence on the sign. The effects of the five elements on the Tiger are described below, together with the years in which the elements were exercising their influence. Therefore all Tigers born in 1950 are Metal Tigers, those born in 1962 are Water Tigers, and so on.

Metal Tiger: 1950
The Metal Tiger has an assertive and outgoing personality. He is very ambitious and, while his aims may change from time to time, he will work relentlessly until he has obtained what he wants. He can, however, be impatient for results and also become highly strung if things do not work out as he would like. He is distinctive in his appearance and is admired and respected by many.

Water Tiger: 1962
This Tiger has a wide variety of interests and is always eager to experiment with new ideas or go off and explore distant lands. He is versatile, shrewd and has a kindly

nature. He tends to remain calm in a crisis, although he can be annoyingly indecisive at times. He communicates well with others and through his many capabilities and persuasive nature he usually achieves what he wants in life. He is also highly imaginative and is often a gifted orator or writer.

Wood Tiger: 1914, 1974

The Wood Tiger has a very friendly and pleasant personality. He is less independent than some of the other types of Tiger and is more prepared to work with others to secure a desired objective. However, he does have a tendency to jump from one thing to another and can get easily distracted. He is usually very popular, has a large circle of friends and invariably leads a busy and enjoyable social life. He also has a good sense of humour.

Fire Tiger: 1926, 1986

The Fire Tiger sets about everything he does with great verve and enthusiasm. He loves action and is always ready to throw himself wholeheartedly into anything which catches his imagination. He has many leadership qualities and is capable of communicating his ideas and enthusiasm to others. He is very much an optimist and can be most generous. He has a likeable nature and can be a witty and persuasive speaker.

Earth Tiger: 1938, 1998

This Tiger is responsible and level-headed. He studies everything objectively and tries to be scrupulously fair in all his dealings. Unlike other Tigers, he is prepared to specialize in certain areas rather than get distracted by other matters, but he can become so involved in what he is doing that he does not always take into account the opinions of those around him. He has good business sense and is usually very successful in later life. He has a large circle of friends and pays great attention to both his appearance and his reputation.

PROSPECTS FOR THE TIGER IN 2001

The Chinese New Year starts on 24 January 2001. Until then, the old year, the Year of the Dragon, is still making its presence felt.

The Year of the Dragon (5 February 2000 to 23 January 2001) will have been a generally favourable one for the Tiger, with the remaining months holding much promise. However, to make the most of these positive trends, the Tiger does need to give thought to what he wishes to accomplish over the rest of the year and then set about his aims in his usual earnest way. As he will find, by working towards something specific he can make this a most constructive and rewarding time.

The prospects are particularly positive as far as work is concerned, with many Tigers being offered the chance to take on additional responsibilities or new positions. The Tiger should also promote any ideas he has, as these could sometimes create interesting opportunities. The Dragon year does very much favour enterprise and this is one of the reasons why the Tiger can make such progress at this time. He has the ideas, talents and skills, and should aim to make the most of them.

The Tiger does, though, need to exercise care when dealing with financial matters and should watch his level of spending. As the Dragon year draws to a close, he will find he has many outgoings and will need to make allowances for these.

The remaining months of the Dragon year will see much activity in the Tiger's personal life. He will be much in demand with his family and friends and can look forward to some enjoyable and sometimes spirited occasions in their company. From mid-November to early 2001 he will have the chance to go to a wide range of social gatherings and will not only have a good time but will also be able to add to his circle of acquaintances.

Overall the Dragon year will be a fine and progressive time for the Tiger and he really should make the most of the favourable aspects that prevail.

The Year of the Snake starts on 24 January and will be an interesting one for the Tiger. Although not all areas of his life may go as well as he may like, the year will still contain its pleasures and the Tiger will make some worthwhile progress. Unlike the more active Dragon year, the Snake year will give the Tiger a chance to consolidate and enjoy what he has achieved as well as contribute to his longer term growth.

In work many Tigers will be content to build on their current position, using their skills and experience to good effect and finding themselves well placed when promotion opportunities arise or new positions become available. With his keen approach, inventive mind and personable nature, the Tiger will have established a fine reputation for himself and this will continue to grow throughout the year. Also, what he learns and accomplishes in 2001 will often prove instrumental in the successes he will enjoy in following years.

For Tigers who are seeking work or a change from their present position, there will be some interesting openings to pursue. Admittedly, these may not be plentiful or always exactly what the Tiger was hoping for, but once he has secured a new position, he will quickly establish himself and sow the seeds for his further progress.

All Tigers, whether in work or seeking it, should also take advantage of any training opportunities that may be available and take steps to obtain any skill they feel it would be useful to learn. The Snake year very much favours self-development and anything that the Tiger can do to extend his abilities would be to his long-term benefit.

As far as financial matters are concerned, this will be a rather tricky year. Family expenses, accommodation and transport could all eat into the Tiger's finances and throughout 2001 it would be worth his while to watch his financial position and budget in advance whenever possible. This is a year which calls for careful financial management as well as a tight control over the purse strings. The Tiger should also be wary of taking undue risks or of committing his money to speculative ventures.

In 2001 money could come and go all too easily and, without care, problems could emerge. Also, if the Tiger is planning on making a large purchase, particularly any items of equipment or furnishings for his home, he should take his time rather than buying too much on impulse. This way he will not only be able to reflect longer on his requirements but could also save himself unnecessary outlay.

In addition, the Tiger needs to deal carefully with any important paperwork he receives over the year, especially any that is related to finance and tax. Although he may despair of all the details required, he does need to give proper attention to this otherwise he could find himself subject to even more correspondence and possibly additional expense. Also, though this will only apply to a few Tigers, should he become involved in any awkward or contentious matter, he would do well to get professional and possibly legal advice. Again, this is not a time to take risks over complex matters.

While the Tiger does need to be careful with his money, one of the more favourably aspected areas of the year is travel and he should aim to set some funds aside for this. Not only will a change of scene be beneficial, but many Tigers will get the chance to visit some interesting destinations, including one they have wanted to see for some time. Also, if the Tiger receives invitations to visit relations or friends living some distance away, he should accept, as again these could lead to an enjoyable time away.

The Tiger will also get much satisfaction from his personal interests, especially those that draw on his creative talents. If there is an interest that he wishes to develop or take up, this would be a good time to do so, as the Snake year is supportive of such enterprises.

As far as his personal life is concerned, this will be an active and often rewarding time for the Tiger, but it could also contain some potentially awkward elements. With care, the Tiger can do much to minimize or prevent difficulties from arising, but generally 2001 should be regarded as a year for tact and diplomacy. Over the year issues in his domestic life could give rise to disagreement and at such times the Tiger should aim to deal with the matter as quickly and amicably as he can. If not, difficulties could emerge which could take some time to heal or resolve. Sometimes these could arise because the Tiger has not fully consulted others or may have jumped to conclusions about how others feel. Tiredness and pressure, too, can lead to tetchiness and this is something the Tiger should watch.

However, while there is a need for care in his personal life, it can still bring him considerable pleasure. By encouraging joint pursuits and involving everyone more readily in activities, Tiger will find that many meaningful occasions can result. Travel and visits to places of interest will also go well and household and outdoor projects (particularly garden alterations) could, if tackled together, help maintain the strong bonds the Tiger so values.

The Tiger can also look forward to an active social life, enjoying the company of friends and attending a wide range of social occasions. The spring and last quarter of the year will be particularly active. There will also be opportunities to add to his social circle. However, while for the most part his personal and social life will go well, the Tiger should not let himself become involved in any situation which he may later come to regret. Tigers, do take note. For the unattached, the prospects are good for romance, although it would be best to let any new friendship form steadily, rather than rushing into a too hasty commitment.

Although the Snake year may contain pitfalls for the Tiger, with care it is certainly possible for him to avoid them and lead a pleasant and fulfilling life. In addition to the satisfaction new and existing interests will bring, developments in his working life will stand him in good stead for the future. Travel is splendidly aspected and provided he remains mindful of the views and feelings of others, the Tiger's personal life will go well, although, as with so much in 2001, care is needed.

As far as the different types of Tiger are concerned, this will be a tricky year for the *Metal Tiger*. With his determined and enterprising nature, he does like to realize his objectives quickly and without too much opposition, and in 2001 this will not always be possible. During the year the Metal Tiger will have to accept that his activities cannot always be hurried and that sometimes more caution and planning would be wise. There will be frustrating times for him, but despite this the year will still contain its rewards. As far as the Metal Tiger's work is concerned, care will be needed. He should aim to build on his recent progress and if he has taken on new duties or is offered any during the year, he should take time to familiarize himself with these and rise to the challenges given. In 2001 he really would do best to build on what he has already attained and concentrate on his proven strengths. He has, after all, considerable experience behind him and he should put this to effective use rather than venturing into less familiar areas. Similarly, those Metal Tigers seeking work should aim for positions in which they can draw on their skills and expertise. Their determination and enterprise will be recognized and will enable many to gain what could prove to be an interesting position. Also, all Metal Tigers should take advantage of any training opportunities they may be offered or spend some of their own time adding to skills. Many could benefit from extending their computer knowledge or learning a skill that would help in the performance of their duties. This will not only be personally satisfying but will also help the Metal Tiger's prospects when opportunities do fall available. The Metal Tiger also needs to exercise care in financial matters. During the year he will face some large expenses, often involving family activities, transport and home furnishings and equipment. In view of this, he would find it helpful to budget in advance for expenses as well as regularly monitor his outgoings. All too easily these could exceed his expectations and without care he could find himself dipping into his savings or using money he had set aside for other purposes. However, while the Metal Tiger will need to manage his money with care, he should still take advantage of any opportunity he gets to travel and take a well-deserved break. His journeys, particularly to destinations he has been wanting to visit for some time, will lead to some highly interesting and enjoyable occasions. This is also a favourable year for the Metal Tiger to develop his hobbies and if he is able to contact fellow enthusiasts, either through a club, society or even a group over the Internet, he will add to his knowledge and make useful contacts. The Metal Tiger should also make sure he pays attention to his well-being over the year, eating a balanced diet and exercising regularly. If he lets himself get too out of condition, he could find his energy levels are not as high as he would like and he could become prone to minor ailments. As far as his domestic life is concerned, some key events could take place, including the possibility of a close relation moving out for the purposes of education or through marriage. As always, the Metal Tiger will play an active role in helping those around him as well as arranging some of the events that take place. This will be much appreciated, but the Metal Tiger must avoid letting his desire to get things done prevent him from fully consulting others. Failure to do so could result in some tensions. Also, some family plans and household projects may not always move as swiftly as the Metal Tiger would like and some parts of the year will call for patience, which is not always his strong point. However, while his domestic life will be busy and sometimes demanding, it will still be a source of much happiness. The Metal Tiger will also enjoy meeting up with friends and the often varied social occasions that he attends over the year. Although his actual rate of progress in 2001 may not always meet his high expectations, what he accomplishes and learns will bring him much satisfaction and have a positive bearing on the next few years.

Enterprising, inquisitive and determined, the *Water Tiger* likes to live life to the full. While 2001 may not be the best or easiest of years for him, he can still gain much. Of all the Tigers, the Water Tiger has the most patience. He is prepared to work steadily towards what he wants rather than expect immediate results. Indeed, rather than expecting rapid advances during the Snake year, most Water Tigers will concentrate on building on their recent achievements, adding to their skills and giving thought to how they would like their career to develop. Some of the ideas the Water Tiger has now could prove particularly important and set him some interesting goals for the next few years. Those Water Tigers seeking work will see some interesting developments, with many securing a position which, although slightly different from what they may have been aiming for, will nevertheless hold considerable potential. For many, the Snake year will set in motion developments that will prove helpful in the years ahead. The Water Tiger will enjoy a modest improvement in his income over the year, although, as with all Tigers, he must keep a watchful eye over his outgoings. Also, if he makes any major purchase, particularly equipment for his accommodation, he should make sure he checks the terms of any obligations he might be placed under as well as keeps the relevant paperwork safe. If not, problems and misunderstandings could result. A more favourably aspected area is travel and all Water Tigers should aim to go away at some time over the year. This will not only do the Water Tiger a considerable amount of good but he could get the chance to visit some impressive destinations. He will also obtain much pleasure from his personal interests, especially those that take him out of doors or allow him to use his skills in both practical and creative ways. With the Snake year favouring self-development, it is an ideal time to extend these interests in some way and perhaps set himself some new and stimulating challenges. As far as his personal life is concerned, the Water Tiger will have much to occupy his time. His home life, in particular, will be busy, and he will do much to assist those around him, in particular helping a close relation who may have some difficulty to overcome. As always, the Water Tiger's support will be greatly valued. There will, though, be occasions when he will feel under pressure and this, combined with his other responsibilities, may leave him tired and on edge. At such times, the Water Tiger should prioritize what needs to be done and share out some of the tasks rather than feel obliged to do so much single-handed. This may mean some projects have to be postponed, but better this than driving himself too hard and running the risk of strained relations as a result. Water Tigers, do take careful note of this – organize domestic tasks and be realistic in the number of commitments you take on. However, while the Water Tiger's home life will be busy, it will still contain many agreeable moments, including time spent on joint interests, travel and following the successes of loved ones. This will also be quite an active year socially, with the Water Tiger attending a wide range of functions and particularly enjoying meeting friends. There will also be opportunities for him to add to his social circle and for the unattached or lonely Water Tiger, the prospects of a major new friendship await, particularly in the first quarter of 2001. Although the Snake year may bring its challenges, it can still be a satisfying time for the Water Tiger. This is very much a year in which he will be preparing himself for the next major upturn in his life, one which he will aim to make rich, rewarding *and* successful.

The *Wood Tiger* will have seen many changes in his life over the last few years. Some of these will have been positive, especially those related to personal matters, but there will have been other areas in which the Wood Tiger will have felt that he could have done better. Some of his more negative feelings will be corrected in 2001, with the year bringing some interesting developments. However, as the Snake year starts, the Wood Tiger would do well to reflect on recent events and his present position and, in the light of this, decide on his chief objectives. These can concern almost any area of the Wood Tiger's life, from personal goals and household matters to taking up new interests and developing his career, but by deciding on what he wants to do next, he will find himself setting about his activities in a much more purposeful way. He will also gain a great deal by talking his ideas over with his loved ones and with those who can offer informed advice. Not only will this bring him welcome support but newer and stronger ideas could well result from more open discussion. Indeed, one of the lasting legacies of the Snake year is that the Wood Tiger will be doing much to prepare the way for his progress over the next few years. In his personal life, he will particularly enjoy the companionship of those around him, pursuing mutual interests as well as encouraging younger relations. He will also enjoy any holidays or breaks he is able to take as well as some more local outings, especially those arranged on the spur of the moment and as something of a surprise. The Wood Tiger will also devote some considerable time to adding to home comforts, including buying new equipment and furnishings as well as changing the décor of certain rooms. However, where practical projects are concerned, he should be wary of starting too many all at once. He will find that the best results will come from concentrating on specific tasks and getting these finished before moving on to the next. Also, he would find it helpful to involve those around him in what he does. This way there can be a general pooling of talents and ideas and this will help to make the finished result more meaningful for all concerned. The Wood Tiger will also get much satisfaction from his social life during the year. Those who are unattached could find themselves swept off their feet by an exciting romance which quite likely stems from a chance encounter early in the year. However, throughout 2001, all Wood Tigers do need to remain their honourable selves in their dealings towards others and to avoid acting in any way that could lead to difficulties. This is a year to enjoy but not to 'play with fire'. It will also be an interesting year as far as the Wood Tiger's work is concerned. He will be able to consolidate his recent progress as well as make impressive use of his skills and strengths. Over the year all Wood Tigers should give some thought to how they would like to see their work developing in the longer term. That way they will become more alert to the type of opportunities they need to follow up and the skills they might need to improve, as well as feel more stimulated by the challenge they have set themselves. The Wood Tiger would also be helped by speaking to those engaged in the type of position he would like and by obtaining advice from professional bodies. As far as his work is concerned, what he sets in motion now will have some beneficial long-term results, with some of his efforts bearing fruit in the closing stages of the Snake year. Those Wood Tigers currently seeking work should remain persistent in their quest. Once they are given a chance, they will quickly impress and so place themselves in line for further progress, particularly in the excellently aspected Year of the Horse which follows. The Wood Tiger will fare reasonably well in financial matters over the year, but with so many expenses to meet he does need to budget carefully and make allowance for any new financial obligations. Overall, 2001 will bring the Wood Tiger considerable satisfaction and by planning and using his time well, he will be pleased with what he accomplishes and will enjoy his personal life as well as do much to prepare the way for the considerable success he will enjoy in the next few years.

This will be a reasonable year for the *Fire Tiger* with certain areas of his life bringing him considerable pleasure. Travel is especially well aspected and the Fire Tiger should take advantage of any travel opportunities as well as accept invitations to visit family and friends living some distance away. Also, if there is some destination he has been longing to visit or revisit, he should see whether this can be arranged. By discussing his ideas with others he could be helped to realize his plans in an unexpected way. For the many Fire Tigers in education, this will be a significant year, with some important project work and exams as well as decisions to take about which subjects to specialize in. Although there may be times when the young Fire Tiger may feel daunted by all that is being expected of him, he can take heart. By organizing his studying time, rising to the challenges set him and giving of his best, he can obtain some good results over the year and build a solid foundation from which to progress. Also, some of the subject and course work that he carries out now will prove useful to him later, sometimes even influencing his choice of future vocation. If over the year he should ever find himself struggling with certain subjects, he should not hesitate to seek further guidance. He will find that those around him can do much to assist. All Fire Tigers will also get great pleasure from their hobbies and interests over the year. Outdoor activities are especially well aspected and for those who follow sport or enjoy exploring the countryside or places of interest, the year will hold many happy moments. In addition, some fresh interest will appeal over the year and the Fire Tiger, ever inquisitive, could find himself thoroughly caught up in a new hobby. Indeed, the Fire Tiger is rarely at a loss for interesting things to do. The main problem in 2001 could be fitting them all in (especially if he has academic work as well) and parts of the year will call for a certain self-discipline and sensible management of his time. Added to this, his social life will be fairly full, with many agreeable times spent with friends. Any Fire Tiger who may feel lonely or would like more companionship would really do well to consider joining a local club or society, or, for the younger Fire Tiger, youth group. There he will soon get to meet others and build some good friendships. As far as financial matters are concerned, the Fire Tiger will have many outgoings and it would be in his interests to keep a watchful eye over spending levels and avoid succumbing to too many spur-of-the-moment indulgences. At times, a certain restraint would not come amiss. The Fire Tiger will, though, be grateful for the support he is given by family members over the year and if ever he feels under pressure or has any problems, he should not hesitate to seek advice. By being forthcoming, he will find that those around him can do much to assist as well as allay some of his concerns. Also, if at any time over the year he experiences any differences of opinion with others, again he should talk these over rather than remaining inflexible. Admittedly the Fire Tiger may possess strong feelings about certain issues, but for the sake of domestic harmony, a certain willingness to compromise would certainly be in the interests of all concerned. Generally, the Fire Tiger will find the Snake year a reasonably satisfying one. However, to make the most of it, he does need to organize his activities well, make good use of his time and remember that should problems arise there are many who are willing to help and advise him.

The *Earth Tiger* can fare reasonably well in the Snake year, particularly as he will now have the chance to develop some ideas that he has been nurturing for some time. By taking positive steps to realize what he has in mind, the Earth Tiger can achieve some satisfying results. Accommodation matters will figure prominently over the year, with some Earth Tigers deciding to move, while others will carry out improvements to certain rooms or add new features to their garden. Practical home projects will take up a great deal of time, but with the help and support of others, the Earth Tiger will be delighted with the outcome. In all he does, however, he should fully involve others. He will find that practical activities in particular will not only benefit from the pooling of skills and ideas but will also lead to some meaningful occasions. The Earth Tiger will also get much pleasure from his own interests over the year and should not only set a regular time aside for these but also extend them, either by developing an existing hobby or taking up a new one. Some Earth Tigers may be tempted to enrol on a course or undertake some personal study. In general, whatever the Earth Tiger can do to improve his skills and knowledge will bring him much satisfaction. Another favourably aspected area is travel and the Earth Tiger should try to ensure that he goes away for a holiday or break over the year as well as follow up any other travel opportunities he may be offered. In 2001 he can look forward to visiting some interesting and in some cases unusual destinations, with his adventurous nature often being amply satisfied. As far as financial matters are concerned, this will be a reasonable year, although domestic and travel expenses could prove costly. To help cope, the Earth Tiger should aim to set regular funds aside for forthcoming expenses as well as watch his general level of spending. With good financial planning any additional expenses can be comfortably dealt with, but overall this is a year for careful financial management. The Earth Tiger always sets great store by his home life and this can provide him with much contentment during the year. In addition to joint projects and interests, he will follow the activities of loved ones with fond interest. Domestically, there will be many pleasurable times, although the year will not be free of anxieties. In particular, a relative will face some challenging decisions and the Earth Tiger will not only feel concern but also be keen that any action or decision that has to be taken is the right one. At such times, he would be helped by discussing his worries with others rather than keeping them to himself and if he feels it appropriate, he should seek the views of those qualified to advise. Over the year he will find much truth in the saying 'a worry shared is a worry halved'. However, although as with all years, problems will arise, these will generally not mar the many happy and meaningful domestic occasions that the Earth Tiger will enjoy. He will also take much satisfaction from his social life, with the spring being an especially active time. For those Earth Tigers who would like more company, positive effort on their part, such as joining group activities or perhaps a society, can certainly help bring this about and lead to some important new friendships. Generally, although the Snake year may not be without its problems, it can still be fulfilling and constructive, allowing the Earth Tiger to further his interests as well as carry out many satisfying pursuits, with travel and home improvements being especially rewarding.

FAMOUS TIGERS

Kofi Annan, Sir David Attenborough, Queen Beatrix of the Netherlands, Victoria Beckham (Posh Spice), Beethoven, Tony Bennett, Tom Berenger, Chuck Berry, Jon Bon Jovi, Richard Branson, Emily Brontë, Garth Brooks, Mel Brooks, Isambard Kingdom Brunel, Agatha Christie, Charlotte Church, Phil Collins, Robbie Coltrane, Sheryl Crow, Tom Cruise, Charles de Gaulle, Leonardo DiCaprio, Emily Dickinson, David Dimbleby, Isadora Duncan, Dwight Eisenhower, Queen Elizabeth II, Enya, Roberta Flack, E. M. Forster, Frederick Forsyth, Jodie Foster, Connie Francis, Crystal Gayle, Elliott Gould, Buddy Greco, Sir Alec Guinness, Ruud Gullit, Prince Naseem Hamed, Ed

Harris, Tim Henman, William Hurt, Derek Jacobi, Jewel, Stan Laurel, Karl Marx, Marilyn Monroe, Demi Moore, Eric Morecambe, Alanis Morissette, Neil Morrissey, Jeremy Paxman, Marco Polo, Beatrix Potter, John Prescott, Renoir, Kenny Rogers, the Princess Royal, Dame Joan Sutherland, Dylan Thomas, Liv Ullman, Jon Voight, Julie Walters, Oscar Wilde, Robbie Williams, Tennessee Williams, Terry Wogan, Stevie Wonder.

29 JANUARY 1903 ~ 15 FEBRUARY 1904   *Water Rabbit*

14 FEBRUARY 1915 ~ 2 FEBRUARY 1916   *Wood Rabbit*

2 FEBRUARY 1927 ~ 22 JANUARY 1928   *Fire Rabbit*

19 FEBRUARY 1939 ~ 7 FEBRUARY 1940   *Earth Rabbit*

6 FEBRUARY 1951 ~ 26 JANUARY 1952   *Metal Rabbit*

25 JANUARY 1963 ~ 12 FEBRUARY 1964   *Water Rabbit*

11 FEBRUARY 1975 ~ 30 JANUARY 1976   *Wood Rabbit*

29 JANUARY 1987 ~ 16 FEBRUARY 1988   *Fire Rabbit*

16 FEBRUARY 1999 ~ 4 FEBRUARY 2000   *Earth Rabbit*

THE
RABBIT

THE PERSONALITY OF THE RABBIT

I know the price of success: dedication, hard work, and
an unremitting devotion to the things you want to see
happen.

Frank Lloyd Wright: a Rabbit

The Rabbit is born under the signs of virtue and prudence.
He is intelligent, well-mannered and prefers a quiet and
peaceful existence. He dislikes any sort of unpleasantness
and will try to steer clear of arguments and disputes. He is
very much a pacifist and tends to have a calming influence
on those around him.

He has wide interests and usually has a good appreciation of the arts and the finer things in life. He also knows
how to enjoy himself and will often gravitate to the best
restaurants and night spots in town.

The Rabbit is a witty and intelligent speaker and loves
being involved in a good discussion. His views and advice
are often sought by others and he can be relied upon to be
discreet and diplomatic. He will rarely raise his voice in
anger and will even turn a blind eye to matters which
displease him just to preserve the peace. The Rabbit likes to
remain on good terms with everyone, but he can be rather
sensitive and takes any form of criticism very badly. He
will also be the first to get out of the way if he sees any
form of trouble brewing.

The Rabbit is a quiet and efficient worker and has an
extremely good memory. He is very astute in business and
financial matters, but his degree of success often depends

on the conditions that prevail. He hates being in a situation which is fraught with tension or where he has to make sudden decisions. Wherever possible he will plan his various activities with the utmost care and a good deal of caution. He does not like to take risks and does not take kindly to changes. Basically, he seeks a secure, calm and stable environment, and when conditions are right he is more than happy to leave things as they are.

The Rabbit is conscientious in most of the things he does and because of his methodical and ever-watchful nature can often do well in his chosen profession. He makes a good diplomat, lawyer, shopkeeper, administrator or priest and he excels in any job where he can use his superb skills as a communicator. He tends to be loyal to his employers and is respected for his integrity and honesty, but if he ever finds himself in a position of great power he can become rather intransigent and authoritarian.

The Rabbit attaches great importance to his home and will often spend much time and money maintaining and furnishing it and fitting it with all the latest comforts – the Rabbit is very much a creature of comfort! He is also something of a collector and there are many Rabbits who derive much pleasure from collecting antiques, stamps, coins, *objets d'art* or anything else which catches their eye or particularly interests them.

The female Rabbit has a friendly, caring and considerate nature, and will do all in her power to give her home a happy and loving atmosphere. She is also very sociable and enjoys holding parties and entertaining. She has a great ability to make the maximum use of her time and although she involves herself in numerous activities, she always manages to find time to sit back and enjoy a good read or a chat. She has a great sense of humour, is very artistic and is often a talented gardener.

The Rabbit takes considerable care over his appearance and is usually smart and very well turned out. He also attaches great importance to his relations with others and matters of the heart are particularly important to him. He will rarely be short of admirers and will often have several serious romances before he settles down. The Rabbit is not the most faithful of signs, but he will find that he is especially well suited to those born under the signs of the Goat, Snake, Pig and Ox. Due to his sociable and easy-going manner he can also get on well with the Tiger, Dragon, Horse, Monkey, Dog and another Rabbit, but will feel ill at ease with the Rat and Rooster as both these signs tend to speak their mind and be critical in their comments, and the Rabbit just loathes any form of criticism or unpleasantness.

The Rabbit is usually lucky in life and often has the happy knack of being in the right place at the right time. He is talented and quick-witted, but he does sometimes put pleasure before work and wherever possible will tend to opt for the easy life. He can at times be a little reserved and suspicious of the motives of others, but generally will lead a long and contented life and one which – as far as possible – will be free of strife and discord.

THE FIVE DIFFERENT TYPES
OF RABBIT

In addition to the 12 signs of the Chinese zodiac, there are five elements and these have a strengthening or moderating influence on the sign. The effects of the five elements on the Rabbit are described below, together with the years in which the elements were exercising their influence. Therefore all Rabbits born in 1951 are Metal Rabbits, those born in 1903 and 1963 are Water Rabbits, and so on.

Metal Rabbit: 1951

This Rabbit is capable, ambitious and has very definite views on what he wants to achieve in life. He can occasionally appear reserved and aloof, but this is mainly because he likes to keep his thoughts to himself. He has a very quick and alert mind and is particularly shrewd in business matters. He can also be very cunning in his actions. The Metal Rabbit has a good appreciation of the arts and likes to mix in the best circles. He usually has a small but very loyal group of friends.

Water Rabbit: 1903, 1963

The Water Rabbit is popular, intuitive and keenly aware of the feelings of those around him. He can, however, be rather sensitive and tends to take things too much to heart. He is very precise and thorough in everything he does and has an exceedingly good memory. He tends to be quiet and at times rather withdrawn, but he expresses his ideas well and is highly regarded by his family, friends and colleagues.

Wood Rabbit: 1915, 1975

The Wood Rabbit is likeable, easy-going and very adaptable. He prefers to work in groups rather than on his own and likes to have the support and encouragement of others. He can, however, be rather reticent in expressing his views and it would be in his own interests to become a little more open and let others know how he feels on certain matters. He usually has many friends, enjoys an active social life and is noted for his generosity.

Fire Rabbit: 1927, 1987

The Fire Rabbit has a friendly, outgoing personality. He likes socializing and being on good terms with everyone. He is discreet and diplomatic and has a very good understanding of human nature. He is also strong-willed and provided he has the necessary backing and support he can go far in life. He does not, however, suffer adversity well and can become moody and depressed when things are not working out as he would like. He has a particularly good manner with children, is very intuitive and there are some Fire Rabbits who are even noted for their psychic ability.

Earth Rabbit: 1939, 1999

The Earth Rabbit is a quiet individual, but he is nevertheless very shrewd and astute. He is realistic in his aims and is prepared to work long and hard in order to achieve his objectives. He has good business sense and is invariably lucky in financial matters. He also has a most persuasive manner and usually experiences little difficulty in getting others to fall in with his plans. He is held in very high esteem by his friends and colleagues and his views are often sought and highly valued.

PROSPECTS FOR THE RABBIT IN 2001

The Chinese New Year starts on 24 January 2001. Until then, the old year, the Year of the Dragon, is still making its presence felt.

The Year of the Dragon (5 February 2000 to 23 January 2001) will not have been a particularly easy one for the Rabbit and in what remains of it he will need to proceed with care. Dragon years are often characterized by activity and change and the Rabbit, who so likes to be in control of events and prefers a settled existence, will have been worried by some of the changes that have taken place. However, the Rabbit can take heart. The Year of the Snake will be a far better one for him and during it he will come to benefit from some of what has occurred recently. As the Rabbit himself acknowledges, change is a necessary part of progress and the upheavals of the Dragon year will be responsible for laying the foundations for some exciting new opportunities in the year ahead.

In what remains of the Dragon year, however, the Rabbit will need to remain vigilant as well as show some flexibility in the face of change. In his work many developments are possible. By making the most of the situations that arise and being adaptable in outlook, the Rabbit can place himself in an excellent position to make headway in the near future. Similarly, some of those Rabbits seeking work could find a position they obtain, although in some cases different from what they were seeking, will prove to be a useful stepping-stone to something better in 2001.

The Rabbit usually handles his finances with care, but throughout the Dragon year he should avoid committing himself to risky undertakings. He could, though, be particularly fortunate in making some useful acquisitions for his home, especially items of an aesthetic nature, in the closing months of 2000.

The Rabbit will also be grateful for the support he receives from both family and friends at this time and should be forthcoming about any concerns he has as well as ask for assistance at busy and demanding moments. As the Dragon year draws to a close he can look forward to a general easing of some of the pressures the year has brought as well as an improvement in the rapport he enjoys with those around him. December 2000, in particular, will produce some meaningful domestic and social occasions which will do much to raise the Rabbit's spirits as the new Chinese year approaches.

The Year of the Snake starts on 24 January and will be a much improved one for the Rabbit. He will feel more at ease with the general trends that prevail and this in turn will inspire him to new heights.

One aspect of the Snake year the Rabbit will especially

appreciate is the chance for him to add to his knowledge and further his abilities. The Snake year is very much one which favours self-development and as it starts the Rabbit would do well to consider what skills he would like to obtain, what interests he is keen to follow up and in what other ways he can further himself. By taking positive steps, he will not only gain much personally but will also help enhance his work prospects. Similarly, whether he is currently in work or seeking work, he should take full advantage of any training opportunities he may be offered. Again, what he learns can be to his advantage and in some cases will open up some exciting new possibilities for him.

Work-wise, many Rabbits will have seen some considerable changes over the last 12 months and will sometimes have felt they have not been making the progress of which they are capable. However, conditions will now become more settled and recent changes will bring forth interesting opportunities, which many Rabbits will be well placed to benefit from. Also, the Rabbit will feel more motivated and inspired than of late and this again will add to his desire to improve on his situation. Once he is determined and has an aim in sight, the Rabbit is indeed capable of making great strides. The periods from January 2001 to mid-March and from September to November are particularly favoured for work matters and will offer some interesting and often exciting opportunities.

Similarly, for those Rabbits seeking work or keen to move from their present position, several excellent openings will emerge over the year, some in a curious and rather fortuitous way. Admittedly, it may take several attempts for the Rabbit to secure the type of position he desires, but with persistence and the favourable aspects on his side, some interesting offers will be made and there will be chances for the Rabbit to show his true worth and capabilities. Once he is given his chance, further progress will beckon later in the year.

Another favourably aspected area is the Rabbit's own personal interests. Again, with the year so favouring self-development, he should aim to extend these, either by learning more about an existing interest or taking up a new one. Over the year, his interests can provide him with great pleasure and he should make sure he sets sufficient time aside for them. Also, any Rabbit who is involved in the creative arts should make every effort to promote any work that he does. He could be considerably heartened by the response he receives and some Rabbits will even find that an interesting opportunity results from something that they produce or show.

As far as financial matters are concerned this will be a positive year for the Rabbit. Many Rabbits will enjoy a noticeable increase in income as well as receive an additional sum of money, perhaps as a gift or as the fruition of an investment or policy. In addition, with some enterprising thinking, some Rabbits might even be able to put one of their interests or skills to profitable use. However, while the Rabbit will welcome this upturn, he could still be faced with some large expenses over the year. When these are known about in advance, he should aim to set funds aside for them rather than having to bear the brunt all at once. In addition, he could find that repair bills, replacing equipment and certain family expenses will cause him to dip into his reserves. With care, problems can be averted –

and, indeed, the Rabbit's financial good sense will help – but throughout 2001, it would be very much in his interests to watch his financial situation and, if he does not already do so, keep a set of household and personal accounts.

The Rabbit's domestic life will be full and active over the year. As always, he will take a fond and caring interest in those around him and others will look to him for guidance and set great store by his judgement. Sometimes matters could arise which could be tricky or embarrassing, but here again the Rabbit's discreet and understanding manner will be valued. However, while he will do so much to assist others, he should not feel that he has to bear the brunt of family matters single-handed. Wherever possible he should encourage open discussion about general family concerns as well as seek advice himself about any matters which may be troubling him. However, while there may be testing moments in family life, there will also be a great deal that will bring the Rabbit happiness. This not only includes his own personal successes and achievements but also those enjoyed by his loved ones. Some of these will be particularly meaningful as they will stem, in part, from advice, encouragement and assistance the Rabbit himself has given. Any Rabbit with young family members in education will find that any support and instruction he is able to offer will be of considerable benefit, with his attentive and yet understanding manner being further appreciated.

The Rabbit's social life will also be busy over the year with a wide range of functions to attend and plenty of chances to meet up with friends as well as extend his social circle. For those who are unattached, there will certainly be opportunities to make new friends and, where affairs of the heart are concerned, significant romances can form as the year unfolds.

However, while the Rabbit's social life can bring him much pleasure, he should be wary of any rumours that he hears. If he is not careful, he could fall victim to someone's mischief and cause himself needless worry. Rabbits, be warned and be circumspect when faced with rumours or gossip.

An area which is favourably aspected over the year, however, is travel and the Rabbit should take advantage of any opportunities that arise as well as try to ensure he has a holiday or break at some time over the year. He will not only benefit from this but could also be particularly taken with some of the destinations he visits.

Generally, this will be an active and successful year for the Rabbit with gains in many areas of his life. By furthering his skills and interests, he can make this a personally satisfying year as well as help to ensure his future progress. This really is a year which holds much promise.

As far as the different types of Rabbit are concerned, this will be a constructive year for the *Metal Rabbit*. As this marks his fiftieth year, he will determine to make something of it and his resolve and ideas will lead to some interesting developments. Indeed, the Metal Rabbit has always been a doer and when there is something he wants, he strives to achieve it. So it will be in 2001. One of the most active areas of the year will concern the Metal Rabbit's work and here good progress is indicated. Over the year many Metal Rabbits will find themselves well placed for promotion, greater responsibilities or a different position, one which will bring fresh challenges and be a real incentive for the Metal Rabbit to make more of himself and his abilities. He will often relish the tasks set him and feel more inspired than for a long time. He will also value the greater freedom the year will bring for him to act on his own initiative and try out some of his ideas. Again, these will produce favourable results. In addition, the Metal Rabbit will benefit from the supportive attitude of those around him and while he may sometimes prefer to keep his thoughts and plans to a select few, he should also seek the opinions of those able to give informed advice. There are many who think highly of the Metal Rabbit and will be glad (and honoured) to help and advise him, should he ask. This also applies to those Metal Rabbits seeking work. Again, if they have contacts that can put in a good word for them or provide advice or openings, they should ask for their assistance. By making the most of the contacts and experience they have as well as the chances the year will bring, these Metal Rabbits really can make excellent progress over the year and will often find that one opportunity can quickly lead to another, such are the favourable aspects that prevail. The Metal Rabbit will also enjoy a noticeable improvement in his income over the year, although he could find much of the increase taken up by additional household and family expenses, and, for a few, by moving. However, the Metal Rabbit will be considerably helped by his generally careful way with money and, by keeping a close watch on his situation, he can do much to avoid problems from occurring. With travel well aspected, he should certainly aim to set some money aside for a break or holiday. He will not only enjoy the destinations he will visit but also the rest and change of scene will do him much good. In addition, for any Metal Rabbit who is a keen collector or is thinking of starting some sort of collection, perhaps as a new hobby, it could be worth his while to keep his eye open for unusual items. One bought over the year could bring particular pleasure as well as possibly grow in worth. As far as the Metal Rabbit's family life is concerned, this will be a busy year with many calls upon his time. As usual he will take a fond interest in the activities of those dear to him and will offer much in the way of practical support and advice. There will also be some family news or an event in the summer which will much please him. However, while his domestic life will go well, some awkward matters could still arise and require care and discretion to resolve. Again, the Metal Rabbit's ability to relate so effectively to others will do much to help, but the main thing is, he should not let differences go unresolved lest they start to cast a shadow over this fine year. The Metal Rabbit will greatly value his social life and will have the chance of attending many different social occasions as well as meeting up with some friends or relations he has not seen for some time. For the unattached Metal Rabbit and any who may be hoping to extend their social circle, the aspects are especially favourable, with at least one new friendship becoming, in time, truly significant. Overall this will be a favourable year for the Metal Rabbit and by taking advantage of the opportunities that the year will bring as well as furthering his plans and ideas, he will have every reason to be pleased with his often considerable accomplishments.

This will be an interesting year for the *Water Rabbit* with pleasing developments in many areas of his life. However, as the Snake year starts, there will be many Water Rabbits who are feeling dispirited as far as their work situation is concerned. This could be because they feel they could be making better use of their skills or consider themselves in a rut. As a result these Water Rabbits, together with those currently seeking work, will resolve to make something of the year and redouble their efforts to move on and make greater headway. Their determination and enthusiasm will enable almost all to progress and to obtain a new and more challenging position. In their quest they should leave no stone unturned, not only pursuing vacancies that may be of interest, but also seeking out those who may know of openings or be able to offer informed advice. Sometimes the Water Rabbit will gain a position through a personal recommendation or a contact he has successfully built up. However, in work matters, good fortune really will favour the determined and it rests with the Water Rabbit to make the most of the favourable aspects that prevail. The early months of the Snake year will be particularly positive for work matters, with chances of further openings occurring in the closing months of the year, especially around October and November. This would also be a good year for the Water Rabbit to extend his skills and he should take advantage of any training opportunities that may be offered. He will not only find this personally satisfying but it could also count for a great deal when he seeks promotion or further advance in his work. The Water Rabbit will also enjoy an upturn in financial matters, although he will find certain parts of the year

expensive. The expense could arise from family events –
for some, a wedding in the family – or transport, travel or
the purchase of new equipment for the home. Fortunately
the Water Rabbit is blessed with good financial sense and
by managing his financial situation carefully, he can do
much to avoid problems. Despite the sometimes large
expenses, almost all Water Rabbits will end the year in a
better financial position. As far as personal matters are
concerned, this will also be an eventful year for the Water
Rabbit. In addition to the possibility of a wedding in the
family, there could also be another cause for celebration,
including the academic and career success of younger
family members, as well as the Water Rabbit's own
progress. However, while there will be much that will bring
the Water Rabbit pride, there could also be a few problems
for him to face. Having such a caring nature, he is sensitive
to a lot of what is happening around him and when difficulties and tensions arise, he feels them keenly.
Admittedly, every year has its difficult moments, but this
year in particular the Water Rabbit does need to keep
things in perspective. If he is ever worried over any matter,
he must tell others. Sometimes keeping problems or
concerns to himself only makes them worse. Water
Rabbits, do remember this and if troubled, do seek advice.
Also, the Water Rabbit should be on his guard against
rumours or scandal-mongering and if in doubt over
anything he hears, he should check the facts himself.
However, despite these notes of caution, there will be much
in his personal life that he will enjoy and socially, too, the
year will be quite active, with many gatherings, parties and
events for the Water Rabbit to attend. There will also be

opportunities to add to his social circle and for any Water Rabbit who may have had some recent sadness and would like more company and new friendships, the Snake year is well aspected. By going out more, especially to places where he is likely to meet others, he will be able to build up some new and important friendships as the year progresses, with the months from March to May being significant. Travel, too, is well aspected and all Water Rabbits will thoroughly enjoy any holiday or breaks they are able to take. In most respects the Water Rabbit will fare well in 2001. Work-wise his prospects are excellent, while personally there will be much to enjoy. The main point he should remember is that if problems arise he must keep them in perspective, seek advice and be prepared to sort them out rather than let them become an unwelcome distraction. If he bears this in mind, then they should not detract from the many positive and personally rewarding times that the year will hold.

Almost as soon as the Snake year begins, the *Wood Rabbit* will renew his determination to make the headway he wants, realizing that he himself should take action rather than wait for the right circumstances to arise. His renewed sense of purpose, together with his fine abilities, will help propel him forward to some interesting new opportunities. Some Wood Rabbits will aim for progression and promotion within their current place of work, bene-fiting from the experience they already have, while others will look for fresh challenges elsewhere. These Wood Rabbits, together with those seeking work, will discover several interesting openings over the year, with many finding that one they successfully follow up will not only mark a change in the type of work that they do but will also allow them to discover a new forte. Work-wise, the Snake year can prove of lasting significance for the Wood Rabbit. Furthermore, the chances he is given will provide an excellent base from which to develop and this, together with his own desire to progress, will often lead him to being offered further responsibilities as the year develops. The Snake year does offer the Wood Rabbit considerable potential and those determined enough can really make great gains. The progress the Wood Rabbit makes will also lead to a significant increase in his income. However, this will prove an expensive year for him, as for all Rabbits, with family and accommodation matters as well as transport drawing heavily on his resources. In addition, some Wood Rabbits will also decide to move and this will prove a major financial undertaking. In all financial matters the Wood Rabbit will need to proceed carefully, making allowances for any new obligations he takes on as well as checking the terms and watching his general level of spending. By remaining his vigilant self, he can do much to prevent problems from occurring and, in some cases, save himself considerable outlay. There will also be some Wood Rabbits who will be able to supplement their income by putting an interest or skill they have to profitable use. For those with practical and/or creative talents it really would be worthwhile investigating freelance possibilities. Also, with the year so favouring learning and self-improvement, the Wood Rabbit should take advantage of any chances he gets to develop himself and his interests, either enrolling on a course or undertaking some studies himself. This will also be a pleasing year for personal matters. The Wood

Rabbit will take much delight in his domestic life, sharing mutual interests as well as spending a great deal of time encouraging the activities of younger relations. He will also busy himself with some household projects over the year and those he carries out with others will be especially gratifying and often fun to do. The Wood Rabbit's social life is also well aspected and he will enjoy meeting up with his many good friends as well as the range of often interesting social functions that he attends. Any Wood Rabbit who may have had some personal sadness or disappointment in recent times will find that 2001 will mark a noticeable upturn and bring new happiness into his life. For these Wood Rabbits a friendship made early in the year could develop in a truly special way. Generally, this is a constructive year for the Wood Rabbit with positive and often far-reaching developments in many areas of his life. However, to take advantage of the favourable aspects, he does need to promote himself and take action. For the determined and enterprising, this really can prove a successful and significant year, and personally it will also be a happy one.

The *Fire Rabbit* will fare well in 2001. For those born in 1987, this will be an important year as far as their education is concerned, often with new subjects and projects to start as well as some important exams to take. By working consistently over the year and giving of his best, the young Fire Rabbit will make good progress as well as enjoy some of the studies and challenges given him. He will also benefit from the supportive attitude of those around him and if he has any uncertainties or difficulties over any academic matter, he should not hesitate to raise these. His family and tutors are really keen to see him make the most of his considerable abilities but in order for him to benefit from their willingness to help, the Fire Rabbit does need to ask. Similarly, if these Fire Rabbits should have any personal worries, they should raise these with others rather than keep their concerns to themselves. As they will find, a worry shared *will* be a worry halved. Also, as with all Rabbits in 2001, the Fire Rabbit should be wary of any rumours or malicious gossip. If he is not careful, there is a chance that he could be misled and cause himself some needless worry. If he has uncertainties over anything he might hear, he should check. The Fire Rabbit always sets great store by his domestic life and will value the support and obvious affection of those close to him. However, there will be occasions when his views might run counter to those around him. At these times, the Fire Rabbit should be prepared to discuss these matters openly rather than maintain too inflexible a stance. Although he may not always appreciate it – particularly when his mind is made up – those around him do have his best interests at heart and often speak with the benefit of considerable experience. In 2001 the Fire Rabbit should bear this in mind. However, despite the occasional awkward moment that may arise (as they do every year), this will generally be a happy year for family matters. In particular, joint activities and projects, trips out and any holiday and breaks that can be arranged will lead to some interesting and enjoyable times. Those Fire Rabbits born in 1927 will also take much joy in following the activities of family members and will often find themselves involved in some family celebration or gathering over the year, including the possible wedding of a loved one or birth of a great grandchild. Again, if the older Fire Rabbit has concerns over any domestic issue or matter affecting a close relation, he should let his views be known rather than keep them to himself. Although he may not wish to appear interfering, his words count for a great deal and those he speaks to will be grateful for his interest and often shrewd insight. Indeed, the senior Fire Rabbit holds a special place in the hearts of many and he will be touched by the respect and affection shown him, especially at times when difficult matters do raise their head. The Fire Rabbit will also enjoy his social life over the year and those born in 1987 will have a particularly lively time meeting up with friends and attending parties and various social occasions. While so much will bring the Fire Rabbit pleasure over the year, there is, however, one word of warning. While he may possess high spirits and be keen on having a good time, he should not let this lead him into mixing with undesirable company. Fortunately these words will only apply to a few Fire Rabbits, but all should bear them in mind. As far as financial matters are concerned, the Fire Rabbit will need to watch his spending. Sometimes there could be the tendency for this to creep up and be greater than he expected or has allowed for. Also he should be careful when completing forms related to finance, as a slip or error could be to his detriment. Fire Rabbits, take note and do remain vigilant. The Fire Rabbit will, however, get great pleasure from any travelling he undertakes over the year, with outdoor pursuits also being well favoured. His personal interests too will bring him much satisfaction, especially those that allow him to draw on his creative talents or bring him into contact with others. Overall, there will be much in 2001 that the Fire Rabbit will enjoy.

However, he does need to remain mindful of the views of others and seek advice should he have any concerns. For the most part, though, this will be a pleasing and fulfilling year.

The Year of the Snake will satisfy the *Earth Rabbit*, particularly as he will have more time and opportunity to develop some of his plans, ideas and interests. As the year starts, he would do well to think over what he hopes to achieve in the next 12 months and discuss his plans with those around him. This will not only help him to clarify his own thoughts but will also result in offers of help for which he will come to be grateful. The Earth Rabbit should be receptive to some of the suggestions made, as these could sometimes prove useful. Some of the activities that he has in mind will concern his accommodation, particularly altering the look, features and even style of certain rooms. By planning these changes with others and considering different ideas, the Earth Rabbit will obtain some pleasing results which can do much to enhance both the décor and comfort of certain areas. Many Earth Rabbits will also decide to spend money on new furnishings and equipment, and by taking their time and considering the ranges available, will be delighted with what they acquire. Some Earth Rabbits will, however, decide to move over the year and live in a totally new location. Much time and energy will be spent looking at various possibilities, but once they have made their choice, these Earth Rabbits will be pleased with their decision, even though the moving process will sometimes be a considerable wrench. However, once installed in their new accommodation, they will come to regard the Snake year as one which has helped usher in a new and positive period in their life. With much physical activity indicated over the year, the Earth Rabbit must, however, be respectful of his own well-being and particularly seek help when lifting or moving heavy weights. He will obtain considerable pleasure from pursuing his own personal hobbies and interests over the year, especially those that allow him to be creative in any way. Activities such as photography, writing, art or craftwork could provide him with many absorbing moments and if he is able to promote or show something he produces, he could receive some particularly encouraging feedback. The computer and, for some, the Internet could provide some interest over the year and by adding to his knowledge and experimenting with certain programs (including perhaps designing his own website), the Earth Rabbit will enjoy many fascinating hours of study and experimentation. By using his time well he can find the Snake year rich and personally rewarding. As always, the Earth Rabbit will play a full part in family activities over the year and will not only enjoy following the progress of those close to him but also the projects in which he becomes involved. He will also do much to encourage others over the year and younger relations will often look to him for advice. As usual, they will set great store by his sound judgement. The Earth Rabbit will also value his social life over the year. This will not only give him the chance to discuss wide-ranging issues (something he greatly enjoys) but will also provide him with some relaxing and convivial occasions. There will, though, be some Earth Rabbits who will start the Snake year in low spirits, having experienced some recent sadness or loneliness. Although it will often require much effort on their part, these Earth Rabbits should aim to immerse themselves in new activities as well as go to places where they will find company. They will not only find this a stimulating use of their time but will be able to strike up some good friendships. However, it does rest with them to make that all-important initial effort. In most respects, 2001 will be a fine year for the Earth Rabbit and by planning his activities and using his time well, he can achieve some very satisfying results. Not only will he carry out pleasing improvements to his home, but he will also get much pleasure from his interests and his domestic and social life.

FAMOUS RABBITS

Bertie Ahern, Drew Barrymore, David Beckham, Harry Belafonte, Ingrid Bergman, Melvyn Bragg, Gordon Brown, Emma Bunton (Baby Spice), James Caan, Nicolas Cage, Lewis Carroll, Fidel Castro, John Cleese, Confucius, Christopher Cross, Marie Curie, Johnny Depp, Albert Einstein, George Eliot, Peter Falk, Fatboy Slim, W. C. Fields, Bridget Fonda, Peter Fonda, James Fox, Sir David Frost, Melanie G. (Scary Spice), James Galway, Cary Grant, Edvard Grieg, Oliver Hardy, Seamus Heaney, Bob Hope, Whitney Houston, John Howard, John Hurt, Anjelica Huston, Chrissie Hynde, Clive James, Henry James, David Jason, Michael Jordan, Garry Kasparov, Michael Keaton, John Keats, Kevin Keegan, Judith Krantz, Danny La Rue, Cheryl Ladd, Julian Lennon, Patrick Lichfield, Gina Lollobrigida, Robert Ludlum, Ali MacGraw, Trevor

McDonald, George Michael, Arthur Miller, Colin Montgomerie, Roger Moore, Mike Myers, Brigitte Nielsen, Christina Onassis, George Orwell, John Peel, Edith Piaf, Sidney Poitier, Romano Prodi, Ken Russell, Mort Sahl, Elisabeth Schwarzkopf, Neil Sedaka, Jane Seymour, Neil Simon, Frank Sinatra, Sting, Jimmy Tarbuck, Sir Denis Thatcher, J. R. R. Tolkien, Arturo Toscanini, Tina Turner, Luther Vandross, Queen Victoria, Orson Welles, Walt Whitman, Robin Williams, Tiger Woods.

16 FEBRUARY 1904 〜 3 FEBRUARY 1905   *Wood Dragon*

3 FEBRUARY 1916 〜 22 JANUARY 1917   *Fire Dragon*

23 JANUARY 1928 〜 9 FEBRUARY 1929   *Earth Dragon*

8 FEBRUARY 1940 〜 26 JANUARY 1941   *Metal Dragon*

27 JANUARY 1952 〜 13 FEBRUARY 1953   *Water Dragon*

13 FEBRUARY 1964 〜 1 FEBRUARY 1965   *Wood Dragon*

31 JANUARY 1976 〜 17 FEBRUARY 1977   *Fire Dragon*

17 FEBRUARY 1988 〜 5 FEBRUARY 1989   *Earth Dragon*

5 FEBRUARY 2000 〜 23 JANUARY 2001   *Metal Dragon*

THE
DRAGON

THE PERSONALITY OF THE DRAGON

Far away there in the sunshine are my highest aspirations. I may not reach them, but I can look up and see their beauty, believe in them and try to follow where they may lead.

Louisa May Alcott: a Dragon

The Dragon is born under the sign of luck. He is a proud and lively character and has a tremendous amount of self-confidence. He is also highly intelligent and very quick to take advantage of any opportunities that occur. He is ambitious and determined and will do well in practically anything he attempts. He is also something of a perfectionist and will always try and maintain the high standards he sets himself.

The Dragon does not suffer fools gladly and will be quick to criticize anyone or anything that displeases him. He can be blunt and forthright in his views and is certainly not renowned for being either tactful or diplomatic. He does, however, often take people at their word and can occasionally be rather gullible. If he ever feels that his trust has been abused or his dignity wounded he can sometimes become very bitter and it will take him a long time to forgive and forget.

The Dragon is usually very outgoing and is particularly adept at attracting attention and publicity. He enjoys being in the limelight and is often at his best when he is confronted by a difficult problem or tense situation. In some respects he is a showman and he rarely lacks an audience. His views and opinions are very highly valued and he invariably has something interesting – and sometimes controversial – to say.

He has considerable energy and is often prepared to work long and unsocial hours in order to achieve what he wants. He can, however, be rather impulsive and does not always consider the consequences of his actions. He also has a tendency to live for the moment and there is nothing that riles him more than to be kept waiting. The Dragon hates delay and can get extremely impatient and irritable over even the smallest of hold-ups.

The Dragon has an enormous faith in his abilities, but he does run the risk of becoming over-confident and unless he is careful he can sometimes make grave errors of judgement. While this may prove disastrous at the time, the Dragon does have the tenacity and ability to bounce back and pick up the pieces again.

The Dragon has such an assertive personality, so much will-power and such a desire to succeed that he will often reach the top of his chosen profession. He has considerable leadership qualities and will do well in positions where he can put his own ideas and policies into practice. He is usually successful in politics, show business, as the manager of his own department or business, and in any job which brings him into contact with the media.

The Dragon relies a tremendous amount on his own judgement and can be scornful of other people's advice. He likes to feel self-sufficient and there are many Dragons who cherish their independence to such a degree that they prefer to remain single throughout their lives. However, the Dragon will often have numerous admirers and many will be attracted by his flamboyant personality and striking looks. If he does marry, the Dragon will usually marry young and will find himself particularly well suited to those born under the signs of the Snake, Rat, Monkey and Rooster. He will also find that the Rabbit, Pig, Horse and Goat make ideal companions and will readily join in with many of his escapades. Two Dragons will also get on well together, as they understand each other, but the Dragon may not find things so easy with the Ox and Dog, as both will be critical of his impulsive and somewhat extrovert manner. He will also find it difficult to form an alliance with the Tiger, for the Tiger, like the Dragon, tends to speak his mind, is very strong-willed and likes to take the lead.

The female Dragon knows what she wants in life and sets about everything she does in a very determined and positive manner. No job is too small for her and she is often prepared to work extremely hard until she has secured her objective. She is immensely practical and somewhat liberated. She hates being bound by routine and petty restrictions and likes to have sufficient freedom to be able to go off and do whatever she wants. She will keep her house tidy but is not one for spending hours on housework – there are far too many other things that she feels are more important and that she prefers to do. Like her male counterpart, she has a tendency to speak her mind.

The Dragon usually has many interests and enjoys sport and other outdoor activities. He also likes to travel and often prefers to visit places that are off the beaten track rather than head for popular tourist attractions. He has a very adventurous streak in him and providing his financial circumstances permit – and the Dragon is usually sensible with his money – he will travel considerable distances during his lifetime.

The Dragon is a very flamboyant character and while he can be demanding of others and in his early years rather precocious, he will have many friends and will nearly always be the centre of attention. He has charisma and so much confidence in himself that he can often become a source of inspiration for others. In China he is the leader of the carnival and he is also blessed with an inordinate share of luck.

THE FIVE DIFFERENT TYPES OF DRAGON

In addition to the 12 signs of the Chinese zodiac, there are five elements and these have a strengthening or moderating influence on the sign. The effects of the five elements on the Dragon are described below, together with the years in which the elements were exercising their influence. Therefore all Dragons born in 1940 and 2000 are Metal Dragons, those born in 1952 are Water Dragons, and so on.

Metal Dragon: 1940, 2000

This Dragon is very strong-willed and has a particularly forceful personality. He is energetic, ambitious and tries to be scrupulous in his dealings with others. He can also be blunt and to the point and usually has no hesitation in speaking his mind. If people disagree with him, or are not prepared to co-operate, he is more than happy to go his own way. The Metal Dragon usually has very high moral values and is held in great esteem by his friends and colleagues.

Water Dragon: 1952

This Dragon is friendly, easy-going and intelligent. He is quick-witted and rarely lets an opportunity slip by. However, he is not as impatient as some of the other types of Dragon and is more prepared to wait for results than to expect everything to happen at once. He has an understanding nature and is prepared to share his ideas and co-operate with others. His main failing, though, is a tendency to jump from one thing to another rather than concentrate on the job in hand. He has a good sense of humour and is an effective speaker.

Wood Dragon: 1904, 1964

The Wood Dragon is practical, imaginative and inquisitive. He loves delving into all manner of subjects and can quite often come up with some highly original ideas. He is a thinker and a doer and has sufficient drive and commitment to put many of his ideas into practice. He is more diplomatic than some of the other types of Dragon and has a good sense of humour. He is very astute in business matters and can also be most generous.

Fire Dragon: 1916, 1976

This Dragon is ambitious, articulate and has a tremendous desire to succeed. He is a hard and conscientious worker and is often admired for his integrity and forthright nature. He is very strong-willed and has considerable leadership qualities. He can, however, rely a bit too much on his own judgement and fail to take into account the views and feelings of others. He can also be rather aloof and it would certainly be in his own interests to let others join in more with his various activities. The Fire Dragon usually gets much enjoyment from music, literature and the arts.

Earth Dragon: 1928, 1988

The Earth Dragon tends to be quieter and more reflective than some of the other types of Dragon. He has a wide variety of interests and is keenly aware of what is going on around him. He also has clear objectives and usually has no problems in obtaining support and backing for any of his ventures. He is very astute in financial matters and is often able to accumulate considerable wealth. He is a good organizer, although he can at times be rather bureaucratic and fussy. He mixes well with others and has a large circle of friends.

PROSPECTS FOR THE DRAGON IN 2001

The Chinese New Year starts on 24 January 2001. Until then, the old year, the Year of the Dragon, is still making its presence felt.

The Year of the Dragon (5 February 2000 to 23 January 2001) will have been an excellent one for the Dragon, enabling him to make good progress as well as lead a fulfilling personal life. The favourable aspects remain strong right to the end of the year, with the following Chinese year allowing the Dragon to build on much of what he has achieved.

In the remaining months of the Dragon year, all Dragons should remain alert for opportunities to pursue in their work, particularly any which offer interesting challenges and the chance to add to their skills. What the Dragon is able to achieve at this time could establish a positive base from which to make greater progress over the next 12 months. September and November 2000 in particular could bring some interesting possibilities for him to pursue.

This is also a positive year for financial matters. However, the upturn almost all Dragons will enjoy should not tempt them to try their luck too far, take risks or become complacent. Also, with the closing months of the year being a traditionally expensive time, it would be in the Dragon's interests to watch what he spends. Without care, his outgoings could be far greater than he had allowed for.

This will also be an active time personally, with the Dragon's family and social life being both busy and rewarding. He will greatly enjoy the socializing that takes place towards the end of the year as well as the chance to meet up with some family and friends he has not seen for some time. As usual, he will thoroughly immerse himself in the many activities that take place, with his diary quickly filling up. For the unattached Dragon or those who would like more company and new friends, the closing months of the year are superbly aspected for meeting others, and the Dragon year often brings the prospects of a major new friendship and romance.

In most respects, the Dragon year will treat its own sign well and it rests with the Dragon himself to take full advantage of the opportunities that the closing months of his own year will bring.

The Year of the Snake starts on 24 January and will be a pleasant and constructive one for the Dragon. Over the year he will be able to build on his more recent achievements as well as see some of his ideas develop in an interesting manner. Overall this is a year which holds much promise.

In the preceding year, many Dragons will have seen changes in their work and they should use the early stages of the Snake year to familiarize themselves with their duties, undertake any training that may be offered, get to know useful personnel and generally build a base from which to develop. What they are able to accomplish early in 2001 will greatly impress others and will often lead to their being considered for further opportunities later in the year. In particular, the month of June and from September to early December will be especially positive periods for making additional progress.

For those Dragons who are seeking work or eager to move from their present position, the year will again hold much potential. However, some will find that positions they are offered have different duties from those they have done before. While this may sometimes be daunting, these Dragons will rise to the task before them and may, in the process, discover strengths they did not know they possessed. Again, by giving of their best, many will find themselves in line for further responsibilities as the year develops.

One area in which the Dragon can score some notable successes is in displaying his inventive and creative talents and he should make every effort to promote his work and ideas. If he does so, his initiative and ingenuity will be recognized and rewarded. The Snake year is an encouraging one for the Dragon, but it does rest with him to make the most of the supportive aspects that prevail.

This is a favourable year for personal development and many Dragons will gain much satisfaction from pursuing their interests. Indeed, the Snake year, with its cultural leanings, will offer the Dragon an excellent chance to add to his knowledge and develop his interests and, in the process, help satisfy his wide-ranging curiosity.

The Dragon will fare well in financial matters over the year with almost all Dragons enjoying a noticeable increase in their income. However, the Dragon should still manage his money well. He would find it helpful to set certain amounts aside for forthcoming expenses and to add, if possible, to his long-term savings. If he is contemplating any major purchase for his home he would do well to take his time considering his requirements and the ranges available rather than rush his purchase. This way he will often obtain something more suitable and offering better value than if he were to act too hastily, as some of the more impulsive Dragons can be apt to do!

The Dragon should also set some money aside for travel over the year, as this will lead to some interesting and enjoyable occasions. If there is a particular destination he is keen to visit, he should investigate the possibility of doing so. Many Dragons will take particular delight in visiting places a little off the usual tourist map.

The Dragon's domestic and social life will go well in 2001, but sometimes the Dragon can become so preoccupied with his own concerns that he is not always as mindful of others as he should be. Even at busy times, he should always ensure he gives adequate attention to those around him and take an informed interest in all that is going on. If others feel his attention and interest are lacking, strains could emerge which, with a bit of forethought, could have easily been avoided. In 2001, the Dragon does need to remain aware of this and avoid becoming so preoccupied that the good relations he enjoys with those around him begin to suffer.

Provided he bears this in mind, however, both his domestic and social life can provide him with considerable pleasure. In his home life he should make a real effort to involve himself in activities that others can share and appreciate. This includes joint interests and any household projects that can be carried out together. Some Dragons might even mount an efficiency drive and have a concerted family effort to smarten up certain rooms or areas, with the end result being pleasing to all. Also, some may like to consider starting courses with their loved ones or taking up a new interest together, something that they can help each other with. Similarly, outings and visits to places of local interest can provide some agreeable occasions. If the

Dragon can participate in and encourage general family activities, the year can contain many fine moments.

The Dragon will also enjoy his social life and throughout 2001 will find himself being invited to a range of gatherings. He will appreciate chances to meet up with friends and will find that his social circle will widen considerably over the year. One new acquaintance in particular could turn into an important friend who will be of great help to him in future years. For the unattached Dragon and those seeking new friends or company, the year will again bring some excellent chances to meet others, with a serious and meaningful romance indicated. The months of March, April, August and December are all particularly favoured for meeting others as well as for much social activity.

Generally, the Year of the Snake offers much promise to the Dragon. In his work there will be excellent chances for him to further his career, with his diligence, enterprise and ideas being appreciated and well rewarded. He will also be satisfied with his own personal development, being especially pleased with some new interests he takes up or skills he learns. His domestic and social life too can be rewarding, provided, that is, the Dragon remains attentive to the interests of others. But overall this will be a satisfying and pleasurable year.

As far as the different types of Dragon are concerned, this will be a pleasant year for the *Metal Dragon*. After the often considerable activity of the previous year, he will be content to build on, as well as enjoy, many of his more recent achievements. Those Metal Dragons who have recently changed their accommodation or intend to do so over the year will enjoy settling into their new home and discovering the amenities their new area offers. In addition, some Metal Dragons will also decide to carry out projects on their accommodation – perhaps by making something, sorting through and reorganizing belongings or buying new equipment and furnishings. Whatever they do will bring them much satisfaction and will be something they will appreciate both in this and future years. Also, in the Snake year the Metal Dragon will have more time to turn his attention to some new activities. For some Metal Dragons these will be outdoor pursuits, sometimes with a sporting or physical element, while others may opt for creative and cerebral activities ranging from artwork and photography to writing or studying a certain subject. Whatever the Metal Dragon does take up is likely to provide him with many absorbing and pleasurable hours. When considering possible new activities, as well as his more general plans for the year, the Metal Dragon would find it helpful to discuss his ideas with those close to him. He will not only be grateful for their co-operation but will also find that some may be able to assist him, for instance by providing introductions, lending equipment or books, or in some other manner. Similarly, as travel is favourably aspected, if there is a destination the Metal Dragon would like to visit, he should discuss the possibility with others and see what emerges. Again, by being forthcoming, he will often be able to benefit from the input of others. The Metal Dragon will also take much pleasure from general family activities over the year, doing much to assist and advise those around him, especially younger relations. Although he may not wish to appear interfering, his advice will be much appreciated and can often be of greater value than he may realize. Also, involving his loved ones more in his own activities will lead to some meaningful occasions as well as help maintain the close bonds the Metal Dragon so values. His social life, too, will go well and he will appreciate meeting up with friends as well as enjoy some of the often varied social occasions he attends. For any Metal Dragons who have recently moved or who would like additional company or to learn more about one of their interests, a local group or society could add a new dimension to the year, providing new friends as well as some pleasurable occasions. However, to help bring this about, the Metal Dragon does need to take the initiative and make the effort to join such groups. The Metal Dragon will also fare well in financial matters over the year and by managing his money with care will be satisfied with his general situation. However, bureaucratic matters could present problems and the Metal Dragon does need to take extra care over any forms he has to complete, especially if they are tax or finance related. Although he may resent some of what is asked of him, to delay or be lax in dealing with them could result in further correspondence and even be to his detriment. Metal Dragons, take note and do handle paperwork promptly and carefully. This warning apart, the Snake year will generally go well for the Metal Dragon and will allow him to accomplish much as well as immerse himself in some often fascinating new interests. In addition, he will greatly value the support and input others are able to give in so much of what he does, as well as the love and affection shown him. Overall this will be a year that will bring him much joy and contentment.

This is a favourably aspected year for the *Water Dragon* and he can look forward to pleasing developments in many areas of his life. His work prospects are particularly encouraging. Over the year he will be able to build on some of his more recent gains and put his ideas and skills to good use. The Water Dragon has a fine reputation and this, together with his abilities and personable nature, will lead him onward. In his work he will be offered the chance to take on new responsibilities or to switch to a more senior position. In some cases, what he is offered may seem daunting, particularly if it represents a big change from what he has been doing, but in his usual determined fashion he will be inspired by the challenges given him. Work-wise, the Snake year is very much a time of opportunity and advance. Similarly, those Water Dragons who are seeking work or anxious to move from their present position can make excellent headway. By actively following up opportunities that arise they will, in time, make the breakthrough and be given a position which will allow them to make effective use of their skills as well as offer the chance of further development. The progress that the Water Dragon makes in his work will also lead to an increase in income over the year. In view of this, many Water Dragons will decide to treat themselves to some items they have been considering for some time, maybe overhauling their wardrobe, buying items for their home or taking a well-deserved break or holiday. The Water Dragon should also try to add to his savings and so make some provision for his longer term future. He will take much satisfaction from his personal interests over the year and while there will be times when he will have a great deal to do, he should ensure that he does leave plenty of time for his own pursuits. In addition to the pleasure his interests bring, they give him the chance to unwind and often provide a good contrast to his usual daily concerns. Many Water Dragons are particularly interested in music and this would be a fine year in which to devote time to this. If the Water Dragon plays an instrument or would like to learn one, he should consider developing this skill. His domestic life will bring him much happiness and he will delight in the progress of family members as well as some exciting family news, including the possible engagement or marriage of a dear relation, or the birth of a grandchild. However, the Water Dragon should guard against becoming so preoccupied with his own activities that the interests of those around him begin to suffer. Fortunately he is usually considerate in this respect but, for some, inattention or feelings of pressure and tiredness, perhaps due to the often considerable developments in their work, could lead to some strains and disagreements. The Water Dragon should watch this and if at any time he does feel tired or anxious about all he has to do he should tell others and, where possible, ask for assistance. In some cases, sharing out household chores could ease some of his burden. The Water Dragon should also make sure that his social life does not suffer due to his other commitments. This will not only be another source of relaxation for him but he will also enjoy meeting up with friends and the chance just to chat and exchange news and views. For those Water Dragons who are unattached, a meeting last year or a chance encounter in the early months of 2001 could now develop in a significant manner and bring considerable happiness. In so many respects this will be a positive year for the Water Dragon with many chances to develop his ideas and considerable talent. However, to make sure the year does go smoothly, the Water Dragon should be careful to balance his various activities and commitments. Too much emphasis one way or another could cause problems. If the Water Dragon bears this in mind then this can be a truly favourable year for him.

This will be an important year for the *Wood Dragon*, one in which he can make good headway and which he will also find personally enjoyable. He knows that with his experience and keen mind he has it within him to make much of his life and in 2001 he will make further strides and reveal some of his considerable potential. As the year starts, he would find it helpful to consider his current position and give some thought to what he wants to accomplish over the next 12 months. This is especially true as far as his work is concerned. Once he has formed some idea of his goals, the Wood Dragon will find himself setting about his activities with greater resolve, becoming more aware of which areas and opportunities to concentrate on as well as being able to take advantage of suitable training opportunities. Also, by concentrating on certain goals, he will find that encouraging developments will soon start to appear, developments that he can turn to his advantage. The Snake year will offer some golden opportunities for the Wood Dragon and he should make the most of them. This also applies to those Wood Dragons currently seeking work. Again, these Wood Dragons should decide on the nature of the work they want and then go *persistently* after the openings that they see. This will require considerable determination and will-power on their part, and they may have disappointments on the way, but their fine indomitable spirit will win through and they will be given an opening which will give them a good chance to prove themselves as well as provide an excellent base for future advances. For work opportunities the months of March and April and last quarter of the year could prove significant. The positive developments the Wood Dragon makes in his work will lead to an increase in his income, although much of this will be taken up with family expenses. Several times in 2001 the Wood Dragon will need to provide additional support for family members, particularly for those involved in education. In view of this and the general household expenses and other commitments he has, it would be worth him taking additional care when dealing with his finances, ideally maintaining a set of personal, family and household accounts. This way he will be better able to manage his budget and keep track of his financial position. Over the year the Wood Dragon will play a much appreciated role in family matters and, despite the often considerable demands on his time, will give much attention to both younger and more senior relations. His care and assistance will be truly appreciated, particularly as those around him set such store by his judgement and value his considerate and understanding manner. However, while the Wood Dragon will do so much to help others, he should not take on too much single-handed. If there are others who can assist him, even just by carrying out additional household chores, he should ask rather than overload himself. The Wood Dragon may be caring and willing, but he must not push himself too far at the expense of his own well-being. However, although some parts of the year will be busy as far as domestic matters are concerned, mutual interests, joint household projects and more pleasurable activities such as outings and breaks will provide some truly happy occasions. Also, the Wood Dragon should make sure he makes time for his social life and interests. These can provide him with much pleasure as well as help him to relax and unwind. As far as his social life is concerned, he will not only enjoy the company of friends both old and new, but also the range of social occasions that he goes to over the year. To keep himself on top form, he should not be neglectful of his well-being and if he does not get much exercise during the day or is reliant on convenience food, he should aim to remedy this. Overall, this will be a pleasing and satisfying year for the Wood Dragon. Not only will he feel more fulfilled by what he achieves, but his progress, particularly work-wise, will often lead to further successes in the future.

This will be an important year for the *Fire Dragon* and one which will not only bring progress but also help shape his future. Being so determined, the Fire Dragon is always keen to take action and make the best of himself. Over the years this attitude will have brought him many worthy achievements but there will be some Fire Dragons who still do not feel fulfilled by their present work and are keen for change. These Fire Dragons, together with those currently seeking work, would do well to give serious thought to just what they wish to achieve in the longer term. The Fire Dragon should discuss his thoughts with those currently in the type of position he may be considering and obtain their informed views and advice. Similarly, contact with professional organizations could provide an indication of the skills the Fire Dragon could need and the way in which he should be developing. By giving thought to his future and getting expert guidance, he will be doing much to prepare the way forward. Once he has decided on his objectives he will, in true Fire Dragon style, set about achieving them and over the year will make useful progress. Admittedly, his early attempts may not go as well as he would like, but at least by trying he will be giving himself the chance to strengthen his approach and presentation and improve his interview technique as well as learn more about what employers may be seeking. All this will stand him in excellent stead for the future and, as so many Fire Dragons will find, progress will often follow shortly after a disappointment or setback. Once the Fire Dragon has been given a chance – as so many will be during the year – he should make the most of it and will not only impress but also mark himself out as someone destined for further advancement. For those Fire Dragons who are currently content with their present role, again a conscientious approach will stand them in good stead for when promotion opportunities arise. Also, all Fire Dragons, whether in work or seeking work, should take advantage of any training opportunities that may be offered. Anything the Fire Dragon can do to enhance his prospects will be to his advantage. As far as finance is concerned, some of the Fire Dragon's recent commitments, especially those relating to accommodation, will draw heavily on his resources, and throughout the year he will need to keep a close watch on his level of spending. By remaining vigilant and prudent he should be able to avoid problems and end the year in a relatively sound position, but some care will be needed. The Fire Dragon's domestic life will keep him busy over the year, with the activities and interests of those close to him taking up much of his time, and there will be occasions when he may despair of all he has to do. At such times, he should not hesitate to ask others for help, particularly with household duties. Also, while sometimes his work activities will pray heavily on his mind, he should try not to let these encroach too much on family life. In 2001 it is essential he maintains a balance between his professional and personal life. However, active though the Fire Dragon's domestic life will be, it will also bring him considerable pride and happiness. Despite his many commitments, he should also make sure his social life does not suffer. This can provide him with some enjoyable occasions as well as help him unwind – something which will be very important over the year. For those Fire Dragons who may be feeling lonely, perhaps because they have moved to a new area or have had some recent personal sadness to bear, the Snake year will bring a major improvement. However, to help bring this about, these Fire Dragons should aim to go out more, especially to places where they are likely to meet others, and perhaps join an interest group or society. Positive effort on their part will certainly be rewarded. Overall, this will be a positive and satisfying year for the Fire Dragon. He knows he is capable of achieving a great deal in life and in the Snake year he will do a lot to prepare the way for the very considerable success that awaits him in future years.

This will be a year that the *Earth Dragon* will enjoy, particularly as it will be more settled than recent years and will give him a better chance to get on with some of his own activities. All Earth Dragons, whether born in 1928 or 1988, will get special satisfaction from pursuing and developing their interests over year and also from taking up new ones. In some cases this will require study or delving deeper into certain subjects, but by making the effort, the Earth Dragon can make this a rich and rewarding process. For those born in 1988 who are keen on sport and outdoor activities, joining a sports group could be a particularly good way to extend their skills, while for those born in 1928, a special interest group would again be worth considering. The Snake year is very much one which favours self-improvement. For Earth Dragons born in 1988 this will be an important year as far as their education is concerned. Over the year many will be given new subjects and projects and by working consistently and giving of their best, they will make some encouraging progress. With his keen and searching mind the Earth Dragon certainly has it in him to make good academic progress and his fine accomplishments will certainly help build his confidence and lead him to further successes in later years. However, if at any time there are aspects of his schoolwork that concern him, he should not hesitate to ask for assistance. Help will be readily forthcoming and will do much to ease his difficulties, but he does need to ask. The Earth Dragon will also value his domestic and social life and will not only appreciate the encouragement and interest shown in his activities but will also enjoy playing a full part in much that goes on. Earth Dragons born in 1928 will delight in assisting younger family members and the important role they play will be greatly appreciated. Those born in 1988 will also become more involved in helping with certain tasks around the home. However, while the young Earth Dragon will enjoy home life, he may sometimes feel a little resentful about certain instructions given him. He should remember that those around do have his best interests at heart and sometimes a more accommodating attitude on his part could lead to a compromise being worked out. Young Earth Dragons, take note! The Earth Dragon's social life will bring him much pleasure over the year and he will enjoy meeting up with friends as well as the various social occasions that he attends. For those Earth Dragons who would like to enlarge their social circle, again joining a local society could be beneficial, while, for the younger Earth Dragon, a youth group could certainly lead to some fun as well as new friends. As far as finance is concerned, this will be a reasonable year. However, as with all Dragons, it would be in the Earth Dragon's interest to watch his general level of spending, as there could be a tendency for this to creep up and be greater than originally allowed for. The more senior Earth Dragon should aim to set some money aside for travel over the year, as any breaks and holidays he is able to take will be beneficial and he may also get to visit some interesting destinations. In most respects, this will be a rewarding year for the Earth Dragon and by developing his interests and ideas, he will be well satisfied with what he is able to accomplish. Overall, it will be a pleasing and fulfilling year.

FAMOUS DRAGONS

Clive Anderson, Maya Angelou, Jeffrey Archer, Joan Baez, Michael Barrymore, Count Basie, Pat Benatar, Maeve Binchy, James Brown, Sandra Bullock, James Coburn, Courteney Cox, Bing Crosby, Roald Dahl, Salvador Dali, Charles Darwin, Lindsay Davenport, Neil Diamond, Bo Diddley, Matt Dillon, Christian Dior, Frank Dobson, Placido Domingo, Fats Domino, Kirk Douglas, Faye Dunaway, Bruce Forsyth, Sigmund Freud, James Garner, Sir John Gielgud, Graham Greene, Che Guevara, David Hasselhoff, Sir Edward Heath, James Herriot, Paul Hogan, Joan of Arc, Tom Jones, Imran Khan, Martin Luther King, Virginie Ledoyen, John Lennon, Abraham Lincoln, Queen Margrethe II of Denmark, Yehudi Menuhin, François Mitterrand, Bob Monkhouse, Andrew Motion, Hosni Mubarak, Florence Nightingale, Nick Nolte, Al Pacino, Elaine Paige, Gregory Peck, Pele, Edgar Allan Poe, Vladimir Putin, Christopher Reeve, Keanu Reeves, Sir Cliff Richard, Harold Robbins, George Bernard Shaw, Ringo Starr, Dave Stewart, Karlheinz Stockhausen, Mr T, Shirley Temple, Andy Warhol, Johnny Weissmuller, Raquel Welch, the Earl of Wessex, Mae West, Frank Zappa.

4 FEBRUARY 1905 ⁓ 24 JANUARY 1906   *Wood Snake*

23 JANUARY 1917 ⁓ 10 FEBRUARY 1918   *Fire Snake*

10 FEBRUARY 1929 ⁓ 29 JANUARY 1930   *Earth Snake*

27 JANUARY 1941 ⁓ 14 FEBRUARY 1942   *Metal Snake*

14 FEBRUARY 1953 ⁓ 2 FEBRUARY 1954   *Water Snake*

2 FEBRUARY 1965 ⁓ 20 JANUARY 1966   *Wood Snake*

18 FEBRUARY 1977 ⁓ 6 FEBRUARY 1978   *Fire Snake*

6 FEBRUARY 1989 ⁓ 26 JANUARY 1990   *Earth Snake*

24 JANUARY 2001 ⁓ 11 FEBRUARY 2002   *Metal Snake*

THE
SNAKE

THE PERSONALITY OF THE SNAKE

My philosophy is that not only are you responsible for
your life, but doing the best at this moment puts you in
the best place for the next moment.

Oprah Winfrey: a Snake

The Snake is born under the sign of wisdom. He is highly
intelligent and his mind is forever active. He is always
planning and always looking for ways in which he can use
his considerable skills. He is a deep thinker and likes to
meditate and reflect.

Many times during his life he will shed one of his
famous Snake skins and take up new interests or start a
completely different job. The Snake enjoys a challenge and
he rarely makes mistakes. He is a skilful organizer, has
considerable business acumen and is usually lucky in
money matters. Most Snakes are financially secure in their
later years provided they do not gamble – the Snake has
the distinction of being the worst gambler in the whole of
the Chinese zodiac!

The Snake generally has a calm and placid nature and
prefers the quieter things in life. He does not like to be in a
frenzied atmosphere and hates being hurried into making a
quick decision. He also does not like interference in his
affairs and tends to rely on his own judgement rather than
listen to advice.

The Snake can at times appear solitary. He is quiet,
reserved and sometimes has difficulty in communicating

with others. He has little time for idle gossip and will certainly not suffer fools gladly. He does, however, have a good sense of humour and this is particularly appreciated in times of crisis.

The Snake is certainly not afraid of hard work and is thorough in all that he does. He is very determined and can occasionally be ruthless in order to achieve his aims. His confidence, will-power and quick thinking usually ensure his success, but should he fail it will often take a long time for him to recover. He cannot bear failure and is a very bad loser.

The Snake can also be evasive and does not willingly let people into his confidence. This secrecy and distrust can sometimes work against him and it is a trait which all Snakes should try to overcome.

Another characteristic of the Snake is his tendency to rest after any sudden or prolonged bout of activity. He burns up so much nervous energy that without proper care he can, if he is not careful, be susceptible to high blood pressure and nervous disorders.

It has sometimes been said that the Snake is a late starter in life and this is mainly because it often takes him a while to find a job in which he is genuinely happy. However, the Snake will usually do well in any position which involves research and writing and where he is given sufficient freedom to develop his own ideas and plans. He makes a good teacher, politician, personnel manager and social adviser.

The Snake chooses his friends carefully and while he keeps a tight control over his finances, he can be particularly generous to those he likes. He will think nothing of buying expensive gifts or treating his friends or loved ones to the best theatre seats in town. In return he demands loyalty. The Snake is very possessive and he can become extremely jealous and hurt if he finds his trust has been abused.

The Snake is also renowned for his good looks and is never short of admirers. The female Snake in particular is most alluring. She has style, grace and excellent (and usually expensive) taste in clothes. A keen socializer, she is likely to have a wide range of friends and has the happy knack of impressing those who matter. She has numerous interests and her advice and opinions are often highly valued. She is generally a calm-natured person and while she involves herself in many activities, she likes to retain a certain amount of privacy in her undertakings.

Affairs of the heart are very important to the Snake and he will often have many romances before he finally settles down. He will find that he is particularly well suited to those born under the signs of the Ox, Dragon, Rabbit and Rooster. Provided he is allowed sufficient freedom to pursue his own interests, he can also build up a very satisfactory relationship with the Rat, Horse, Goat, Monkey and Dog, but he should try to steer clear of another Snake as they could very easily become jealous of each other. The Snake will also have difficulty in getting on with the honest and down-to-earth Pig, and will find the Tiger far too much of a disruptive influence on his quiet and peace-loving ways.

The Snake certainly appreciates the finer things in life. He enjoys good food and often takes a keen interest in the arts. He also enjoys reading and is invariably drawn to subjects such as philosophy, political thought, religion or the occult. He is fascinated by the unknown and his enquiring mind is always looking for answers. Some of the world's most original thinkers have been Snakes, and – although he may not readily admit it – the Snake is often psychic and relies a lot on intuition.

The Snake is certainly not the most energetic member of the Chinese zodiac. He prefers to proceed at his own pace and to do what he wants. He is very much his own master and throughout his life he will try his hand at many things. He is something of a dabbler, but at some time – usually when he least expects it – his hard work and efforts will be recognized and he will invariably meet with the success and financial security he so much desires.

THE FIVE DIFFERENT TYPES OF SNAKE

In addition to the 12 signs of the Chinese zodiac, there are five elements and these have a strengthening or moderating influence on the sign. The effects of the five elements on the Snake are described below, together with the years in which the elements were exercising their influence. Therefore all Snakes born in 1941 and 2001 are Metal Snakes, those born in 1953 are Water Snakes, and so on.

Metal Snake: 1941, 2001
This Snake is quiet, confident and fiercely independent. He often prefers to work on his own and will only let a

privileged few into his confidence. He is quick to spot opportunities and will set about achieving his objectives with an awesome determination. He is astute in financial matters and will often invest his money well. He also has a liking for the finer things in life and has a good appreciation of the arts, literature, music and good food. He usually has a small group of extremely good friends and can be generous to his loved ones.

Water Snake: 1953

This Snake has a wide variety of interests. He enjoys studying all manner of subjects and is capable of undertaking quite detailed research and becoming a specialist in his chosen area. He is highly intelligent, has a good memory, and is particularly astute when dealing with business and financial matters. He tends to be quietly spoken and a little reserved, but he does have sufficient strength of character to make his views known and attain his ambitions. He is very loyal to his family and friends.

Wood Snake: 1905, 1965

The Wood Snake has a friendly temperament and a good understanding of human nature. He is able to communicate well with others and often has many friends and admirers. He is witty, intelligent and ambitious. He has numerous interests and prefers to live in a quiet, stable environment where he can work without too much interference. He enjoys the arts and usually derives much pleasure from collecting paintings and antiques. His advice is often very highly valued, particularly on social and domestic matters.

Fire Snake: 1917, 1977

The Fire Snake tends to be more forceful, outgoing and energetic than some of the other types of Snake. He is ambitious, confident and never slow in voicing his opinions – and he can be very abrasive to those he does not like. He does, however, have many leadership qualities and can win the respect and support of many with his firm and resolute manner. He usually has a good sense of humour, a wide circle of friends and a very active social life. The Fire Snake is also a keen traveller.

Earth Snake: 1929, 1989

The Earth Snake is charming, amusing and has a very amiable manner. He is conscientious and reliable in his work and approaches everything he does in a level-headed and sensible way. He can, however, tend to err on the cautious side and never likes to be hassled into making a decision. He is extremely adept at dealing with financial matters and is a shrewd investor. He has many friends and is very supportive towards the members of his family.

PROSPECTS FOR THE SNAKE
IN 2001

The Chinese New Year starts on 24 January 2001. Until then, the old year, the Year of the Dragon, is still making its presence felt.

The Year of the Dragon (5 February 2000 to 23 January 2001) will have been a variable one for the Snake. Being methodical and generally of a quiet disposition, he likes to set about his activities in his own way and at his own pace and this will not always have been possible during the sometimes volatile Dragon year.

For what remains of the year, the Snake will need to remain alert and make the best of the situations in which he finds himself. Admittedly, these may not be ideal, but the Dragon year affords the Snake a wonderful chance to learn and extend his experience. In addition, the Snake will often find positive developments emerging as a result of recent events and the decisions he has had to make. Progress and success often follow on from more challenging times and the Dragon year will do much to open the way for the opportunities that await the Snake in his own year.

In view of the impending upturn, the Snake would do well to give some thought to what he would like to achieve over the next 12 months, particularly how he would like his career to develop. By forming ideas now and letting them take root, he will gain a greater sense of direction as well as an added incentive to realize his ambitions. In addition, in the latter stages of the Dragon year, the Snake could find it helpful to make a concerted effort to deal with

THE SNAKE

any outstanding matters he might have, including any jobs and correspondence he might have been putting to one side. By dealing with these now the Snake will not only not only be relieved that they are out of the way but will also find himself freer to enjoy the holiday period at the end of the year and start 2001 reasonably up to date.

Personally, the latter part of the Dragon year will go well for the Snake, with many agreeable occasions indicated in both his domestic and social life. Travel, too, is favourably aspected and the Snake should take full advantage of any opportunities to go away at this time. However, when dealing with financial matters, he must not let his usual vigilance slip. The Dragon year is not a time to get involved in risky or speculative ventures or for overspending.

Although the Dragon year will be a challenging one for the Snake he will emerge from it wiser, more experienced and superbly placed to benefit from the exciting times that now await him.

The Year of the Snake starts on 24 January and is one which is almost tailor made for the Snake. It is a year in which he will not only make considerable progress but also be able to realize some of his key ambitions. The Snake will have worked a long time to achieve some of these, but his persistence and patience will be well rewarded. These successes can relate to almost any area of the Snake's life – his personal life, relationships, hobbies, interests and work – but in 2001 almost all Snakes will achieve results or see developments which will truly delight them. This will be a year to savour.

In view of the auspicious aspects, it really would be worth the Snake redoubling his efforts to secure some of his most fervent desires. Admittedly, circumstances may not always have been in his favour over the last 12 months and some Snakes will have become disillusioned, but now is very much the time to leave the past behind, focus on the present and build for the future. This is, after all, the Snake's own Chinese year and by making the effort he will soon notice how quickly circumstances begin to turn in his favour.

As far as the Snake's work is concerned, this will be an especially rewarding year, with many Snakes deciding the time has come to make more effective use of their skills and experience. As a result they will keep alert for opportunities to pursue as well as start to make enquiries about possible openings. By taking action, they will find that some ideal opportunities will soon arise. For any Snake who has entrepreneurial aspirations, an idea could develop in a significant way, although again, to benefit from the favourable aspects, the Snake does need to take action and follow through his ideas.

For those Snakes seeking work this will be a positive year with many finding their persistence rewarded. To help in their search, these Snakes should consider their experience and skills and the various ways in which these can be put to good use. Some enterprising thinking could widen the scope of positions they could try for or lead to some ideas that are worth developing. If the Snake has been seeking work for some time, it could also be in his interests to investigate training opportunities that may be available and consider learning new skills. For some, this will open up new possibilities as well as enable them to discover strengths that they never appreciated they had.

Almost all the year is favourably disposed for work matters, but the months of February and March could see some pleasing developments, with the last quarter of the year also bringing chances for further progress.

The Snake can also look forward to a noticeable improvement in his financial situation over the year. However, when dealing with his finances, he could find it helpful to set regular amounts aside for specific purposes, including furnishings and equipment for his home, travel and recreational pursuits, as well as adding to his long-term savings. Many Snakes will decide to invest in themselves over the year, improving their wardrobe, enrolling on courses and buying books, software and sometimes a new personal computer. By managing his money and planning his purchases, the Snake will be pleased with his general financial situation as well as with what he is able to acquire. The one thing that he should guard against is spending any bonus payment or additional sum of money too hastily. His best purchases will come as a result of deliberation than from being too impulsive.

Another favourably aspected area concerns the Snake's personal interests and he should make sure he sets time aside for both developing existing interests and taking up new ones. Some of these will provide an ideal contrast to his usual preoccupations and help him relax, and one could take on special significance. For those Snakes who are creatively inclined, some work they produce could be particularly well received and in some cases even provide an additional source of income. As the Snake will find, the year offers so many possibilities.

The Snake's domestic life is well aspected and throughout the year he will be considerably heartened by the support and affection of his loved ones. While the Snake may have a tendency to be one of the more independent signs, it would be very much to his advantage to discuss his ideas more openly. Not only is he likely to get more support that way, but he will be able to benefit from the input that those around can give. In addition to his own successes, family events will be a source of much joy and the Snake will enjoy any family breaks and holidays he is able to take over the year.

The Snake will also gain a great deal from his social life and will enjoy meeting up with friends and the various functions he attends. Some Snakes do tend to keep themselves to themselves, preferring a more solitary existence, and these Snakes will find that by making the effort to go out more and meet others, they will be able to inject something special into their life, something they may not realize has been lacking for some time. Any Snakes who may have had some recent sadness or would like a more active social life should try to do likewise. Although this may be difficult for some, by making a positive effort they really can bring some happiness back into their lives. For Snakes who are unattached and possibly seeking a partner, romance is superbly aspected. The year will see many Snakes getting engaged or married, such are the auspicious aspects that prevail.

In almost all respects this is a year which holds wonderful prospects for the Snake, allowing him to make progress as well as realize some of his long-held goals. However, to truly benefit from his own year, the Snake must seize the opportunities that it will bring. This is a time when enterprise and initiative will be rewarded and provided the Snake is prepared to go after what he wants (rather than just think about it), his accomplishments could surpass his expectations. For the Snake, his own year is one of the best.

As far as the different types of Snake are concerned, this is the *Metal Snake's* own year and will be an important one for him. It is almost as if the Metal Snake will shed one of his famous Snake skins and take on another, and with it will come new opportunities, new situations and new hope. As this marks their sixtieth year, many Metal Snakes will decide that the time has now come to make a concerted effort to realize some of their ideas, and their determination will help make this a year to remember. Quite a few Metal Snakes will decide to move house during 2001 and although the moving process may initially be slow, once they have found what they are looking for, it will gather a momentum of its own, with the Metal Snake then facing several months of hectic activity, sorting, packing and preparing for his new home. Once installed, these Metal Snakes will feel invigorated by what is almost a fresh start, with a new area and amenities to discover and the opportunity to build up a new social life. Even those who do not move will make some significant changes to their home. These will include altering the look of certain rooms, replacing some furnishings and equipment and generally making their home more comfortable. Again, what the Metal Snake accomplishes will bring him much satisfaction. Throughout the year he will be well supported by his family and while much of what takes place (especially accommodation-wise) will in fact involve everyone, whenever the Metal Snake feels in need of additional help or advice he should not hesitate to ask. As he will find, those around him will be glad to assist and over the year he will gain much from their input and practical help. Also, if he has any personal concerns he should raise these rather than dwell on them by himself. Again, by being forthcoming, he will find that others can do much to help and put his mind at ease. In addition to all that he accomplishes regarding his accommodation, there will also be events in the Metal Snake's domestic life that will bring him considerable joy. These could include the birth of a grandchild or great grandchild or some success enjoyed by a dear and close relation. The Metal Snake will also enjoy joint family activities and some may decide to take up a new interest or project with a loved one, something they can help each other with. By spending time with others and following meaningful pursuits, the Metal Snake can make this a most fulfilling year. His social life, too, also holds much promise and, while the Metal Snake can sometimes keep himself to himself, meeting up with friends will provide some very pleasurable occasions. The summer is particularly well aspected for this, with the Metal Snake's social life being busier than it has been for some time. For those who may have faced some personal sadness in recent years or who would like additional company, the year holds some glittering prospects and, by going out more, someone they meet – often by chance – could become special as the year unfolds. As far as finance is concerned, however, the Metal Snake will need to remain his usual vigilant self. With some large expenses likely, especially involving accommodation, he will need to monitor his outgoings carefully otherwise he could find these greater than he had allowed for. Also, when entering into sizeable transactions, it would be prudent for him to check the terms of any obligations as well as keep the paperwork safely. Financial matters and paperwork do need care and scrutiny if problems or misunderstandings are to be avoided later. Metal Snakes, take note. With travel favourably aspected, however, the Metal Snake should make sure he takes a proper holiday or break over the year, as he could have the chance to visit some appealing destinations. In most respects, this will be a splendid year for him and one which will mark the start of a new and positive phase in his life.

This is the year the *Water Snake* has long been waiting for. While he may have a patient disposition and has worked hard for what he has achieved so far, he still has many goals that he is keen to reach. In 2001 some of these will be realized and over the year the Water Snake can look forward to some tremendous personal successes. His faith in his own ideas and abilities will now be well rewarded. For most Water Snakes, the key successes will come in their professional life and here many will be given the opportunity (and in some cases recognition) they have long been waiting for. This could include promotion or being offered the type of position they have sought for so long. Alternatively, one of the Water Snake's many ideas could now strike a positive response and develop in an exciting manner. However, for him to reap the considerable benefits that this year can bring, the Water Snake really does need to take action to promote himself. For the bold and enterprising, this can be a wonderful year. Those Water Snakes who are currently seeking work or anxious to move from their present position should again pursue any opportunities that the year will bring, but also be adventurous in what they try for. The Water Snake does, after all, have many abilities and a little imaginative thinking could result in some interesting possibilities. The progress that the Water Snake makes will often lead to an increase in income and, by the close of the year, his finances will be much improved. However, while he usually handles his finances with care, he should not let this upturn lead him into complacency or undue extravagance. If tempted by something on the spur of the moment, he would sometimes do better to pause and reflect rather than act too hastily. If not, he could come to regret some of the more impulsive purchases made over the year. He should also consider adding to his savings over the year, particularly with a view to the longer term. The Water Snake's personal life will bring him much happiness and he will greatly value the support and affection shown him by his loved ones. They, too, will share his delight at the personal successes he will enjoy. Bearing in mind that those around him know him well – including his weaknesses! – the Water Snake should remain mindful of any advice they give. In 2001 he can benefit greatly from their input as well as be encouraged by their support. Also, at particularly busy times, he should not hesitate to ask for assistance with some of the things he has to do, particularly the usual household tasks. Although he may feel some of these are his own preserve, asking for a helping hand would be preferable to putting himself under sometimes unnecessary strain. The Water

Snake will also take particular pleasure in the success of a younger relation over the year and if this relation is in education, any encouragement or assistance he feels able to give could make an important difference. He will also enjoy activities he can share with his loved ones, including any joint interests and family holidays. Being so involved in his work and other interests and often possessing a quiet disposition, the Water Snake may not always be as active a socializer as some. However, in 2001, he should make sure he does not neglect his social life for this can also bring him some rewarding times over the year. Parties and other gatherings could be especially enjoyable as well as give him a good chance to relax and unwind. There will be opportunities for him to strike up some important new friendships and for the unattached or lonely Water Snake, one of these could become significant and in some cases transform his life. The aspects for the Water Snake are just so encouraging that throughout the year if there is something that he wants, whether a personal or professional goal, a romance or a new friendship, he should make every effort to secure it. With a positive approach and determined attitude, the rewards for the Water Snake in 2001 can be truly considerable.

A substantial amount will have happened to the *Wood Snake* over the last 12 months and while at the time some of these events will have given rise to uncertainty, in 2001 some of the benefits will now begin to emerge. Indeed, the last year will have done much to usher in the changes necessary for progress. However, as the year starts, the Wood Snake would do well to clarify just what he wishes to accomplish over the next 12 months. This way he will find himself advancing in a more purposeful manner as well as introducing an element of challenge (and excitement) to the year. In his work the Wood Snake should aim to build on his present position and recent accomplishments. This includes pursuing any opportunities for promotion within his current organization or transferring to a better position elsewhere. There will also be some Wood Snakes who have been contemplating a complete change of career. These Wood Snakes should now think carefully about just what it is they wish to do. They will find it helpful to talk their ideas over with both their loved ones and those experienced in the area they are considering. Then, once they have made their decision, they should take positive steps to try and get what they want. Admittedly, not all their early attempts may go their way, but with resolve, many will eventually make the breakthrough they need and establish an excellent base from which to develop. For many Wood Snakes, the winds of change will blow strongly and favourably over the year. For those seeking work, the year holds great promise and by pursuing openings that interest them, many Wood Snakes will succeed in being given a position which will allow them to make effective use of their skills. Almost all the year could bring interesting opportunities, but especially well aspected are the first and last quarters of 2001. The Wood Snake can also look forward to success in financial matters. In addition to a rise in income he could also receive an additional sum of money over the year. This could be the result of putting a skill or interest he has to some profitable use, a gift, the fruition of a policy or even through a stroke of luck. As usual, the Wood Snake will handle his finances with care and will often use this upturn to add to his home, as well as buying some personal treats and setting a sum aside for a holiday. There are many Wood Snakes who enjoy collecting and have an eye for art and the unusual. During the year, many will delight in adding to their collection, with their fine taste and ability to spot a good buy serving them well. All Wood Snakes should also aim to make some savings over the year and will find that a carefully chosen investment could yield much in the future. The Wood Snake's personal life, too, will bring him considerable pleasure. He will play a full part in family activities, encouraging and advising those around as well as tackling some interesting projects in his home. However, while his domestic life will go well, there could be some busy times, particularly involving the activities of both younger and more senior family members. Whenever he feels under pressure, the Wood Snake would find it helpful to prioritize his various activities, keep his commitments to a manageable level and avail himself of the willingness of others to assist him. Effective management of his time can certainly help a great deal over the year, both in his personal and professional life. The Wood Snake should also make sure that he allows time for his own recreational pursuits. These will not only help him to unwind but any that provide him with additional exercise could also be helpful to his well-being. His social life is well aspected and although other commitments may mean he is not able to meet up with his friends as regularly as he would like, he will thoroughly enjoy the times he does spend socializing. For those Wood Snakes who are unattached or who may have been feeling low, the year will bring a pleasing upturn, with a new friendship made in the early months of 2001 becoming meaningful. The Year of the Snake holds considerable potential for the Wood Snake and it rests with him to seize the chances the year will bring as well as make the most of his considerable talents. For the enterprising, this can be a truly successful year.

This is a year of considerable opportunity for the *Fire Snake* and one which will see positive developments in most areas of his life. Personally it is especially well aspected, with relations with others bringing much joy and contentment. For many this will be a year of celebration, with some Fire Snakes becoming engaged, married or seeing an addition to the family, such are the auspicious aspects that prevail. For any Fire Snake who is seeking romance or who would like to build up his social life, again the prospects are excellent. Indeed, almost as soon as the Snake year starts, many Fire Snakes will sense that this is 'their year' and this positive feeling will help give them a greater determination to bring about what they want, particularly in their personal life. In addition, the Fire Snake will greatly value the love and affection shown to him by others and this will also do much to encourage him. It would, though, be in his interests to remain mindful of any advice given him over the year, especially from those more senior, who are able to advise with the benefit of experience. There will be much wisdom in what the Fire Snake is told, with some of it becoming especially pertinent as the year unfolds. This will also be a positive year for vocational matters, with the Fire Snake being able to make effective use of his skills and experience. With his knowledge, industry and enthusiasm he will greatly impress and over the year be offered the chance to take on new responsibilities, be promoted or decide to switch to a company which offers better prospects. Work-wise, the Snake year will hold some interesting opportunities for the Fire Snake and it rests with him to make the most of them. The Fire Snake is blessed with a determined and shrewd nature and this will certainly serve him well throughout 2001. The one note of caution that does need to be sounded, though, is the Fire Snake must not allow his desire for progress lead him into taking risky or ill thought out decisions. If he has doubts over any action he is considering, he should pause, reflect and seek appropriate advice. Here again the advice of others will guide him well. Fire Snakes who start the year seeking work will often find that their quest will lead to an opening which holds much potential and can prove an ideal base from which to make further progress later in the year. The Fire Snake will also derive much satisfaction from his personal interests over the year and for some these could develop in an exciting manner, even possibly providing an additional source of income. Those who enjoy writing, art or some other creative skill could find that if they promote their work their talents will be well received and rewarded. The outdoor enthusiast will also fare well, the sportingly inclined will enjoy some memorable moments and the keen traveller will have the chance to visit some interesting destinations. The Fire Snake will also see an improvement in his income over the year but will need to remain prudent and watch his spending, especially in view of some of the recent obligations he may have taken on. He would find that maintaining a set of personal accounts would help keep his finances in good order. In addition, the Fire Snake needs to be careful when dealing with any important paperwork and forms he receives. Although he may feel some of these are unnecessarily bureaucratic, he must not let his sometimes stubborn nature get the better of him and be dilatory in sending back information that may be required, otherwise he could find himself embroiled in extra correspondence. Fire Snakes, do take note! In most respects, though, this will be a year the Fire Snake will savour. He has the personality and talents to do well and over the year he will be able to use his many fine abilities to excellent effect. Both professionally and personally this is a year which holds great promise.

This will be an interesting year for the *Earth Snake* and one which will bring him much pleasure and satisfaction. The Earth Snake has wide interests and the sheer variety of what he does will keep him well occupied and personally fulfilled. Over the year he will decide to extend some of his current interests, perhaps by learning about new aspects or tackling more ambitious projects. He will delight in the challenges he sets himself and will spend many absorbing hours pursuing them. The Earth Snake could also find it beneficial to get in contact with fellow enthusiasts, perhaps by joining a club or, if he is able, a group on the Internet. That way he will not only extend his knowledge but also enjoy exchanging views and making some new friends and useful contacts. For those born in 1989, this will be an important year as far as education is concerned. The young Earth Snake will sometimes feel daunted by what is being expected of him, especially as he may have recently changed schools and taken up new subjects. However, by giving of his best he will acquit himself well and become more confident. He will also value the support he is given and if he has any problems or is experiencing difficulty in a subject, he should raise his concerns with others. He will find that assistance and, importantly, reassurance can quickly be obtained. Both the younger and more senior Earth Snakes will much appreciate their social life over the year, enjoying meeting up with friends and any parties and social occasions they may attend. The summer will be an especially active and pleasurable time. Any Earth Snake who may feel alone or who has had some recent adversity to bear should try to focus his attention firmly on the present and aim to go out more and meet others. Admittedly, in some cases this may require much effort, but the Earth Snake can do much to bring some brightness back into his life, with new interests and friendships proving important. Those Earth Snakes born in 1929 will also take much delight in following the activities of family members and, while the Earth Snake may not like to appear interfering, the help and advice he is able to offer younger relations will be greatly appreciated. Similarly, he too will value the affection and support he is shown over the year and if he has any personal concerns, he would be helped by raising these with others rather than keeping them to himself. All Earth Snakes, whether born in 1929 or 1989, will enjoy any holidays or breaks they take over the year, with many being fascinated by some of the places they visit, both near and far. Financially, this will be a generally positive year. However, when making any large purchase, the Earth Snake should make sure he keeps the paperwork carefully as well as check the terms of any new obligation he takes on. Without care and reading the small print, problems and misunderstandings could arise later. Earth Snakes, take note. However, in most respects, this will be a satisfying year for the Earth Snake and one in which he will enjoy his many interests and activities. Overall, it will be a year that will bring him much personal contentment.

FAMOUS SNAKES

Muhammad Ali, Ann-Margret, Yasser Arafat, Paddy Ashdown, Lord Baden-Powell, Ehud Barak, Ronnie Barker, Kim Basinger, Bjork, Tony Blair, Heinrich Böll, Michael Bolton, Brahms, Pierce Brosnan, Stephen Byers, Casanova, Chubby Checker, Tom Conti, Randy Crawford, Alistair Darling, Jim Davidson, Len Deighton, Bob Dylan, Elgar, Sir Alex Ferguson, Sir Alexander Fleming, Henry Fonda, Mahatma Gandhi, Greta Garbo, Art Garfunkel, J. Paul Getty, Dizzy Gillespie, W. E. Gladstone, Goethe, Princess Grace of Monaco, Stephen Hawking, Audrey Hepburn, Jack Higgins, Howard Hughes, Tom Hulce, Liz Hurley, Eddie Irvine, Rev. Jesse Jackson, James Joyce, Stacy Keach, Ronan Keating, Howard Keel, J. F. Kennedy, Carole King, James Last, Cindi Lauper, Lennox Lewis, Courtney Love, Dame Vera Lynn, Peter Mandelson, Mao Tse-tung, Henri Matisse, Robert Mitchum, Nasser, Bob Newhart, Alfred Nobel, Ryan O'Neal, Mike Oldfield, Aristotle Onassis, Jacqueline Onassis, Pablo Picasso, Mary Pickford, Brad Pitt, Michael Portillo, André Previn, Franklin D. Roosevelt, Jean-Paul Sartre, Franz Schubert, Brooke Shields, Paul

Simon, Delia Smith, John Thaw, Madame Tussaud, Dionne Warwick, Charlie Watts, Ruby Wax, Oprah Winfrey, Victoria Wood, Virginia Woolf, Susannah York.

25 JANUARY 1906 ∽ 12 FEBRUARY 1907   *Fire Horse*

11 FEBRUARY 1918 ∽ 31 JANUARY 1919   *Earth Horse*

30 JANUARY 1930 ∽ 16 FEBRUARY 1931   *Metal Horse*

15 FEBRUARY 1942 ∽ 4 FEBRUARY 1943   *Water Horse*

3 FEBRUARY 1954 ∽ 23 JANUARY 1955   *Wood Horse*

21 JANUARY 1966 ∽ 8 FEBRUARY 1967   *Fire Horse*

7 FEBRUARY 1978 ∽ 27 JANUARY 1979   *Earth Horse*

27 JANUARY 1990 ∽ 14 FEBRUARY 1991   *Metal Horse*

THE

HORSE

THE PERSONALITY OF THE HORSE

> I think luck is the sense to recognize an opportunity and
> the ability to take advantage of it. Everyone has bad
> breaks, but everyone also has opportunities. The man who
> can smile at his breaks and grabs his chances gets on.
>
> *Samuel Goldwyn: a Horse*

The Horse is born under the signs of elegance and ardour.
He has a most engaging and charming manner and is
usually very popular. He loves meeting people and likes
attending parties and other large social gatherings.

The Horse is a lively character and enjoys being the
centre of attention. He has considerable leadership qualities
and is much admired for his honest and straightforward
manner. He is an eloquent and persuasive speaker and has
a great love of discussion and debate. He also has a particularly agile mind and can assimilate facts remarkably
quickly.

He does, however, have a fiery temper and although his
outbursts are usually short-lived, he can often say things
which he will later regret. He is also not particularly good
at keeping secrets.

The Horse has many interests and involves himself in a
wide variety of activities. He can, however, get involved in
so much that he can often waste his energies on projects
which he never has time to complete. He also has a
tendency to change his interests rather frequently and will
often get caught up with the latest craze or 'in thing' until
something better or more exciting turns up.

The Horse also likes to have a certain amount of freedom and independence. He hates being bound by petty rules and regulations and as far as possible likes to feel that he is answerable to no one but himself. But despite this spirit of freedom, he still likes to have the support and encouragement of others in his various enterprises.

Due to his many talents and likeable nature, the Horse will often go far in life. He enjoys challenges and is a methodical and tireless worker. However, should things work against him and he fail in any of his enterprises, it will take a long time for him to recover and pick up the pieces again. Success to the Horse means everything. To fail is a disaster and a humiliation.

The Horse likes to have variety in his life and he will try his hand at many different things before he settles down to one particular job. Even then, he will probably remain alert to see whether there are any better opportunities for him to take up. The Horse has a restless nature and can easily get bored. He does, however, excel in any position which allows him sufficient freedom to act on his own initiative or which brings him into contact with a lot of people.

Although the Horse is not particularly bothered about accumulating great wealth, he handles his finances with care and will rarely experience any serious financial problems.

The Horse also enjoys travel and he loves visiting new and far-away places. At some stage during his life he will be tempted to live abroad for a short period of time and due to his adaptable nature he will find that he will fit in well wherever he goes.

The Horse pays a great deal of attention to his appearance and usually likes to wear smart, colourful and rather distinctive clothes. He is very attractive to the opposite sex and will often have many romances before he settles down. He is loyal and protective to his partner, but, despite his family commitments, still likes to retain a certain measure of independence and have the freedom to carry on with his own interests and hobbies. He will find that he is especially well suited to those born under the signs of the Tiger, Goat, Rooster and Dog. The Horse can also get on well with the Rabbit, Dragon, Snake, Pig and another Horse, but he will find the Ox too serious and intolerant for his liking. The Horse will also have difficulty in getting on with the Monkey and the Rat – the Monkey is very inquisitive and the Rat seeks security, and both will resent the Horse's rather independent ways.

The female Horse is usually most attractive and has a friendly, outgoing personality. She is highly intelligent, has many interests and is alert to everything that is going on around her. She particularly enjoys outdoor pursuits and often likes to take part in sport and keep-fit activities. She also enjoys travel, literature and the arts, and is a very good conversationalist.

Although the Horse can be stubborn and rather self-centred, he does have a considerate nature and is often willing to help others. He has a good sense of humour and will usually make a favourable impression wherever he goes. Provided he can curb his slightly restless nature and keep a tight control over his temper, he will go through life making friends, taking part in a multitude of different activities and generally achieving many of his objectives. His life will rarely be dull.

THE FIVE DIFFERENT TYPES OF HORSE

In addition to the 12 signs of the Chinese zodiac, there are five elements, and these have a strengthening or moderating influence on the sign. The effects of the five elements on the Horse are described below, together with the years in which the elements were exercising their influence. Therefore all Horses born in 1930 and 1990 are Metal Horses, those born in 1942 are Water Horses and so on.

Metal Horse: 1930, 1990
This Horse is bold, confident and forthright. He is ambitious and also a great innovator. He loves challenges and takes great delight in sorting out complicated problems. He likes to have a certain amount of independence and resents any outside interference in his affairs. The Metal Horse has charm and a certain charisma, but he can also be very stubborn and rather impulsive. He usually has many friends and enjoys an active social life.

Water Horse: 1942
The Water Horse has a friendly nature, a good sense of humour, and is able to talk intelligently on a wide range of topics. He is astute in business matters and quick to take advantage of any opportunities that arise. He does, however, have a tendency to get easily distracted and can change his interests – and indeed his mind – rather frequently, and this can sometimes work to his detriment.

He is nevertheless very talented and can often go far in life. He pays a great deal of attention to his appearance and is usually smart and well turned out. He loves to travel and also enjoys sport and other outdoor activities.

Wood Horse: 1954

The Wood Horse has a most agreeable and amiable nature. He communicates well with others and, like the Water Horse, is able to talk intelligently on many different subjects. He is a hard and conscientious worker and is held in high esteem by his friends and colleagues. His opinions and views are often sought and, given his imaginative nature, he can quite often come up with some very original and practical ideas. He is usually widely read and likes to lead a busy social life. He can also be most generous and often holds high moral viewpoints.

Fire Horse: 1906, 1966

The element of Fire combined with the temperament of the Horse creates one of the most powerful forces in the Chinese zodiac. The Fire Horse is destined to lead an exciting and eventful life and to make his mark in his chosen profession. He has a forceful personality and his intelligence and resolute manner bring him the support and admiration of many. He loves action and excitement and his life will rarely be quiet. He can, however, be rather blunt and forthright in his views and does not take kindly to interference in his own affairs or to obeying orders. He is a flamboyant character, has a good sense of humour and will lead a very active social life.

Earth Horse: 1918, 1978

This Horse is considerate and caring. He is more cautious than some of the other types of Horse, but he is wise, perceptive and extremely capable. Although he can be rather indecisive at times, he has considerable business acumen and is very astute in financial matters. He has a quiet, friendly nature and is well thought of by his family and friends.

PROSPECTS FOR THE HORSE IN 2001

The Chinese New Year starts on 24 January 2001. Until then, the old year, the Year of the Dragon, is still making its presence felt.

The Year of the Dragon (5 February 2000 to 23 January 2001) will have been an interesting one for the Horse, with the closing months being a generally positive time. The Dragon year very much rewards enterprise and initiative and this will suit the Horse's personality well. Always keen to make the most of himself, the Horse will have made good progress over the year. As it draws to a close, he should remain active in pursuing any attractive opportunities that he sees, with further headway being likely in both September and November 2000. Those Horses currently seeking work could also be successful in gaining an interesting position at this time, even if, for some, this may be on a temporary or part-time basis.

However, while prospects are encouraging for work matters, the Horse does need to take care when dealing with

finance. In the Dragon year there could be many temptations to spend and it would certainly be in the Horse's interests to watch his outgoings, otherwise these could exceed
expectations. This is especially important with the latter
part of the year being traditionally more expensive.

The Horse's personal life will be active at this time and
in view of this, he would find it helpful to organize his
various activities and be realistic about his commitments.
To take on too much or try to 'burn the candle at both
ends' could leave the Horse feeling tired and unable to
make the most of himself or enjoy the various events that
take place.

Provided the Horse takes things sensibly, however, the
closing months of the year can be most pleasurable, with
many convivial occasions with both family and friends. In
addition, many Horses will have the opportunity to travel
late in 2000 and any visits to those the Horse may not have
seen for some time could go particularly well.

Generally, the Dragon year will be an active one for the
Horse and if he takes the time to look back over the last 12
months, he will be surprised at just how much he has
achieved.

The Year of the Snake starts on 24 January and will be a
tricky one for the Horse. Although there will be parts of
the year that will go well, there are other elements that
could cause problems.

One of these areas concerns the Horse's relations with
others and here he must exercise great care. The Horse not
only possesses an independent spirit but can also be very
determined and resolute. While such traits can serve him

well – and are qualities others admire in him – they could, if not watched, also present problems. In the Snake year in particular, the Horse should make sure his attitude does not bring him into conflict with others and so jeopardize some of the good relationships he has built up. When he has ideas or plans, he should take time to discuss them with others and remain mindful of their views rather than carry on regardless. Neither should he automatically assume he has support for some of what he proposes. This is very much a year when the Horse will need to act in conjunction with others rather than go his own way.

Also, with some of the pressures that the year will bring, there will be times when the Horse will feel tetchy and strained. He should avoid taking his frustrations out on others, particularly if he wishes to preserve domestic harmony. Admittedly, this can sometimes be difficult, but rather than provoke an argument or be too snappy, the Horse should be more forthcoming about his feelings and talk over any concerns he might have. He will find this far better than bottling up his aggravations and he may well be helped by the advice and assistance others are able to give.

Admittedly, in all relationships there are good and bad times, but in 2001, the Horse really must be mindful of others. Also, there may be a few Horses who are tempted to act in a manner that leaves them open to censure, particularly in forming inappropriate friendships. If they succumb to temptation, these Horses could find themselves facing some very difficult problems. Horses, take serious note and do not 'play with fire'!

Provided the Horse heeds these warnings, he can do much to avoid some of the pitfalls the year could bring and will enjoy some of the brighter aspects. In his domestic life various activities and occasions will bring him much pleasure, including the often considerable achievements of loved ones. Many Horses will decide to tackle various household projects over the year and these too will be satisfying. They could include redecorating and adding new features to the home as well as sorting through accumulated belongings and paperwork and improving the organization of the household. In carrying out these activities, again the Horse should involve others, as joint effort will not only make many of these tasks easier but will also help to maintain rapport and understanding. In addition, the Horse would do well to encourage mutual interests and hobbies and, with the aspects for travel being good, aim to take a family holiday or break. The Horse's input into family life will prove important in the Snake year as well as provide some meaningful occasions.

The Horse's social life will also be active, with a wide variety of social occasions to attend and many chances to meet up with old friends as well as make new ones. However, here again the Horse does need to handle his relations with others with care and those Horses seeking romance should let any new friendship develop gradually rather than rush into a hasty commitment.

As far as the Horse's work is concerned, he should aim to build on his present position and if he has recently taken on new duties, he should familiarize himself with these. In 2001 he will fare best by concentrating on the familiar and using his experience to good effect. However, with the variable aspects that prevail, the Horse does need to remain alert to all that is happening at his place of work as well as the views of his colleagues. This is not a year in which he can afford to be too independent in attitude. If he is, he could find himself vulnerable to change or could undermine some of the good work he has done in the past.

Those Horses who are seeking work or keen to move from their present position should actively pursue openings that interest them, especially those in which they can use and develop their skills. However, any Horse who may have been seeking work for some time might find it in his interests to investigate any training opportunities that are available. By learning new skills, he could not only find securing a position that much easier but also that it opens up some exciting possibilities for him in the future.

Although the Horse's progress may not be all he would like over the year, the experience he does gain will stand him in excellent stead for the magnificent opportunities that await him next year.

As far as financial matters are concerned, this will be a reasonable year for the Horse. He would, though, find it in his interests to take greater control over his finances and keep watch over his outgoings rather than proceed on too much of an ad hoc basis. Also, he should be wary of taking undue risks and should carefully check the details and obligations of any new agreement that he enters into. Extra vigilance would certainly not come amiss.

One of the more favourably aspected areas of the year, however, is travel and in 2001 the Horse should take up any travel opportunities that arise as well as ensure that he takes a holiday or break. He could get the chance to visit some interesting destinations and will greatly benefit from the rest and change of scene. In addition, despite his many commitments, he should also allow time for his hobbies and other personal interests. Again, these will help him unwind and provide him with some fulfilling times. In 2001 it is important that the Horse gives himself the chance to let off steam and to relax, and travel and his interests are excellent ways for him to do this.

Provided the Horse maintains a balance in his life and remains careful in his various activities, he can do much to negate the more awkward aspects of the year. Admittedly, this may mean tempering his more impulsive and independent ways and remaining particularly mindful of others, but better this than jeopardizing what he has already achieved. However, while the Snake year may contain its awkward elements, the Horse can still learn a great deal from it and do a tremendous amount to prepare for the excellent times that await him in his own year, 2002.

As far as the different types of Horse are concerned, this will be a challenging year for the *Metal Horse*. The Metal Horse possesses many fine abilities and over the years these will have allowed him to accomplish a great deal. He is certainly not one to shrink from taking action. However, another of the Metal Horse's traits is his tendency to go his own way. He is resolute, but sometimes stubborn, and if he is not careful these particular traits could work against him. Throughout 2001, he does need to remain especially mindful of the views of others. In his home life, whenever he has activities he is keen to carry out, he should make sure he fully consults those around him and involves them in his plans. At times, he would find it helpful to encourage joint activities, including any mutual interests, as well as suggesting occasions all would enjoy, such as having friends round or visiting places of interest. By positive input into family life, the Metal Horse will not only help to prevent possible differences from arising but also maintain and even strengthen his bonds with those around him. This is something he will need to work at, but the effort will be worthwhile and can help produce many meaningful occasions over the year. If any differences do arise, the Metal Horse should try to sort them out as quickly and as amicably as he can and so prevent them from escalating or lingering in the background. Once again, this is very much a year when the Metal Horse must remain mindful of others and work at preserving the good rapport he normally enjoys with those around him. For Metal Horses born in 1990, the difference between their views and those of more senior relations may sometimes cause problems, but these are certainly not insurmountable. Again, compromise and a willingness to talk would help. With the prospects of changing schools, being in different classes and starting new subjects, there will be times when the young Metal Horses will feel anxious about all that is happening. Rather than worry about their situation, they would find it reassuring to talk to others. Also, if they are experiencing problems with certain subjects, by asking for assistance they can be given much useful guidance. As far as the young Metal Horse's social life is concerned, he can look forward to striking up some new and good friendships. However, while he might like to be one of the 'in crowd', at no time should he allow himself to become involved in any situation with which he feels uncomfortable. Again, if he has concerns over any personal or social matter, he should speak to others. As far as finance is concerned, those Metal Horses born in 1930 will have a reasonable year, although they will need to take care over any important forms or correspondence they receive. Although they may sometimes be irritated by certain bureaucratic matters, to ignore them or be dilatory in their response could be to their detriment. Also, if the Metal Horse does become involved in any complex bureaucratic matter, he would do well to seek advice and, in some cases, professional guidance. Although the aspects may be challenging over the year, provided the Metal Horse remains mindful of others, heeds any advice given and makes a determined effort to involve others more in what he does, he will improve his prospects considerably. It is very much in his own hands which course he decides to steer – if he chooses wisely, this could be a highly interesting and pleasant year for him.

This will be an important year for the *Water Horse* and one in which he will make some far-reaching decisions. In view of this, the year may not necessarily be easy or smooth, but some of the Water Horse's ideas and actions will do much to contribute to the superb upturn that awaits him next year. In 2001 almost all areas of his life will see some activity, but his work will be particularly important. It is here that some interesting and sometimes surprising developments are likely. For some Water Horses this could include being offered the chance to take up different responsibilities – sometimes unexpectedly – and so give their career an almost new lease of life. Others could take the opportunity to leave their present position and retire or aim to do something they have been considering for a long time. In almost all cases, the decisions that the Water Horse will take will require much soul-searching. However, he can help make the decision-making process easier by discussing his options with his loved ones as well as seeking out those who have already made a similar decision to the one he is faced with. He will find that talking to others will help clarify his thoughts. However, while much good can come as a result of the Water Horse's actions over the year, some of the decisions he has to take will pray heavily on his mind, with the result that his patience will sometimes be low and there will be times when he will feel tetchy. Over the year he must make allowance for this and if tempted to be critical or snappy, check himself and think before he speaks. Words said in haste could come to be regretted later. Also, at busy or demanding times, it would be in the Water Horse's interests to make sure he allows himself time to relax and unwind as well as pay attention his well-being. Some appropriate exercise, such as additional walking, swimming or cycling, could prove helpful. Any holiday or break will also be beneficial and all Water Horses should try to go away at some point over the year. They will not only enjoy the rest and change of scene but could also have the opportunity to visit some attractive destinations. The Water Horse's home life will be busy, with many Water Horses deciding to carry out practical projects and some to move to new accommodation. However, mixed in with the considerable activity, there will be some rich and rewarding times, including celebrating both the successes of loved ones and some of the Water Horse's own decisions. However, throughout the year, the Water Horse does need to stay particularly mindful of others and could also find it helpful to encourage family activities that all can enjoy. This, too, can help preserve the good rapport that he so values. The Water Horse's social life will also provide some interesting occasions and he will enjoy meeting up with friends and attending various events. There will also be opportunities for him to widen his social circle, but once again he should be careful not to become embroiled in any situation he may later come to regret. Financial matters will go reasonably well, although the Water Horse should avoid taking unnecessary risks and be sure to check the terms of any large transaction he enters into. Indeed, this need for caution is very much the keynote for the Water Horse throughout the year. Provided he is his careful self, however, he will not only lessen the impact of some of the more difficult aspects that prevail but also be pleased with what he manages to accomplish. These achievements will help to place him in an excellent position to benefit from the significantly better times that await in 2002.

The *Wood Horse* is always keen to give of his best and sets about his various activities with commendable resolve and commitment. However, while his abilities will have helped him to accomplish much over the years, there will be many Wood Horses who currently feel that recently things have not been going as well as they could. In particular, certain ideas will not have developed as well as expected, some of the Wood Horses' efforts could have been overlooked and their progress may not have been all they hoped for. In many cases, the earnest and well-intentioned Wood Horse will have been left feeling dispirited. However, while 2001 will not be the easiest of years for him, there is excellent reason for him to take heart. His prospects are about to receive a tremendous boost and in 2002 he will be able to realize some of his fondest ambitions and be able to make the progress he has wanted for so long. In the Snake year he will do much to prepare for this forthcoming success. As far as his work is concerned, he should continue to give of his best, rising to the challenges set him as well as developing and promoting his ideas. In addition, he should keep himself fully informed of all that is happening around him as well as take note of the views of his colleagues. This is not a year in which he can ignore or distance himself from events or remain too independent in his views and actions. However, by remaining his usual conscientious and diligent self, what the Wood Horse accomplishes and some of the ideas he develops will help to place him in a superb position to make headway in the near future. Also, whether in work or seeking work, the Wood Horse should take full advantage of any training opportunities that may be offered, particularly those that could be helpful to his future aspirations. In some cases, training or retraining could open up many new possibilities for him. In addition, any position that those seeking work are able to secure could provide an ideal foothold within a company or a way of getting valuable experience. In 2001 so many Wood Horses will sow the seeds that will reap an abundant harvest in later years. Financial matters will, however, require vigilance, particularly as there will be many temptations to spend. In some cases, it would be in the Wood Horse's interests to take time to reflect over some of the purchases he is considering rather than succumb to too many impulsive buys. Without some caution and restraint, he could come to rue some of his hasty purchases. He should, though, aim to set some funds aside for a holiday or break over the year, as he will greatly benefit from the rest as well as enjoy the chance to see some often interesting places. As with all Horses in 2001, the Wood Horse's relations with others do, however, require great care. He should remain mindful of the opinions of his loved ones as well as show a willingness to discuss his own thoughts and plans. There may be a temptation for him to keep some of these to himself, but in many cases he will feel so much better for discussing them openly and sometimes getting his worries off his chest. This way he will also be able to benefit from the views and often sound advice that others are able to give. In addition, the Wood Horse should make sure that he sets sufficient time aside for general family activities rather than remaining too wrapped up with his own concerns. If not, he could find tensions arising which, with some forethought, could have been avoided. Usually the Wood Horse is careful in his relations with his loved ones, but he should aim to pay particular attention to them over the year. His social life will be generally pleasant in 2001 and he will enjoy meeting up with friends as well as some of the social occasions he attends. However, as with all Horses, the Wood Horse should be wary of becoming involved in any situation he may come to later regret. The key word for him throughout 2001 has to be 'care'. Provided he remains aware of the pitfalls the Snake year can present, however, he can do much to avoid them and to set himself firmly on course for some great successes in 2002.

The *Fire Horse* has many fine qualities and is much admired by others for his strength of purpose, zeal and integrity. However, despite his best intentions, this will not be an easy year for him or one that suits his active temperament. Instead, caution, reflection and planning are called for. However, while the Fire Horse may have to temper some of his activities, he can still gain much of value from the year. In his work he should concentrate on building on his present position and if he has recently taken on new duties or has the chance to do so, he should familiarize himself with these. He should also be prepared to show some flexibility in his attitude, particularly if asked to adapt to new procedures or take on tasks at short notice. If he appears unaccommodating or too entrenched in his ways, then he could find himself losing out on future opportunities. This is very much a year in which the Fire Horse needs to tread carefully, co-operate and show himself an active and willing team member rather than remain too independent. Also, in view of the impending upturn that awaits him next year, he should give some thought to how he would like his career to develop over the next few years, and if, in order to progress, it would be helpful to undertake some training and learn new skills, this would be an excellent year in which to do so. For those Fire Horses seeking employment, any positions they are able to obtain – even if sometimes different from what they were hoping for – can prove a useful base from which to develop, enabling them to broaden their skills and, in some cases, find an area that leads to future success. As far as finance is concerned, this will be a demanding year with the Fire Horse facing some large expenses, especially in connection with the activities of family members. When these are known about in advance, the Fire Horse should try to make ample and early provision for them. To help him keep better track of his finances, he would find it useful to maintain a set of personal and household accounts. If he takes the trouble to manage his money, he will fare much better as a result. The Fire Horse's domestic life will generally be busy over the year with a variety of family matters requiring his attention. Some of these will bring pleasure and be a source of much pride – especially the progress enjoyed by some younger relations – but there could be some more demanding issues requiring important decisions and action. At such times the Fire Horse should seek the help of others rather than take on too much single-handed. Also, in view of some of the pressures he may face, he could find there will be times when he has little patience and feels tired and tetchy. Rather than take this out on others, he should see whether those around him can help take some of the pressures off him, for instance by doing more around the house. In addition, the Fire Horse should make sure that he regularly gives himself the chance to rest and unwind. His interests, especially any that he can carry out with his loved ones, will be of great help in this respect, not only doing him some good but also leading to some enjoyable occasions. The Fire Horse would also benefit from any holiday or breaks he is able to take over the year. With so many activities to occupy him in 2001, it is important that he looks after himself as well as maintains some sort of balance to his life. However, while the year can prove challenging, provided the Fire Horse remains careful in his activities and mindful of others, then he will not only negate some of the more difficult aspects but will also find that what he accomplishes will serve him splendidly in the future. The Snake year is, in many ways, a year of preparation for the more fulfilling and successful times that lie ahead.

This will be an important year for the *Earth Horse* and one which will have a significant bearing on his future. The year may not always be easy or smooth, but the Earth Horse can emerge from it with real gains to his credit, especially as far as his work is concerned. Indeed, there will be many Earth Horses who start 2001 with uncertainties over their current work situation, even though some will have made creditable progress in recent times. Some Earth Horses could be wondering if they have made the right choice of career, while others may feel their efforts are not being appreciated or that they could be making better use of their skills elsewhere. In addition, there will be those who start the year seeking work and feeling concerned about their prospects. The Snake year will resolve many of these worries and will set a large number of Earth Horses off on a new track, one that will help them find their true forte and greater fulfilment. Often the developments that take place will arise in a fortuitous manner and throughout 2001 the Earth Horse should investigate some of the opportunities that arise with an open mind, surprising though some may be. This is very much a time when the Earth Horse should be adaptable in his outlook and willing to give any work offers a try. The months of April, May and the last quarter of the year could bring some particularly interesting developments. Those Earth Horses currently in work should again be alert to any changes that may be in the offing as well as any chances to show their skills and promote their ideas. Despite the variable aspects, this is still a year for the Earth Horse to push forward and keep faith with himself. By doing so, he will not only gain valuable experience but will also do much to prepare the way for future advances. Financial matters will loom large over the year with many Earth Horses facing considerable expenses, particularly relating to accommodation. Some Earth Horses will move over the year and this, plus various household purchases they will need to make, will involve considerable outlay. In view of this it would certainly be in the Earth Horse's interests to keep a close watch on his outgoings. In addition, he should thoroughly check the details and small print of new agreements he enters into as well as avoid committing himself to any risky ventures. This is very much a year for vigilance. This will also be an important year for personal matters, though, like all other Horses, the Earth Horse needs to pay close attention to the views and feelings of others. Fortunately, his considerate nature and ability to empathize will help, but care is certainly needed over the year. Also, when important matters arise or decisions need to be taken, the Earth Horse should make sure he fully involves others, particularly if he wishes to prevent misunderstandings from arising later. At busy times or whenever he may feel under pressure, he would also find it helpful to tell others rather than struggle on unaided. By being forthcoming he could be given much useful assistance. However, while problems and difficulties will arise, as they do every year, there will be much that will bring the Earth Horse pleasure. In particular he will enjoy the activities he can share with others, as well as carrying out home improvements and getting his home as he and those around would like. Earth Horses who may be seeking friends or romance will have many chances to meet others, but where matters of the heart are concerned, the Earth Horse would do best to let any new romance develop gradually rather than rush into an early commitment. This will help place the relationship on a sounder footing. Overall, despite the variable aspects, this will still be a reasonable year for the Earth Horse and while it may not always develop as he had envisaged, he will end it considerably wiser, more experienced and excellently placed to benefit from the exciting prospects that await him in 2002.

FAMOUS HORSES

Neil Armstrong, Rowan Atkinson, Samuel Beckett, Ingmar Bergman, Leonard Bernstein, Sir John Betjeman, Cherie Blair, Helena Bonham Carter, James Cameron, Ray Charles, Chopin, Sean Connery, Billy Connolly, Catherine Cookson, Ronnie Corbett, Elvis Costello, Kevin Costner, Cindy Crawford, Michael Crichton, James Dean, Clint Eastwood, Thomas Alva Edison, Britt Ekland, Chris Evans, Harrison Ford, Aretha Franklin, Sir Bob Geldof, David Ginola, Samuel Goldwyn, Billy Graham, Gene Hackman, Rolf Harris, Rita Hayworth, Jimi Hendrix, Bob Hoskins, Janet Jackson, Neil Kinnock, Calvin Klein, Lenin, Annie Lennox, Desmond Lynam, Sir Paul McCartney, Nelson Mandela, Princess Margaret, Thabo Mbeki, Spike Milligan, Ben Murphy, Sir Isaac Newton, Louis Pasteur, Ross Perot, Harold Pinter, J. B. Priestley, Puccini, Lou Reed, Rembrandt, Ruth Rendell, Jean Renoir, Anita Roddick,

Theodore Roosevelt, Helena Rubenstein, Adam Sandler, Peter Sissons, Lord Snowdon, Alexander Solzhenitsyn, Igor Stravinsky, Barbra Streisand, Kiefer Sutherland, Patrick Swayze, John Travolta, Kathleen Turner, Mike Tyson, Vivaldi, Robert Wagner, Denzil Washington, Billy Wilder, Andy Williams, Boris Yeltsin, Michael York.

13 FEBRUARY 1907 ⁓ 1 FEBRUARY 1908   *Fire Goat*

1 FEBRUARY 1919 ⁓ 19 FEBRUARY 1920   *Earth Goat*

17 FEBRUARY 1931 ⁓ 5 FEBRUARY 1932   *Metal Goat*

5 FEBRUARY 1943 ⁓ 24 JANUARY 1944   *Water Goat*

24 JANUARY 1955 ⁓ 11 FEBRUARY 1956   *Wood Goat*

9 FEBRUARY 1967 ⁓ 29 JANUARY 1968   *Fire Goat*

28 JANUARY 1979 ⁓ 15 FEBRUARY 1980   *Earth Goat*

15 FEBRUARY 1991 ⁓ 3 FEBRUARY 1992   *Metal Goat*

THE
GOAT

THE PERSONALITY OF THE GOAT

The world is a looking glass and gives back to every man
the reflection of his own face. Frown at it and it will in
turn look sourly upon you; laugh at it and with it, and it
is a jolly, kind companion.

William Makepeace Thackeray: a Goat

The Goat is born under the sign of art. He is imaginative,
creative and has a good appreciation of the finer things in
life. He has an easy-going nature and prefers to live in a
relaxed and pressure-free environment. He hates any sort
of discord or unpleasantness and does not like to be bound
by a strict routine or rigid timetable. The Goat is not one to
be hurried against his will, but despite his seemingly
relaxed approach to life, he is something of a perfectionist
and when he starts work on a project he is certain to give
of his best.

The Goat usually prefers to work in a team rather than
on his own. He likes to have the support and encouragement of others and if left to deal with matters on his own
he can get very worried and tends to view things rather
pessimistically. Wherever possible he will leave major decision-making to others while he concentrates on his own
pursuits. If, however, he feels particularly strongly about a
certain matter or has to defend his position in any way, he
will act with great fortitude and precision.

The Goat has a very persuasive nature and often uses his
considerable charm to get his own way. He can, however,
be rather hesitant about letting his true feelings be known

and if he were prepared to be more forthright he would do much better as a result.

The Goat tends to have a quiet, somewhat reserved nature but when he is in company he likes he can often become the centre of attention. He can be highly amusing, a marvellous host at parties and a superb entertainer. Whenever the spotlight falls on him, his adrenalin starts to flow and he can be assured of giving a sparkling performance, particularly if he is allowed to use his creative skills in any way.

Of all the signs in the Chinese zodiac, the Goat is probably the most gifted artistically. Whether in the theatre, literature, music or art, he is certain to make a lasting impression. He is a born creator and is rarely happier than when occupied in some artistic pursuit. But even in this the Goat does well to work with others rather than on his own. He needs inspiration and a guiding influence, but when he has found his true *métier*, he can often receive widespread acclaim and recognition.

In addition to his liking for the arts, the Goat is usually quite religious and often has a deep interest in nature, animals and the countryside. He is also fairly athletic and there are many Goats who have excelled in some form of sporting activity or who have a great interest in sport.

Although the Goat is not particularly materialistic or concerned about finance, he will find that he will usually be lucky in financial matters and will rarely be short of the necessary funds to tide himself over. He is, however, rather indulgent and tends to spend his money as soon as he receives it rather than make provision for the future.

The Goat usually leaves home when he is young but he will always maintain strong links with his parents and the other members of his family. He is also rather nostalgic and is well known for keeping mementoes of his childhood and souvenirs of places that he has visited. His home will not be particularly tidy but he knows where everything is and it will also be scrupulously clean.

Affairs of the heart are particularly important to the Goat and he will often have many romances before he finally settles down. Although he is fairly adaptable, he prefers to live in a secure and stable environment and will find that he is best suited to those born under the signs of the Tiger, Horse, Monkey, Pig and Rabbit. He can also establish a good relationship with the Dragon, Snake, Rooster and another Goat, but he may find the Ox and Dog a little too serious for his liking. Neither will he care particularly for the Rat's rather thrifty ways.

The female Goat devotes all her time and energy to the needs of her family. She has excellent taste in home furnishings and often uses her considerable artistic skills to make clothes for herself and her children. She takes great care over her appearance and can be most attractive to the opposite sex. Although she is not the best organized of people, her engaging manner and delightful sense of humour create a favourable impression wherever she goes. She is also a good cook and usually gets much pleasure from gardening and outdoor pursuits.

The Goat can win friends easily and people generally feel relaxed in his company. He has a kind and under-standing nature and although he can occasionally be stub-born, with the right support and encouragement he can live a happy and very satisfying life. The more he can use his creative skills, the happier he will be.

THE FIVE DIFFERENT TYPES OF GOAT

In addition to the 12 signs of the Chinese zodiac, there are five elements, and these have a strengthening or moderating influence on the sign. The effects of the five elements on the Goat are described below, together with the years in which the elements were exercising their influence. Therefore all Goats born in 1931 and 1991 are Metal Goats, those born in 1943 are Water Goats, and so on.

Metal Goat: 1931, 1991

This Goat is thorough and conscientious in all that he does and is capable of doing very well in his chosen profession. Despite his confident manner, he can be a great worrier and he would find it helpful to discuss his concerns with others rather than keep them to himself. He is loyal to his family and employers and will have a small group of extremely good friends. He has good artistic taste and is usually highly skilled in some aspect of the arts. He is often a collector of antiques and his home will be very tastefully furnished.

Water Goat: 1943

The Water Goat is very popular and makes friends with remarkable ease. He is good at spotting opportunities but does not always have the necessary confidence to follow them through. He likes to have security both in his home life and at work and does not take kindly to change. He is articulate, has a good sense of humour and is usually very good with children.

Wood Goat: 1955

This Goat is generous, kind-hearted and always eager to please. He usually has a large circle of friends and involves himself in a wide variety of different activities. He has a very trusting nature but he can sometimes give in to the demands of others a little too easily and it would be in his own interests if he were to stand his ground a little more often. He is usually lucky in financial matters and, like the Water Goat, is very good with children.

Fire Goat: 1907, 1967

This Goat usually knows what he wants in life and he often uses his considerable charm and persuasive personality in order to achieve his aims. He can sometimes let his imagination run away with him and has a tendency to ignore matters which are not to his liking. He is rather extravagant in his spending and would do well to exercise a little more care when dealing with financial matters. He has a lively personality, many friends and loves attending parties and social occasions.

Earth Goat: 1919, 1979

This Goat has a very considerate and caring nature. He is particularly loyal to his family and friends and invariably creates a favourable impression wherever he goes. He is reliable and conscientious in his work but he finds it difficult to save and never likes to deprive himself of any little luxury which he might fancy. He has numerous interests and is often very well read. He usually gets much pleasure from following the activities of various members of his family.

PROSPECTS FOR THE GOAT IN 2001

The Chinese New Year starts on 24 January 2001. Until then, the old year, the Year of the Dragon, is still making its presence felt.

The Year of the Dragon (5 February 2000 to 23 January 2001) will not have been an especially easy one for the Goat. He will have faced pressures and changes in certain areas of his life as well as found progress sometimes difficult. However, despite the unsettling nature of the Dragon year, what has happened, together with what the Goat has accomplished, can often do much to prepare the way for the splendid prospects that lie ahead.

In particular, much value can come from the last quarter of the Dragon year and at this time the Goat should pay close attention to developments in his work, particularly any proposals under consideration or openings that he may learn about. Many Goats will find that something started in the closing stages of 2000 can prove significant in the forthcoming year. The Goat should also take advantage of any training opportunities he may be offered or any chances to take on duties that could usefully extend his experience. By showing willing he can do much to help his future prospects.

As far as financial matters are concerned, the Goat will need to proceed with care and watch his outgoings. With the latter part of the year being a more tradition-ally expensive time, his level of spending could easily exceed what he had allowed for. Also, he should be wary of taking unnecessary financial risks during the Dragon year.

More positive, however, are the Goat's relations with others and over the year he will have good cause to value the support given by those around him. Even in the closing stages of the year, if there is some matter troubling him, he should not hesitate to seek the views or assistance of others. He will also enjoy the various social occasions he attends at this time and at one could find himself being given advice by a relative or long-standing friend. He should listen well, for there will be much wisdom in what he is told and it could prove especially significant in view of the encouraging trends soon to emerge.

The Year of the Snake starts on 24 January and will be a favourable one for the Goat. Free from the often consider-able activity of the Dragon year, the Goat will feel more at ease and will both prosper and enjoy himself. In 2001 his prospects are indeed excellent, although as the year starts he would do well to give some thought to just what he would like to accomplish over the next 12 months, particu-larly the direction he would like his work to take. By having some goals to aim for he will find himself setting about his activities with a greater sense of purpose as well as accomplishing more as a result.

Especially well aspected is the Goat's work. In 2001 he will be given the chance to put his experience and abilities to more effective use and, as a result, will find greater fulfilment in what he does. Throughout the year he will find he is well placed to follow up the opportunities which arise, and by making the most of them, many Goats will be able to improve substantially on their present position. This is very much a year for making headway, with the Goat's efforts and talents being recognized and rewarded. The months of March, April and October are especially well aspected for career advancement.

Those Goats who start the year seeking work or who have decided the time has come to move from their present position, perhaps because they feel staid or have accomplished all they can, should also actively seek out opportunities to pursue. Sometimes these could arise in a chance manner and, by being in the right place at the right time, many Goats will be given a position which they are eminently suited for. As so many will find, work-wise, 2001 will be a year for new starts, new roles, improved prospects and greater satisfaction.

One of the Goat's strengths is his creativity and those Goats whose work allows them to draw on their ideas and talents can look forward to some particularly pleasing successes. During the Snake year they should make every effort to promote what they do. This especially applies to those Goats involved in design, communication, education, the arts or media.

The progress that the Goat makes will also lead to an improvement in his financial situation, something he will find most welcome. The Goat is one who very much appreciates money and he will enjoy buying himself and his loved ones some treats as well as improving his wardrobe, making purchases for his home and his interests, and spending money on socializing and breaks. Indeed, the Goat will have no shortage of ideas about what to spend his money on, but throughout the year he would still be wise to keep a tight control over his purse strings. If he is considering expensive purchases, he would do well to consider the options available rather than buying too hastily. This way he could often save himself unnecessary outlay as well as obtain something more suitable as a result. He should also aim to make some savings over the year; in time money saved now could grow into a useful asset.

Another area which is well aspected is travel and all Goats should aim to go away for a break or holiday over the year, perhaps visiting a destination they have had in mind for a while. For many, a holiday taken in 2001 could prove to be one of the best for some time.

The Goat always sets great store by his relations with others and in the Snake year his personal life will bring him much happiness. His family life will be especially rewarding, with him playing a full part in domestic matters as well as participating in the various family activities that take place. His own successes, together with those of his loved ones, will give a lift to the year and produce some special moments. The late summer is especially well aspected. However, while the Goat's domestic life will go well, there will be parts of the year which will be quite busy and if he feels he has too much to do and some household tasks are falling behind, he should not hesitate to ask for assistance rather than feel obliged to struggle on single-handed.

In addition to a pleasing domestic life, the Goat will also thoroughly enjoy his social life. Over the year he will receive various invitations to parties and gatherings and at many of these he will be on top form, impressing those he meets as well as adding to his circle of friends and acquaintances. For those Goats who are unattached and seeking romance, the Snake year is splendidly aspected, with many meeting their future partner. The month of April and the summer will be particularly positive times for social matters.

For any Goat who may start the Snake year feeling low or who has had some personal sadness to bear, this is very much a time to look to the present and future. By immersing himself in a range of different activities as well as going out more and meeting others, he really can do much to bring some happiness back into his life.

In so many respects, this will be a good year for the Goat. However, to benefit from the favourable aspects, he does need to go after the opportunities the year will bring as well as promote himself. Sometimes, due to his retiring nature, he will need to make an extra effort, but he will find it worthwhile. For the enterprising and determined Goat, this is a year which really does hold much potential and it will be one he will thoroughly enjoy.

As far as the different types of Goat are concerned, this will be a year that will suit the *Metal Goat*. After the often considerable activity of the Dragon year, the more settled Snake year will be something he will appreciate. It will not only give him the chance to adjust to some of the changes that have recently occurred but also allow him to set about his activities more in his own way. Admittedly, for some, the disruptive influences of the Dragon year may linger a little into the Snake year, particularly with regard to accommodation matters, but for the most part this will be a satisfying year. For those Metal Goats who have recently moved or who intend to do so, once installed, they will find themselves quickly settling into their new home. With their artistic leanings and eye for detail, many Metal Goats, whether they move or not, will take pleasure in adding refinements and features to their home, enhancing both its looks and comfort. Many will also decide to replace some equipment and furnishings over the year and will enjoy selecting these. The Metal Goat could also be particularly thrilled with some knick-knacks that he acquires and, for some, an item bought in 2001 could mark the start of a collection. The Metal Goat will also take much satisfaction from his hobbies and interests, and again those that allow him to use his creative talents will bring him especial pleasure. Also, if there has been a subject that he has been wanting to find out more about, this would be an excellent year in which to do so, either by enrolling on a course, joining a society or by personal study. In addition, those who enjoy craftwork, writing or some other creative pursuit should take the opportunity to show their work to others. They could be considerably encouraged by the response and inspired to do much more. As the Metal Goat will find, the Snake year will be supportive of anything related to self-development. For those Metal Goats born in 1991 this will be an important year in their education, with much material to be covered and many projects to undertake as well as some keynote tests. Although the young Metal Goat may not always feel comfortable with the demands placed upon him, by working steadily and giving of his best he will learn much as well as impress others. As always, if ever he feels he is struggling with a certain subject, he should not hesitate to ask rather than carry on unaided. As he will find, others can do much to support and reassure him. All Metal Goats, whether born in 1931 or 1991, will also value the interest shown in their activities by their loved ones and in addition to the encouragement they receive, they can look forward to many happy domestic occasions over the year. Those born in 1931 will take much interest in following the progress of family members as well as reciprocate the assistance they are given by helping others at various times. They will also enjoy any interests they can share with their loved ones as well as any breaks or holidays they take. Indeed, as this will mark their seventieth year, many more senior Metal Goats will decide to take a special holiday or visit a place that holds some significance for them. The Metal Goat's social life, too, is well aspected and he will enjoy meeting up with friends both old and new. Any Metal Goat who would like additional company would do well to consider joining a local group and so meet others of similar age and interests. Positive effort on his part will be very much rewarded. In most respects this will be a pleasurable year for the Metal Goat, with his activities and interests going well and many happy times indicated with both family and friends.

This will be a positive year for the *Water Goat* and one which will almost represent the start of a new chapter in his life. Coming after the often challenging times of the Dragon year, it will offer new opportunities, ones which the Water Goat is well qualified and placed to pursue. This is a time for progress and the enterprising Water Goat should make the most of the positive aspects that prevail and not feel fettered or encumbered by recent reversals or mistakes. These have happened. Now is the time to concentrate on the present and seize the chances that the year presents. Headway is possible at almost any time of the year, but particularly well aspected are the first and last quarters. For those Water Goats who are keen to move from their present position or are seeking work, the year will bring some interesting offers which may sometimes arise in an unexpected manner. Some Water Goats will find that the positions offered are unlike anything they have done before, but they will often feel inspired by their new tasks and will acquit themselves well. In contrast, some Water Goats will be offered the chance of early retirement. Although this may prove a difficult decision, by talking it over with their loved ones and looking carefully at their options, those Water Goats who do accept retirement can regard this as a new opportunity. By putting their extra time to practical use, these Water Goats really can turn this into a satisfying year. Whether retired or not, this is an excellent year for the Water Goat to attend to his various interests, maybe starting new projects, learning about different aspects of one of his hobbies or taking up a new one. The Water Goat's interests can bring him great pleasure, especially if they allow him to satisfy his creative yearnings. This will also be a positive year for financial matters, with many Water Goats seeing an increase in their income or receiving an additional sum. Many will decide to spend their money on both themselves and their home, often buying new clothes and furnishings as well as equipment. However, while the Water Goat will be pleased with many of his purchases, he should not be in too great a hurry to spend any additional funds he might receive. By planning his purchases and taking the time to compare the ranges and terms available, he will often fare much better. In addition, he would do well to set some money aside for a holiday or break and consider adding to his savings. This will also be a pleasing year in the Water Goat's personal life. As always, he will take a fond interest in the activities of those around him and his views and advice will be keenly sought. Indeed, the Water Goat may not always be aware of the high regard he is held in by others, but this will be brought home to him over the year and will greatly hearten him. There will also be cause for some family celebrations over the year, including possibly the birth of a grandchild. For any Water Goat who may have experienced some recent sadness or be feeling lonely, the year certainly holds brighter prospects. However, to benefit, these Water Goats should aim to go out more, especially to places where they can meet others. A local group or society could prove ideal. It does, though, rest with the Water Goat to take the initiative. Difficult though it might sometimes be, by making the effort he can do much to bring about a pleasing upturn in his social life. In most respects, this will be a favourable year for the Water Goat and by using his time well he will find that good fortune really will be on his side.

Almost as soon as the Snake year starts, the *Wood Goat* will sense that this is a year which will contain fine prospects for him and that by making an extra effort he will be able to accomplish a great deal. However, to make the most of the positive trends that prevail, the Wood Goat should give some thought to just what he wants to achieve over the next 12 months and decide on his objectives. As he will find, the clearer his target, the better chance he has of achieving it! He will also find it helpful to discuss his thoughts with those around him and, where work matters are concerned, by seeking out those with experience. He could then be given advice, information, leads and contacts which could prove useful. The Wood Goat should also actively pursue any openings that he sees and will often find himself ideally placed to benefit from these. In addition, some of the opportunities that arise will give him the chance to make more effective use of his skills and this, too, will help bring out his best. The months of February, March, September and October could be particularly promising for work matters, but overall the Snake year is a time of advance and the Wood Goat really should make the most of the opportunities that become available. Those Wood Goats who are seeking work, or who decide to switch jobs or careers over the year, will also enjoy pleasing developments. Again, they should actively follow up any openings that interest them and could be helped by considering different ways in which they could use their skills and experience. Once given a chance, they will rise to the challenges given them and quickly impress. Another important feature of the Snake year is that it will do much to restore the Wood Goat's faith in himself and abilities, and this too will help him progress. The positive developments that take place in the Wood Goat's work will lead to an increase in his income and financial matters will go well. However, to make the most of the favourable aspects that prevail, the Wood Goat should aim to be methodical, setting aside certain amounts for forthcoming expenses rather than proceeding on an ad hoc basis. This way he will be more aware of what he has available to spend and will often find himself able to give himself and his loved ones some additional treats over the year. For many Wood Goats these could include some items for their home, wardrobe and hobbies, as well as travel. Indeed, the Wood Goat will enjoy any breaks or holidays he is able to take during the year, not only benefiting from the rest and change of scene but also relishing the chance to visit some interesting and, in some cases, memorable destinations. The Wood Goat will also obtain much contentment from his domestic and social life. As always he will play a full part in family life, helping his loved ones and following their progress. There will be moments of considerable activity within his household, possibly including the marriage of a family member or someone moving out, perhaps for work or education. Again, the Wood Goat will play a helpful part in this, with those around him often coming to him for advice, assistance and sometimes reassurance. The Wood Goat may not always realize the important role he plays in the lives of so many, but this will become evident as the year unfolds. His social life, too, will bring him much pleasure and he will really enjoy meeting up with his friends, particularly when exchanging news and views. He can also look forward to attending some interesting social occasions during the year, with the chance to add to his circle of friends and acquaintances. For those who are unattached and maybe seeking romance, this will prove an exciting time, with someone they meet becoming important as the year progresses. In so many respects this really is a year that holds much promise for the Wood Goat. However, to truly benefit from the positive aspects that prevail, he must decide just what he wants to accomplish over the year and then set about his aims in earnest. For the determined and enterprising Wood Goat, the rewards and long-term significance of the year can be considerable.

This will be a year the *Fire Goat* will greatly enjoy, with positive developments occurring in many areas of his life. His domestic life will be especially rewarding, and where younger relations are concerned, the encouragement and any instruction the Fire Goat can give will not only be appreciated but often of lasting benefit. Indeed, the Fire Goat's ability to relate well to others will be truly valued over the year and he will often be pleased with the positive response his assistance brings. The Fire Goat will also busy himself with various projects in his home and garden, and will use his creative and practical talents to good effect, as, indeed, will so many Goats in the Snake year. Many Fire Goats will redecorate and sometimes redesign certain rooms and although at the time this may cause considerable disruption, everyone will be satisfied with the finished result. There is, though, one word of warning. When using potentially dangerous equipment or tackling any particularly complex activity, the Fire Goat must follow safety procedures and, if need be, seek advice. Similarly, if he has to move or lift heavy weights, he should obtain assistance. This is not a year in which to compromise his safety or risk what could be a nasty strain. In addition to the practical projects the Fire Goat carries out, he will also enjoy any interests and hobbies he can share with others. If there is an interest he would like to develop further, this would be a good year in which to do so, perhaps by enrolling on a suitable course, joining a society or studying by himself. By extending his knowledge and satisfying his curiosity, the Fire Goat can make this a personally rewarding time and what he learns will often be of value in the future. This is also an excellent year for work matters, with the Fire Goat being able to build on his present position and experience. Throughout 2001 he should keep alert for promotion possibilities or for ways in which he can develop his present role. His skills and ideas, together with his personable nature, will really impress others and this, too, will help him to make the progress he desires. In particular, those Fire Goats in positions which allow them to use their abilities to communicate or their creative talents can look forward to some notable successes and should make every effort to promote what they do. For the enterprising and determined, the year really does hold excellent prospects. Those Fire Goats who are seeking work or contemplating changing their present position should remain active in their quest and many will find themselves being offered a position which has potential for longer term development. Again, the Fire Goat will need to be active in making enquiries, but his initiative will be rewarded and will often bring him the chance he has been seeking for some time. The Fire Goat will also see an improvement in his financial situation over the year, though he still needs to manage his finances well. He does, after all, have many obligations to meet, particularly relating to accommodation, and he needs to budget for these. However, the improvement he enjoys will ease some of the pressures he may have been under and allow him to buy some items for himself and his loved ones as well as have a holiday later in the year. The Fire Goat values his social life and 2001 will find him in fine form and enjoying the various events he attends. He will make many new acquaintances over the year and for those Fire Goats who are looking for new friendships and romance, the year holds tremendous prospects. For the unattached, the months of March and April are especially well aspected for meeting someone who could, in time, become quite special. Overall, the year holds great prospects for the Fire Goat and by making good use of his skills and aiming to further his position, he can look forward to making excellent headway as well as finding greater fulfilment. Personally, too, this will be a splendid year, with the Fire Goat's domestic and social life bringing him much happiness.

This will be a memorable year for the *Earth Goat* with many positive developments taking place. Especially well aspected is his personal life. Romance and love will be to the fore, with many Earth Goats meeting someone who will become special to them or deciding to get engaged or married. Also, those who may have had some misfortune in personal relationships of late will find either that an existing relationship will pick up again, with both sides having learnt much from what has happened, or that a new person will enter their life. With his charm and friendly nature, the Earth Goat really revels in company and personally he will be in fine form throughout the year and will benefit from the superb aspects that prevail. There will, though, be some Earth Goats who, because of their work or education, find themselves having to move over the year. While they may not know anybody in the area they go to, even they will be surprised at how quickly their social life becomes active again. Indeed, the positive nature of the Snake year helps the Earth Goat come out of himself, with those who may be shy or reserved becoming more open and better able to enjoy social events. The year will also be positive for work matters and will give the Earth Goat the chance to use his skills in a more effective way than of late. For those Earth Goats who start the Snake year seeking work or with misgivings about their current situation, very early in 2001 opportunities will arise which will lead to them obtaining the type of position they have been wanting or transferring to a better position within the organization in which they are currently based. By remaining alert, almost all Earth Goats will be able to improve on their present situation and help their future prospects. With work matters being so positive, the Earth Goat should also take advantage of any training opportunities he may be offered or any ways in which he can extend his skills. Even if this requires him studying a course in his own time, anything he can do to enhance his prospects will be to his advantage. The advances that the Earth Goat makes in his work will bring an upturn in his financial situation, but with many demands upon his resources and the new obligations he will take on over the year, he should manage his money carefully rather than muddle through, as some might be tempted to do. By handling his finances with care, the Earth Goat will find he is able to put his money to better use as well as avoid some of the problems that could otherwise arise. Although care is called for in 2001, all Earth Goats should aim to treat themselves to a holiday or break over the year, particularly as travel is so well aspected. For any Earth Goat who is keen to extend his language skills, this could be a good year to consider the possibility of lengthy overseas travel or working in another country. Overall this will be a splendid year for the Earth Goat, one which will bring much happiness to his personal life and also open up many exciting possibilities for him, particularly work-wise. The Snake year will also help to reveal, both to himself and others, his considerable potential and this will give him the confidence to rise to greater heights over the next few years. The Earth Goat is growing in stature and really starting to carve his own future, and a promising future it looks to be.

FAMOUS GOATS

Pamela Anderson, Isaac Asimov, W. H. Auden, Jane Austen, Anne Bancroft, George Benson, Cilla Black, Mary Black, George Burns, Lord Byron, Leslie Caron, John le Carré, Coco Chanel, Mary Higgins Clark, Nat 'King' Cole, Harry Connick Jr, Angus Deayton, Catherine Deneuve, John Denver, Charles Dickens, Angie Dickinson, Ken Dodd, Sir Arthur Conan Doyle, Daphne Du Maurier, Douglas Fairbanks, Dame Margot Fonteyn, Anna Ford, Noel Gallagher, Bill Gates, Mel Gibson, Paul Michael Glaser, Whoopi Goldberg, Mikhail Gorbachev, John Grisham, Oscar Hammerstein, George Harrison, Sir Edmund Hillary, John Humphrys, Billy Idol, Julio Iglesias, Mick

Jagger, Nicole Kidman, Ben Kingsley, David Kossoff, Doris Lessing, Franz Liszt, John Major, Michelangelo, Joni Mitchell, Rupert Murdoch, Mussolini, Randy Newman, Robert de Niro, Des O'Connor, Sinead O'Connor, Lord Olivier, Michael Palin, Eva Peron, Marcel Proust, Keith Richards, Julia Roberts, William Shatner, Jerry Springer, R. L. Stine, Lana Turner, Mark Twain, Rudolph Valentino, Vangelis, Barbara Walters, John Wayne, Fay Weldon, Bruce Willis, Debra Winger, Tom Wolfe, Paul Young.

2 FEBRUARY 1908 ～ 21 JANUARY 1909 *Earth Monkey*

20 FEBRUARY 1920 ～ 7 FEBRUARY 1921 *Metal Monkey*

6 FEBRUARY 1932 ～ 25 JANUARY 1933 *Water Monkey*

25 JANUARY 1944 ～ 12 FEBRUARY 1945 *Wood Monkey*

12 FEBRUARY 1956 ～ 30 JANUARY 1957 *Fire Monkey*

30 JANUARY 1968 ～ 16 FEBRUARY 1969 *Earth Monkey*

16 FEBRUARY 1980 ～ 4 FEBRUARY 1981 *Metal Monkey*

4 FEBRUARY 1992 ～ 22 JANUARY 1993 *Water Monkey*

THE
MONKEY

THE PERSONALITY OF THE MONKEY

Those who are the most persistent, and work in the true spirit, will invariably be the most successful.

Samuel Smiles: a Monkey

The Monkey is born under the sign of fantasy. He is imaginative, inquisitive and loves to keep an eye on everything that is going on around him. He is never backward in offering advice or trying to sort out the problems of others. He likes to be helpful and his advice is invariably sensible and reliable.

The Monkey is intelligent, well read and always eager to learn. He has an extremely good memory and there are many Monkeys who have made particularly good linguists. The Monkey is also a convincing talker and enjoys taking part in discussions and debates. His friendly, self-assured manner can be very persuasive and he usually has little trouble in winning people round to his way of thinking. It is for this reason that the Monkey often excels in politics and public speaking. He is also particularly adept at PR work, teaching and any job which involves selling.

The Monkey can, however, be crafty, cunning and occasionally dishonest, and he will seize on any opportunity to make a quick gain or outsmart his opponents. He has so much charm and guile that people often don't realize what he is up to until it is too late. But despite his resourceful nature, the Monkey does run the risk of outsmarting even himself. He has so much confidence in his abilities that he rarely listens to advice or is prepared to accept help from anyone. He likes to help others but prefers to rely on his own judgement when dealing with his own affairs.

Another characteristic of the Monkey is that he is extremely good at solving problems and has a happy knack of extricating himself (and others) from the most hopeless of positions. He is the master of self-preservation.

With so many diverse talents the Monkey is able to make considerable sums of money, but he does like to enjoy life and will think nothing of spending his money on some exotic holiday or luxury which he has had his eye on. He can, however, become very envious if someone else has got what he wants.

The Monkey is an original thinker and despite his love of company, he cherishes his independence. He has to have the freedom to act as he wants and any Monkey who feels hemmed in or bound by too many restrictions can soon become unhappy. Likewise, if anything becomes too boring or monotonous, the Monkey soon loses interest and turns his attention to something else. He lacks persistence and this can often hamper his progress. He is also easily distracted, a tendency which all Monkeys should try to overcome. The Monkey should concentrate on one thing at a time and by doing so will almost certainly achieve more in the long run.

The Monkey is a good organizer and, even though he may behave slightly erratically at times, he will invariably have some plan at the back of his mind. On the odd occasion when his plans do not quite work out, he is usually quite happy to shrug his shoulders and put it down to experience. He will rarely make the same mistake twice and throughout his life he will try his hand at many things.

The Monkey likes to impress and is rarely without followers or admirers. There are many who are attracted by his good looks, his sense of humour or simply because he instils so much confidence.

Monkeys usually marry young and for it to be a success their partner must allow them time to pursue their many interests and indulge in their love of travel. The Monkey has to have variety in his life and is especially well suited to those born under the sociable and outgoing signs of the Rat, Dragon, Pig and Goat. The Ox, Rabbit, Snake and Dog will also be enchanted by the Monkey's resourceful and outgoing nature, but he is likely to exasperate the Rooster and Horse, and the Tiger will have little patience with his tricks. A relationship between two Monkeys will work well – they will understand each other and be able to assist each other in their various enterprises.

The female Monkey is intelligent, extremely observant and a shrewd judge of character. Her opinions are often highly valued and, having such a persuasive nature, she invariably gets her own way. She has many interests and involves herself in a wide variety of activities. She pays great attention to her appearance, is an elegant dresser and likes to take particular care over her hair. She can also be a caring and doting parent and will have many good and loyal friends.

Provided the Monkey can curb his desire to take part in all that is going on around him and can concentrate on one thing at a time, he can usually achieve what he wants in life. Should he suffer any disappointments, he is bound to bounce back. The Monkey is a survivor and his life is usually both colourful and very eventful.

THE FIVE DIFFERENT TYPES OF MONKEY

In addition to the 12 signs of the Chinese zodiac, there are five elements and these have a strengthening or moderating influence on the sign. The effects of the five elements on the Monkey are described below, together with the years in which the elements were exercising their influence. Therefore all Monkeys born in 1920 and 1980 are Metal Monkeys, those born in 1932 and 1992 are Water Monkeys, and so on.

Metal Monkey: 1920, 1980

The Metal Monkey is very strong-willed. He sets about everything he does with a dogged determination and often prefers to work independently rather than with others. He is ambitious, wise and confident, and is certainly not afraid of hard work. He is very astute in financial matters and usually chooses his investments well. Despite his somewhat independent nature, the Metal Monkey enjoys attending parties and social occasions and is particularly warm and caring towards his loved ones.

Water Monkey: 1932, 1992

The Water Monkey is versatile, determined and perceptive. He has more discipline than some of the other Monkeys and is prepared to work towards a certain goal rather than be distracted by something else. He is not always open about his true intentions and when questioned can be particularly evasive. He can be sensitive to criticism but also very persuasive and usually has little trouble in getting others to fall in with his plans. He has a very good understanding of human nature and relates well to others.

Wood Monkey: 1944

This Monkey is efficient, methodical and extremely conscientious. He is also highly imaginative and is always trying to capitalize on new ideas or learn new skills. Occasionally his enthusiasm can get the better of him and he can get very agitated when things do not quite work out as he had hoped. He does, however, have a very adventurous streak and is not afraid of taking risks. He also loves travel. He is usually held in great esteem by his friends and colleagues.

Fire Monkey: 1956

The Fire Monkey is intelligent, full of vitality and has no trouble in commanding the respect of others. He is imaginative and has wide interests, although sometimes these can distract him from more useful and profitable work. He is very competitive and always likes to be involved in everything that is going on. He can be stubborn if he does not get his own way and he sometimes tries to indoctrinate those who are less strong-willed than himself. The Fire Monkey is a lively character, popular with the opposite sex and extremely loyal to his partner.

Earth Monkey: 1908, 1968

The Earth Monkey tends to be studious and well read, and can become quite distinguished in his chosen line of work. He is less outgoing than some of the other types of Monkey and prefers quieter and more solid pursuits. He has high principles, a very caring nature and can be most generous to those less fortunate than himself. He is usually successful in handling financial matters and can become very wealthy in old age. He has a calming influence on those around him and is respected and well liked by those he meets. He is, however, especially careful about whom he lets into his confidence.

PROSPECTS FOR THE MONKEY IN 2001

The Chinese New Year starts on 24 January 2001. Until then, the old year, the Year of the Dragon, is still making its presence felt.

The Year of the Dragon (5 February 2000 to 23 January 2001) will have been a fine year for the Monkey and one which will have suited his resourceful and enterprising nature.

During the Dragon year the Monkey will have felt inspired to make the most of his talents and ideas, often with pleasing results. Many Monkeys will have been able to make good headway in their work, taking on new and sometimes more remunerative duties. Some may even have decided to switch to a different type of work and will have enjoyed rising to the fresh challenges this will have brought. For any Monkey currently looking for work or wanting to make further progress, the aspects remain favourable right to the end of the year. The Dragon year certainly favours the determined and enterprising, and the Monkey is this and more! Also, if he has any ideas he is still yearning to try, whether personal, work related or connected with his interests, he should consider setting these in motion. 'Nothing ventured, nothing gained', as the saying goes, and by venturing the Monkey does stand to gain a great deal.

The positive developments in the Monkey's working life will also bring an increase in his income, but he does need to watch his level of spending. Without some control, he could find his outgoings exceeding expectations. This particularly applies to the last quarter of 2000, which can prove an expensive time.

The Monkey's personal life will go well, with both his domestic and social life bringing many pleasurable occasions. For the unattached and those who would like more company, the prospects for meeting others and striking up what can become an important friendship remain high to the end of the year. November and December 2000 are especially well aspected months for personal matters, with much socializing and many enjoyable times indicated.

The Year of the Snake starts on 24 January and while sometimes lacking the activity of the Dragon year, it will still be a reasonable one for the Monkey. The Monkey is blessed with an adaptable nature and this allows him to adjust better than some to the conditions that prevail. He will be keenly aware of many of the undercurrents and trends of the Snake year and will often be able to turn them to his advantage.

As far as his work is concerned, the Monkey will be able to consolidate and build on his present situation and continue to make steady progress. Those who have recently taken on new duties, or do so over the year, should aim to familiarize themselves with the different aspects of their work as well as take advantage of any training that may be offered. By making the most of his current situation and showing himself willing and keen, the Monkey will not only impress others but also extend his experience and this will be to his advantage when new opportunities do emerge.

The Monkey should also remain keenly aware of the views of his colleagues over the year as well as of any new proposals under consideration. He is usually a past master at this, however, and is able to adapt easily and make the most of new situations as they arise. During 2001, his versatility and resourcefulness will again serve him well.

Work-wise, the Snake year will offer all Monkeys the chance to progress, but they will need to work towards it rather than having opportunities dropping into their lap. Those Monkeys who are seeking work or wanting to move from their current position should give serious consideration to what they want to do. By having some firm ideas, they will find themselves becoming more focused on the type of openings they should pursue as well as better able to prepare themselves. Carrying out appropriate research into the relevant position or company before an interview is something which will impress others and can help swing the interview in the Monkey's favour. The months of May and June as well as the period from September to early December could see some interesting career developments.

In addition to benefiting from any vocational training, this is also an excellent year for the Monkey to consider extending his own skills and interests. If there is something he has been keen to learn, he should make every attempt to do so, either by personal study or enrolling on a suitable course. The Monkey is blessed with a most inquisitive mind and the Snake year will certainly satisfy his thirst for knowledge as well as his desire to extend his abilities. Also, for those with musical talents, this would be an especially fine year in which to learn an instrument, further their skills and promote what they do.

The Monkey's money-making abilities will also be in good form over the year, with most Monkeys enjoying an increase in their income. Some may be able to add to this by putting one of their skills to enterprising use. However, as always, the Monkey should avoid pushing his luck too far and taking any unnecessary risks. Occasionally, in his enthusiasm to improve his situation, he can become careless and overlook certain details, and this is something he must guard against. This also applies to any important long-term obligations he takes on. The Monkey should check the small print carefully and make the appropriate allowances in his budget. However, by managing his money well, he will find this a generally encouraging year for financial matters and almost all Monkeys will end the year in a considerably improved financial position.

The Monkey's domestic life is another area which will go well but again does require some care. As usual, the

Monkey will play a full part in family life and will assist and encourage others. There will be many memorable occasions with his loved ones to enjoy, with the activities and progress of family members bringing much pleasure, as will any projects that can be carried out together. However, while so much can go well, some problems and tensions could still occur and the Monkey should watch this. In some cases difficulties could arise due a lack of consultation over arrangements or through tetchiness, perhaps caused by tiredness or preoccupation over some matter. If the Monkey senses tensions brewing, he really should take steps to ease them or talk them through before they start to take the edge off what can be an agreeable year. In addition, if the Monkey has any problems, rather than keeping them to himself (as he is prone to do), he would find it helpful to discuss them. He will find this will often help to put the matter into perspective as well as lead to an easing or resolution of his difficulty. Monkeys, do remember this.

The Monkey will also lead an interesting social life over the year, particularly valuing meeting up with his friends, including some he may not have seen for some time. Over the year, he will find that certain friends will give him advice, which he would do well to heed. Knowing the Monkey as they do, his friends speak with his best interests at heart and some of what they tell him can be of great help to him. Monkeys, again, do take note and listen to the well-meaning advice you are given.

As usual, the Monkey will enjoy the various social occasions that he attends, with the younger Monkey's social life being particularly busy, especially over the summer.

For the unattached, affairs of the heart will play an important part in the Snake year, though they may not always run smoothly. Again, the Monkey should remain keenly aware of the views and feelings of others and allow time for any new relationship to develop rather than rush into too hasty a commitment. Once again, the Monkey's relations with others can bring happiness in 2001, but care and understanding are required.

Overall, the Snake year will be a positive time for the Monkey, with the chance to build on his achievements as well as to extend his interests. Resourceful as ever, he will make the best of what the year produces and will emerge from it wiser and with some pleasing gains to his credit.

As far as the different types of Monkey are concerned, this will be an interesting and generally successful year for the *Metal Monkey*. Admittedly, not all his plans and ideas may work out as he had envisaged, but the year will present him with some fine opportunities and, resourceful as ever, he will be able to turn many of these to his advantage. Whether in work or seeking work, this will be a positive year for him. The Metal Monkey is always keen to make the most of himself and his enthusiasm and commitment will show through and impress those around him. As a result, many Metal Monkeys will be given additional duties as the year progresses. By rising to all that is asked of them and more, they will usefully extend their experience as well as do much to enhance their prospects both for later in the year and for the future. Also, some of those Metal Monkeys seeking work could find themselves being offered duties different from what they have done before, and again by showing willing and tackling the tasks given, they will not only broaden their experience but could also discover a new strength that they are able to develop. Whether in work or seeking it, by being flexible in attitude, the Metal Monkey will find some interesting possibilities opening up, some of which will have a significant bearing on his long-term future. With its cultural overtones, this is also a positive year for academic matters and those Metal Monkeys involved in study can look forward to obtaining some satisfying results. However, these Metal Monkeys should aim to set about their studies in a planned and systematic way, allowing themselves plenty of time for exam revision and course work rather than cramming a lot in all at once. Good organization will not only lead to better results but could also ease some of the pressure. This will be a positive year for personal matters, with love, romance and an active social life all well aspected. For those Metal Monkeys in a relationship, the year can bring much happiness, including, for some, the possibility of engagement and marriage. However, as with all Monkeys in 2001, the Metal Monkey must pay close attention to the views of partners and close friends and remain aware of their feelings. If he bears this in mind, then his personal life can bring him great joy and contentment. For those Metal Monkeys seeking new friends and perhaps romance, the Snake year holds excellent prospects, with someone they meet – often by chance – becoming significant. For socializing, the summer will be an especially active and auspicious time. As far as financial matters are concerned, while this is not an adverse year, care is required and the Metal Monkey should keep account of all he spends as well as any funds he has to borrow. Fortunately his generally careful and shrewd approach will help, but this is a year which does require careful financial management and some juggling of his resources. Also, while the Metal Monkey may be interested in improving his financial lot, he should avoid taking undue risks or committing himself to dubious or 'get rich quick' schemes. All may not be as it seems and vigilance is needed. Although the Metal Monkey will have much to occupy him, he should also set time aside for his own personal interests over the year. Not only will these provide him with some rewarding occasions, especially those that take him out of doors and allow him to meet others, but they also give him the chance to have a break from his usual preoccupations. Those who are sportingly inclined can look forward to some particularly memorable and exciting moments. Generally, this will be a positive year for the Metal Monkey and provided he is prepared to be adaptable in his outlook and make full use of the opportunities that occur, he can do much to pave the way for the often considerable progress he will make in the next few years. Personally, too, this will be a significant year, with love and romance making it all the more special.

This will be a satisfying year for the *Water Monkey* and with his wide interests, he will find himself becoming involved in a multitude of different activities. One particularly rewarding area concerns his interests, especially those that allow him to draw on his creative talents. Those Water Monkeys who enjoy pursuits such as music, art, photography, designing or some other creative activity would do well to further their interest, possibly experimenting with new ideas and techniques or tackling some more challenging projects. Those who enjoy writing could consider writing about one of their interests and passing on their knowledge to fellow enthusiasts, perhaps through a specialist magazine or even, if they are able, over the Internet. Some might decide to research and write about something more personal, such as their experiences through the years or their family history. This or any other activity or project the Water Monkey chooses to develop can make this a rich and personally fulfilling year. There are also many Water Monkeys who are keen gardeners and they too will take much pleasure from what they carry out over the year, although they should be careful when digging or lifting heavy weights. If not, a resultant strain could not only cause discomfort but also some frustration, as it could prevent the Water Monkey from completing all he wants to do. Water Monkeys, do take note. The Water Monkey always sets much store by his home life and over the year he will do much to encourage the activities of those dear to him. However, although he may aim to act in the interests of all, it is important that he keeps others informed of any arrangements he has in mind. If not, misunderstandings could result. In addition, the Water Monkey has a secretive streak to his nature and keeping his thoughts too much to himself could cause problems. This is something he needs to watch, particularly if he is to preserve domestic harmony. Those Water Monkeys born in 1992 will very much appreciate the support they are given by those around them, but there could be occasions when their views will clash with those of others. At such times, rather than dig his heels in, the young Water Monkey should show willingness to explain his own viewpoint and also listen very carefully to what those more senior have to say. Young Water Monkeys, take note and try not to let often small differences sour what could be a very pleasant home life. These Water Monkeys will, however, be satisfied with how their schoolwork progresses over the year and could become particularly inspired by some topic work that they have to do. If they have uncertainties over any areas of their work, they should not hesitate to seek additional help. As they will find, others can do much to ease some of their concerns. One other area that is favoured is travel and all Water Monkeys should take advantage of any opportunity to go away. Visits to relations and friends not seen for some time can go particularly well. Overall, this will be a pleasant and constructive year for the Water Monkey and provided he handles his relations with others with care, it will contain many happy and rewarding occasions. The Water Monkey should make sure he devotes ample time to developing his own personal interests, as these are especially well aspected and can bring him much personal satisfaction.

These will be interesting times for the *Wood Monkey* and by adapting to the situations in which he finds himself and being his resourceful self, he will find that much good can come from the Snake year. Many Wood Monkeys will have seen considerable change in their work during the often active Dragon year and the legacy of this will linger on. As a result, further changes are likely and these will provide some interesting opportunities for the Wood Monkey to pursue. Openings may arise as a result of recent developments or through the Wood Monkey's own ideas, but when they do occur, they should be followed up. Many Wood Monkeys will find themselves able to move to the type of position they have been wanting for a long time. For those Wood Monkeys who may be seeking work, the Snake year is also capable of springing some surprises. Sometimes, if the Wood Monkey finds himself eligible for training, he could find that the acquisition of a new skill could lead to a job offer which will bring with it an interesting personal challenge. Again, his enterprising spirit will serve him well, with his 'give it a go' attitude winning him many plaudits and leading to impressive results. Some Wood Monkeys may also be able to put one of their interests or hobbies to profitable use, especially if it allows them to create certain pieces of work. This will also be a favourable year for financial matters, with many Wood Monkeys receiving a sum for work they have done or seeing a general improvement in their income. However, while he may be grateful for these additional funds, the Wood Monkey should still handle his money with care. Particularly where expensive purchases are concerned, he would be wise to take his time and examine the ranges and options on offer rather than proceed too hastily. This way he will often end up with something more suitable as well as saving himself some unnecessary outlay. Also, with his love of travel, the Wood Monkey should aim to set some money aside for a holiday or break, as he will not only enjoy this but it could do him considerable good. He will draw much pleasure from his domestic life in 2001, particularly from encouraging the activities of family members, and will offer some practical support to someone dear to him. His efforts will be greatly appreciated, but while so much in his domestic life can go well, there could be matters which might cause him concern or give rise to a difference of opinion. At such times, particularly if the Wood Monkey senses problems looming, he should talk matters over and aim for some sort of understanding or agreement before tensions start to cast a shadow over family life. The Snake year is very much a time when the Wood Monkey should remain keenly aware of the feelings of others and be prepared to take a more accommodating attitude in order to preserve domestic harmony. He can, however, look forward to an interesting and enjoyable social life over the year. If he is a member of a society or group, or decides to join one over the year, he could find himself playing an active part. Generally, the Snake year will be a fine one for the Wood Monkey and while he may sometimes have to modify his plans to fit in with changing circumstances or the views of others, he will find that his achievements will bring him a great deal of personal satisfaction.

Although the *Fire Monkey* will have achieved a great deal in recent years, he will generally find the Snake year a more fulfilling time than of late. In his work he may well decide that rather than looking to make major advances or switching to different duties, he will build on his current position, concentrating on his present duties and the areas he knows best. By doing this he will be able to achieve some impressive results as well as do much to further his longer term prospects. He will also find his work much more satisfying than in recent months and this will help to keep him motivated. In addition to concentrating on his duties, the Fire Monkey should not hold back from advancing any ideas he has and when opportunities arise for him to take on additional duties or become involved in new projects or proposals, he should accept them. Opportunities taken in the Snake year often have a habit of developing in a meaningful way in the future. For those Fire Monkeys who are seeking work, the Snake year will also bring some offers and by taking advantage of these the Fire Monkey will be able to impress others and build a base from which to develop. The Fire Monkey knows that he is capable of a great deal and the Snake year will not only give him the chance to put his abilities to effective use but also set him firmly on course for more substantial progress over the next few years. The months of May and June and last quarter of the year could see some interesting career developments. This will be a reasonable year for financial matters, although the Fire Monkey could face some large expenses. These could be due to a major family occasion, assisting a relation in education or accommodation and transport costs. The Fire Monkey would be helped by making allowance for these as soon as he is able. By managing his money well he can do much to avoid or minimize some of the problems the more expensive parts of the year can bring. The Fire Monkey's domestic life will be active and generally pleasurable over the year, and he will do much to help, advise and support those around him. At certain times there will, though, be a great deal for him to do. At especially busy periods, he should prioritize his tasks and if need be postpone or defer certain projects. He will find this better than trying to fit in just too much. In addition, the Fire Monkey must make sure he consults others over any arrangements rather than just proceeds with what he assumes they would like. To jump to conclusions or make plans without consultation could lead to disagreements and this is something the Fire Monkey should watch. He will, however, enjoy his social life over the year, particularly meeting up with friends and the various social events he attends. The summer promises to be both busy and interesting! With all the activities of the year, though, it is important that the Fire Monkey does not ignore his own well-being. He should make sure he takes regular exercise and has a balanced and healthy diet. To do all he wants in 2001, he must aim to keep himself in good shape! Overall, this will be a positive and interesting year for the Fire Monkey and what he accomplishes in his work will often have an important bearing on his future. His domestic and social life, too, will be quite active, with both bringing him considerable pleasure.

For the *Earth Monkey* this will be a year of surprises and interesting developments. Although much will have happened in his life of late, significant changes are still very much in the offing. In his work the Earth Monkey will be given the chance to extend his current duties and will find himself well placed to make advances. Several of these opportunities could occur in an unexpected manner, for instance when colleagues suddenly leave or new proposals create further openings. In addition, the Earth Monkey should pursue any opportunities that particularly interest him and should promote his ideas. During the Snake year he will greatly impress, not only with his considerable abilities but also his keen and innovative approach. His reputation and stature are set to grow a considerable amount in 2001! Whether in work or seeking work, the Earth Monkey should also take advantage of any training he is eligible for and will find that adding to his skills will help his prospects. Earth Monkeys seeking work will find that once they manage to get a foothold in a company or organization, they will be able to build on this. As all Earth Monkeys will find, the Snake year will present some interesting opportunities and it rests with them to make the most of them. It is also possible that a few Earth Monkeys may be able to put one of their interests or skills to profitable use, and it may even give rise to an employment opportunity. For those with an enterprising disposition, it would certainly be worth furthering their ideas and seeing what results. Although many Earth Monkeys will enjoy an increase in their income over the year, there will still be many obligations to meet and the Earth Monkey could also face some additional expenses, particularly in relation to accommodation and transport. In view of this, he would do well to manage his finances with his usual skill and keep a close watch over his general level of spending. Careful monitoring of his financial position can do much to prevent problems from arising as well as enable him to put his money to more effective use. The Earth Monkey's personal life over the year will be busy and rewarding. Domestically, there will be many demands upon his time and he will do much to support both younger and more senior relations. What he does will be greatly valued, although if at any time there is any matter particularly concerning him he should aim to talk things over with others rather than keep his thoughts to himself. Also, while the Earth Monkey may be willing to take a lot upon himself, with family matters and the usual household duties as well as all his own activities he will find some parts of the year demanding. At such times, he should try to share out some of the responsibilities and chores. He will find others willing to help, but they may sometimes need to be prompted into action! However, despite all the activity, there will still be much in his domestic life that will bring the Earth Monkey a great deal of pleasure. This includes making improvements to his home and garden, pursuing mutual interests and going on outings with his loved ones. The Earth Monkey's social life will also be active, with an often wide and interesting range of social occasions to attend. For those who are unattached or who want to enlarge their social circle, there will be splendid opportunities for meeting others and establishing what can become good and important friendships. The spring and late summer are especially well aspected for this. Overall, there is much that will go in the Earth Monkey's favour in 2001, but throughout the year he must be receptive to the opportunities on offer as well as aim to make full use of his considerable talents. For the positive and enterprising Earth Monkey, this is a year which will not only allow him to make headway but also set him on course for even more substantial progress in the future.

FAMOUS MONKEYS

Gillian Anderson, Francesca Annis, Michael Aspel, J. M. Barrie, Jacqueline Bisset, Victor Borge, Dave Brubeck, Julius Caesar, Johnny Cash, Jacques Chirac, Chelsea Clinton, Joe Cocker, Colette, John Constable, Alistair

Cooke, David Copperfield, Patricia Cornwell, Joan Crawford, Leonardo da Vinci, Timothy Dalton, Bette Davis, Danny De Vito, Bo Derek, Jonathan Dimbleby, Celine Dion, Jason Donovan, Michael Douglas, Mia Farrow, Carrie Fisher, F. Scott Fitzgerald, Ian Fleming, Dick Francis, Fiona Fullerton, Paul Gauguin, Mika Häkkinnen, Jerry Hall, Tom Hanks, Martina Hingis, Harry Houdini, Nasser Hussain, P. D. James, Pope John Paul II, Lyndon B. Johnson, Buster Keaton, Edward Kennedy, Nigel Kennedy, Don King, Gladys Knight, Patti LaBelle, Leo McKern, Bob Marley, Walter Matthau, Kylie Minogue, Jack Nicklaus, Jana Novotna, Peter O'Toole, Anthony Perkins, Robert Powell, Lisa Marie Presley, Debbie Reynolds, Sir Tim Rice, Little Richard, Mickey Rooney, Diana Ross, Boz Scaggs, Gerhard Schröder, Michael Schumacher, Tom Selleck, Omar Sharif, Wilbur Smith, Rod Stewart, Jacques Tati, Elizabeth Taylor, Dame Kiri Te Kanawa, David Trimble, Harry Truman, Venus Williams.

22 JANUARY 1909 ~ 9 FEBRUARY 1910   *Earth Rooster*

8 FEBRUARY 1921 ~ 27 JANUARY 1922   *Metal Rooster*

26 JANUARY 1933 ~ 13 FEBRUARY 1934   *Water Rooster*

13 FEBRUARY 1945 ~ 1 FEBRUARY 1946   *Wood Rooster*

31 JANUARY 1957 ~ 17 FEBRUARY 1958   *Fire Rooster*

17 FEBRUARY 1969 ~ 5 FEBRUARY 1970   *Earth Rooster*

5 FEBRUARY 1981 ~ 24 JANUARY 1982   *Metal Rooster*

23 JANUARY 1993 ~ 9 FEBRUARY 1994   *Water Rooster*

THE
ROOSTER

THE PERSONALITY OF
THE ROOSTER

If I were to wish for anything, I should not wish for wealth and power, but for the passionate sense of the potential, for the eye which, ever young and ardent, sees the possible ... what wine is so sparkling, so fragrant, so intoxicating, as possibility!

Søren Kierkegaard: a Rooster

The Rooster is born under the sign of candour. He has a flamboyant and colourful personality and is meticulous in all that he does. He is an excellent organizer and wherever possible likes to plan his various activities well in advance.

The Rooster is highly intelligent and usually very well read. He has a good sense of humour and is an effective and persuasive speaker. He loves discussion and enjoys taking part in any sort of debate. He has no hesitation in speaking his mind and is forthright in his views. He does, however, lack tact and can easily damage his reputation or cause offence by some thoughtless remark or action. The Rooster also has a very volatile nature and he should always try to avoid acting on the spur of the moment.

The Rooster is usually very dignified in his manner and conducts himself with an air of confidence and authority. He is adept at handling financial matters and, as with most things, he organizes his financial affairs with considerable skill. He chooses his investments well and is capable of achieving great wealth. Most Roosters save or use their money wisely, but there are a few who are the reverse and are notorious spendthrifts. Fortunately, the Rooster has great earning capacity and is rarely without sufficient funds to tide himself over.

Another characteristic of the Rooster is that he invariably carries a notebook or scraps of paper around with him. He is constantly writing himself reminders or noting down important facts lest he forgets – the Rooster cannot abide inefficiency and conducts all his activities in an orderly, precise and methodical manner.

The Rooster is usually very ambitious, but can be unrealistic in some of what he hopes to achieve. He occasionally lets his imagination run away with him and while he does not like any interference from others, it would be in his own interests if he were to listen to their views a little more often. He also does not like criticism and if he feels anybody is doubting his judgement or prying too closely into his affairs, he is certain to let his feelings be known. He can also be rather self-centred and stubborn over relatively trivial matters, but to compensate for this he is reliable, honest and trustworthy, and this is very much appreciated by all who come into contact with him.

Roosters born between the hours of five and seven, both at dawn and sundown, tend to be the most extrovert of their sign, but all Roosters like to lead an active social life and enjoy attending parties and big functions. The Rooster usually has a wide circle of friends and is able to build up influential contacts with remarkable ease. He often belongs to several clubs and societies and involves himself in a variety of different activities. He is particularly interested in the environment, humanitarian affairs and anything affecting the welfare of others. The Rooster has a very caring nature and will do much to help those less fortunate than himself.

He also gets much pleasure from gardening and, while he may not always spend as much time in the garden as he would like, his garden is invariably well kept and extremely productive.

The Rooster is generally very distinguished in his appearance and if his job permits, he will wear an official uniform with great pride and dignity. He is not averse to publicity and takes great delight in being the centre of attention. He often does well at PR work or any job which brings him into contact with the media. He also makes a very good teacher.

The female Rooster leads a varied and interesting life. She involves herself in many different activities and there are some who wonder how she can achieve so much. She often holds very strong views and, like her male counter-part, has no hesitation in speaking her mind or telling others how she thinks things should be done. She is supremely efficient and well organized and her home is usually very neat and tidy. She has good taste in clothes and usually wears smart but very practical outfits.

The Rooster usually has a large family and as a parent takes a particularly active interest in the education of his children. He is very loyal to his partner and will find that he is especially well suited to those born under the signs of the Snake, Horse, Ox and Dragon. Provided they do not interfere too much in the Rooster's various activities, the Rat, Tiger, Goat and Pig can also establish a good relation-ship with him, but two Roosters together are likely to squabble and irritate each other. The rather sensitive Rabbit will find the Rooster a bit too blunt for his liking, and the Rooster will quickly become exasperated by the ever-inquisitive and artful Monkey. He will also find it difficult to get on with the anxious Dog.

If the Rooster can overcome his volatile nature and exercise more tact, he will go far in life. He is capable and talented and will invariably make a lasting – and usually favourable – impression almost everywhere he goes.

THE FIVE DIFFERENT TYPES OF ROOSTER

In addition to the 12 signs of the Chinese zodiac, there are five elements and these have a strengthening or moderating influence on the sign. The effects of the five elements on the Rooster are described below, together with the years in which the elements were exercising their influence. Therefore all Roosters born in 1921 and 1981 are Metal Roosters, those born in 1933 and 1993 are Water Roosters, and so on.

Metal Rooster: 1921, 1981
The Metal Rooster is a hard and conscientious worker. He knows exactly what he wants in life and sets about everything he does in a positive and determined manner. He can at times appear abrasive and he would almost certainly do better if he were more willing to reach a compromise with others rather than hold so rigidly to his firmly held beliefs.

He is very articulate and most astute when dealing with financial matters. He is loyal to his friends and often devotes much energy to working for the common good.

Water Rooster: 1933, 1993

This Rooster has a very persuasive manner and can easily gain the co-operation of others. He is intelligent, well read and gets much enjoyment from taking part in discussions and debates. He has a seemingly inexhaustible amount of energy and is prepared to work long hours in order to secure what he wants. He can, however, waste much valuable time worrying over minor and inconsequential details. He is approachable, has a good sense of humour and is highly regarded by others.

Wood Rooster: 1945

The Wood Rooster is honest, reliable and often sets himself high standards. He is ambitious, but also more prepared to work in a team than some of the other types of Rooster. He usually succeeds in life, but does have a tendency to get caught up in bureaucratic matters or attempt too many things all at the same time. He has wide interests, likes to travel and is very considerate and caring towards his family and friends.

Fire Rooster: 1957

This Rooster is extremely strong-willed. He has many leadership qualities, is an excellent organizer and is most efficient in his work. Through sheer force of character he often secures his objectives, but he does have a tendency to be very forthright and not always consider the feelings of others. If the Fire Rooster can learn to be more tactful he can often succeed beyond his wildest dreams.

Earth Rooster: 1909, 1969

This Rooster has a deep and penetrating mind. He is extremely efficient, very perceptive and is particularly astute in business and financial matters. He is also persistent and once he has set himself an objective, he will rarely allow himself to be deflected from achieving his aim. The Earth Rooster works hard and is held in great esteem by his friends and colleagues. He usually enjoys the arts and takes a keen interest in the activities of the various members of his family.

PROSPECTS FOR THE ROOSTER IN 2001

The Chinese New Year starts on 24 January 2001. Until then, the old year, the Year of the Dragon, is still making its presence felt.

The Year of the Dragon (5 February 2000 to 23 January 2001) will have been a positive one for the Rooster, with the second half of the year being especially favourable. In what remains of the Dragon year the Rooster can accomplish much, but to get the best results he does need to decide upon his priorities and concentrate on them. In this, his fine organizational skills will be much to his advantage.

In work matters this is a positive time, with the Rooster being given every chance to put his ideas, skills and strengths to effective use. As usual, he will impress, and for those keen to move on and make additional progress, the last quarter of the Dragon year will hold some good opportunities. Many of those Roosters seeking work could also be successful in gaining a position at this time, sometimes in an unexpected manner. Although his new duties may be different from those he is used to, they will often allow the Rooster to discover new strengths as well as provide him with a base from which to develop.

The Dragon year is also well aspected for personal matters, with the Rooster leading an active family and social life. He will find himself much in demand with others and will not only busy himself with various family activities, but will also find his social life becoming more active as the year draws to a close. Again, good planning will allow him to fit in a lot as well as enjoy himself. However, the Rooster should still be wary of over-committing himself otherwise he could find some of the free time he so values has all but disappeared.

In general, though, the Dragon year will be a favourable one, enabling the Rooster to make good progress as well as lead a rewarding personal life.

The Year of the Snake starts on 24 January and will be another pleasing one for the Rooster. More settled than the preceding year, it will allow him to build on what he has achieved as well as find greater fulfilment in his activities.

Over the last Chinese year many Roosters will not only have made good progress but also been able to widen their experience and enhance both their reputation and prospects. This, together with their current activities, will lead them onward and work-wise there will be interesting opportunities to follow up over the year as well as chances to take on more challenging responsibilities. For those Roosters who are especially keen on promotion or who want to switch to a different type of work, there will be some excellent openings to pursue, especially in April, May and the late summer.

However, in order to benefit from the positive aspects that prevail, the Rooster should make sure that others are aware of the important contribution that he makes and that he gets credit for all he does. This is not a year in which he can undersell himself, especially if he wants to get on. This also applies to those Roosters who are seeking work or who want to change jobs. Rather than being modest about their skills and achievements, they should make sure these are brought out in any job application or interview. This is a year when the Rooster *must* make sure he does himself justice. The Snake year really will provide many interesting opportunities for him and it rests with him to take full advantage of them.

This is also an excellent year for the Rooster to add to his skills. He should not only take advantage of any training that might be offered but also investigate any courses that interest him. Even if he follows such courses privately, perhaps through studying textbooks or taking an evening class, he could find what he learns will not only be of future value to him but also be satisfying to do. With the Snake year so favouring cultural activities and personal growth, this is something all Roosters should seriously consider.

In addition, the Rooster's interests will bring him considerable pleasure and if he has a hobby he would like to learn more about, he should take steps to do so. By finding out more and, if appropriate, tackling a more ambitious project or activity, he will set himself a fascinating personal challenge and make good use of his time.

This will be a reasonable year for financial matters and provided the Rooster manages his money well, he will be generally content with how he fares. Over the year many Roosters will see an increase in their income and in view of this, if they are able to add to their savings or perhaps start a regular savings policy, they could find this will be something they are grateful for in years to come. There are, though, some Roosters who do tend to be rather more spendthrift, and these really should pause and reflect before making too many spur of the moment purchases. If not, money that could be put to better purpose could all too easily be spent. Roosters, do take note.

The Rooster's personal life will be interesting over the year and as usual he will find himself involved in a myriad of activities. At home he will do much to help and encourage others, and in view of his fine ability to organize, he will find himself arranging various activities and household matters. His contribution will be greatly appreciated. Also, the Rooster will often find himself being approached by loved ones for advice or help over certain matters. Again, his kind, considerate and level-headed approach will be valued. However, if any particularly complex matter should arise, rather than feeling obliged to keep it to himself or tackle it alone, the Rooster should seek guidance, if need be from professionals. Although he might be willing to sort things out himself, there could be times when someone else's input and expertise could really help.

Also, because of the often central role that the Rooster plays in family life, he must make sure that he fully consults others over forthcoming activities. He may be keen to get on and arrange these, but he must not let his eagerness run away with him and will find that discussion will not only lead to better results but also prevent possible misunderstandings from arising. Roosters, do remember this!

This will, however, be a fine and active year for social matters, with the Rooster attending a wide variety of events. At many of these he will be on sparkling form, often revelling in the opportunity to meet others. Over the year there will be ample chance for him to add to his social circle, with some he meets becoming firm friends. Romance, too, is splendidly aspected with many of those Roosters currently unattached meeting someone who will become especially important in the years ahead. The period from April to late summer is especially well favoured for socializing and meeting others.

For any Rooster who may start the year in low spirits, perhaps because he has had some personal misfortune, the Snake year will certainly help to bring some happiness and hope back into his life. However, these Roosters should take advantage of the promising social occasions that the year offers and aim to go out more. As they will find, positive input on their part, even though this may sometimes be difficult, *will* be rewarded.

However, while so much can go well in the Rooster's personal life, there is one word of warning: during the Snake year he should be wary of rumours or information from dubious sources. If not, there is just a chance he could fall victim to someone's mischief. Roosters, take note!

Travel is well aspected over the year and all Roosters should try to go away at some point. They will not only benefit from having a rest and break from their usual routine but also enjoy some of the places they get to see.

Overall, the Snake year holds much promise for the Rooster and by making the most of himself and his wide-ranging talents, he will benefit from its supportive trends. He will not only be able to make progress in his work but also be able to use his skills to good effect. Personally, too, the year will go well, with the Rooster's domestic and social life bringing him a great deal of pleasure.

As far as the different types of Rooster are concerned, the Snake year will be a happy and positive one for the *Metal Rooster*. Over the year there will be much happening in his personal life as well as chances for him to improve on his current position at work. However, in order to benefit from the promising aspects that the year offers, the Metal Rooster must show a certain flexibility in his attitude and approach. Although he may have set ideas on what he wants to achieve in 2001, he must take advantage of the opportunities that exist rather than those he may wish for. Sometimes what he is hoping for may be a long time in coming or cannot be attained without him first getting more experience. However, as far as his work is concerned, this will be a year of many surprising developments. Whether in work or seeking work, the Metal Rooster will find his career developing in an unexpected manner. Those in work may, for instance, be offered the chance to move to a different section of the organization they are currently in. While they may have mixed feelings about this, by taking advantage of the opportunity they will not only widen their experience but considerably enhance their prospects. Alternatively, some of these Metal Roosters will decide to build on what they have already learnt and try for a different and more responsible post. While they will often be successful, the duties they may be given may not quite be what they were anticipating, but again, this will be an excellent chance for them to develop new skills and move several rungs up the career ladder. The important lesson many Roosters will learn in 2001 is that by being accommodating in attitude and willing to 'have a go' rather than adhering to set ideas, they will not only progress but also discover more about the world of work and grow in confidence. This also applies to those Metal Roosters currently seeking work. By taking advantage of what is offered, even if this is different from what they were hoping for, they will be able to establish a base from which to progress. All Metal Roosters would also benefit from any training opportunities that they may be offered, or if there is a skill they would like to learn, they should take steps to obtain it. There will also be many Metal Roosters who will decide to undertake some travelling over the year and this will lead to some memorable experiences, especially for those who decide to venture further afield.

However, for the more adventurous Metal Rooster, it really would be in their interests to read up about their chosen destination before they leave and so set out better prepared. This will help make their time away more interesting and agreeable. This will be a favourable year for personal matters and for those Metal Roosters who are currently seeking to build up their social life, their lively and sociable manner, together with their wide interests, will allow them to get to know many people over the year, with one new friendship becoming especially significant. Indeed, romance will figure prominently in the lives of many Metal Roosters over the year, with quite a few settling down with their partner and enjoying some truly happy and memorable times. The Metal Rooster will also do much to help a more senior relation over the year and his support will be particularly valued, more so than he may realize. As far as financial matters are concerned, the Metal Rooster will need to proceed carefully, however. Over the year there will be many expenses to meet and he may want to do a great deal on often limited resources. If he has to borrow, he must remain aware of his obligations and the likely interest charges. He must also avoid unnecessary risks, as a misjudgement could rebound on him. While this may be a challenging year financially, the Metal Rooster knows that as he progresses his position will change from one of comparative weakness to strength. For the present, however, it is important that he handles his finances as carefully as he can. Generally, though, this will be a fine and happy year for the Metal Rooster and he should take advantage of the opportunities that it will bring as well as enjoy the friendship and love of those close to him.

The *Water Rooster* thrives on setting himself interesting and often challenging things to do and over the year his various activities will bring him much satisfaction. However, as the Snake year starts, he would do well to consider what he would like to accomplish over the next 12 months. This could include completing existing projects as well as starting new activities. The Water Rooster would do well to remember that the Snake year does favour self-development and if he wishes to learn a new skill or undertake some other aspect of personal growth, he should pursue this. As he will find, following up new subjects will be a stimulating and enjoyable use of his time. He will also delight in putting his more creative talents to practical use. These could include redesigning certain areas in his home or garden. Whatever he undertakes, by setting his ideas in motion, the Water Rooster can make this a rewarding and fulfilling year. There will also be some Water Roosters who decide to move over the year. For those that do, this could turn out to be a major upheaval, particularly if they decide to move into smaller accommodation. The Water Rooster would be helped by starting to prepare for the move as soon as he can. This includes sorting through material that he might no longer need and reviewing what he wants to take. The more preparation he is able to do beforehand, the less pressured the actual move will be. In all he does, though, the Water Rooster should actively involve others rather than feel obliged to take on too much single-handed. He should also seek help if he has any particularly physical or strenuous task to carry out, including moving heavy items. As far as his well-being is concerned, this is not a year for taking risks. However, whether the Water Rooster moves or remains where he is, this will be a generally rewarding year for domestic matters. In addition to playing a full and positive role in family activities, the Water Rooster will find that others will look to him for advice and will value his good judgement and wide experience. Indeed, his ability to empathize and relate effectively to others really will prove a blessing over the year. In addition, the Water Rooster will do much to help a younger relative, with his assistance being of considerable value. He will also enjoy carrying out various projects with those around him, not only because of the satisfaction they bring but also because of the close rapport they help engender. Local outings and visits to places of interest can provide some particularly fine family occasions. The Water Rooster's social life will also work out well over the year and he can look forward to some enjoyable times meeting up with friends and attending a wide variety of social events. The summer will be a particularly active time. Over the year there will be opportunities to travel, including invitations to visit some people the Water Rooster has not seen for some time. The travelling he does undertake will lead to some pleasant times away. As usual, the Water Rooster will manage his finances with care, although he does need to be careful when completing forms that are related to finance, tax or other benefits. An oversight could be to his detriment and lead to some additional correspondence which he will feel he could well do without! In most respects this will be a positive year for the Water Rooster and by using his time well, he will be satisfied with what he is able to accomplish.

The Snake year will contain some important developments for the *Wood Rooster*, many of which will have a significant bearing on his future. In particular, one area which will see much activity will be his work. Although many Wood Roosters will have already seen considerable change in what they do in recent times, further developments are likely in 2001. Some Wood Roosters will be offered the chance to switch to different duties which will allow them to make more effective use of their skills and experience, while for others, promotion possibilities could arise in an unexpected manner. Alternatively, some will be offered the chance of early retirement or will decide that they have accomplished all they can in their present line of work and that now is the right time for a change. For these Wood Roosters some of the year will bring pressures and uncertainties, but once the changes have taken place, many will feel a sense of relief, as if they are free from past encumbrances and now able to do something more of their choosing. For them, this will be a significant time but it is also one they should not waste. If they let time and opportunity slip by there is a risk they could fall into a malaise which could take some time to reverse. Wood Roosters, take note. Often exciting new opportunities do occur in the Snake year but they have to be sought out and then acted upon. For the determined Wood Rooster, however, this can be a personally *very* rewarding year. The Wood Rooster will be encouraged by the supportive attitude of those around and whenever important decisions need to be taken, he should seek the views of both loved ones and those able to offer informed advice. If he does so he will not only be offered much helpful guidance but sometimes practical assistance too. There will also be some Wood Roosters who decide to move over the year, sometimes because of events connected with their work. Although this will often result in several months of intense activity, once these Wood Roosters have settled into their new accommodation, they will feel satisfied with what has taken place and the opportunities that a change will bring. As so many Wood Roosters will find, the Snake year will precipitate some significant changes, but these will often be to the Wood Rooster's benefit and once they have happened, they will lead to more settled times. As far as his finances are concerned, this will be a reasonable year for the Wood Rooster, but with his many outgoings, possibly including moving costs, he should still keep track of what he spends as well as his financial obligations. Generally, the more control and organization the Wood Rooster can bring to money matters, the better he will fare. The Wood Rooster is always one who values his domestic and social life and in the Snake year this will not disappoint. The Wood Rooster will particularly enjoy following the activities of those around him and assisting others, particularly those both much younger and more senior to himself. He will also be encouraged by the support others are able to give him. The Wood Rooster does have a special place in the heart of many and this will certainly be evident over the year. This will also be an active year socially, with the Wood Rooster having the chance to attend a wide range of functions. He will enjoy meeting up with friends as well as having the opportunity to make some new ones. For those Wood Roosters who would like to build up their social life or are hoping to strike up a new and important friendship, the Snake year will give them the opportunity, often in a surprising way. The summer is especially well aspected for social matters. Also, with the Wood Rooster's love of travel, all Wood Roosters should take advantage of the opportunity to go away at some point in 2001. Travel is favourably aspected and can provide the Wood Rooster with some enjoyable as well as memorable occasions. Generally, this will be a significant year for the Wood Rooster, with some often important changes taking place which will not only enable him to pursue some of his own ideas and activities but also usher in a more settled and personally fulfilling period.

This will be a positive year for the *Fire Rooster* and one which will allow him to make good use of his experience and build on some of his more recent achievements. Indeed, the Snake year is one that tends to reward the Fire Rooster well and to inspire him to even greater heights. Those Fire Roosters who have recently taken on new duties or who transfer to new ones in 2001 should not only aim to familiarize themselves with their new role but also take full advantage of any training opportunities they may be offered and should put forward any ideas that occur to them. By giving of his best and showing initiative, the Fire Rooster will impress others and this will place him in a favourable position for when further opportunities arise, as they will during the middle and closing parts of the year. Also, as the Fire Rooster himself realizes, the way to make progress is to remain active, persistent and conscientious, and he will show all three qualities to good effect over the year. Those Fire Roosters seeking work will also enjoy pleasing developments over the year and these could often arise in a surprising way. Although the Fire Rooster may have a clear idea of the type of work he wishes to pursue, by chance he could be offered the opportunity to take on something different. This may not only have potential for the future but also allow him to usefully extend his skills. In 2001 Fire Roosters should be open to such possibilities, surprising though some may be, and take advantage of them. The Fire Rooster will also obtain much satisfaction from his personal interests and for the sportingly inclined the year will certainly contain some memorable moments. It is also a good year for the Fire Rooster to follow up any subject or interest that may appeal to him. Anything that contains an element of personal development can be to his long-term benefit. Travel, too, is favoured, with any breaks and holidays the Fire Rooster is able to take often being both enjoyable and beneficial. The Fire Rooster's domestic life will be fairly busy over the year, though by organizing himself well he will be able to accomplish a great deal. If at any time his tasks do start to get too daunting, he should prioritize and if need be cut back on certain commitments or projects. Due to the pressures of a busy life, there may be occasions when the Fire Rooster and those around him get tired and irritable and tempers start to fray. At such times, the Fire Rooster would find it helpful to suggest activities all could enjoy, even if it is just sitting down together to watch a favourite film or to have a special meal. Such suggestions will sometimes work wonders and throughout the year the Fire Rooster should try not to let everyday pressures take the edge off what can be a happy and satisfying home life. He will also enjoy meeting up with his friends over the year and attending a range of social occasions. Any Fire Rooster who may start the year in low spirits will find that by making the effort to go out more and getting to meet others, perhaps through a special interest group, he can do much to improve his social life. Again, the Snake year will encourage those prepared to take action to get what they want. Financially, this will be a reasonable year, and by handling his money in an efficient way and budgeting for any large expenses, the Fire Rooster will generally be content with his situation. Overall, this will be a satisfying year for him. He knows he has it within him to do well and in 2001 his determined and conscientious approach will impress others and allow him to make pleasing headway. However, the year will be busy and, throughout, the Fire Rooster should make sure he balances his various activities and commitments. If he can manage this, then it can be a very good year for him.

This will be a pleasing year for the *Earth Rooster* with a lot going in his favour. Over the year he will be able to put his skills and experience to good use as well as enjoy a contented personal life. It will also be a more settled year than some and this will allow the Earth Rooster to concentrate on his activities and ideas. However, as the Snake year begins, the Earth Rooster would do well to give some thought to how he would like his life to develop over the next 12 months. By giving himself some objectives to work towards, he will find he is becoming more focused as well as generally achieving more as a result. Also, throughout the year, he will find his efficient and methodical manner will be to his advantage, with others often marvelling at just how much he is able to do. As far as work matters are concerned, the Earth Rooster can look forward to achieving some pleasing results. By using his experience well he will greatly impress and the good work he does will often lead to him being given some interesting challenges and duties. He will particularly relish some of these as they will give him the chance to show what he is capable of, and by rising to the challenges he will do much to enhance both his standing and future prospects. The positive aspects that prevail also apply to those Earth Roosters seeking work. By actively pursuing any openings that they see, many will be given the chance they have long been wanting. As they will find, once they have a place in a company or organization, no matter how small this may be to start with, it will at least give them a base from which to make further progress. This is a year which will give the Earth Rooster the chance to show his potential and sow the seeds for future growth. He can also look forward to a gradual improvement in his financial situation as the year progresses. In addition to the increase in income many Earth Roosters will enjoy, some could find they are able to supplement this by putting an interest or skill they have to profitable use. An element of chance and good fortune combined with enterprise will, for quite a few, help their financial situation. With travel favourably aspected, the Earth Rooster should also try to make sure he takes a holiday or break over the year. He will not only benefit from the rest this will bring but could also have the chance to visit some impressive destinations. The Earth Rooster's personal life is also well favoured. As usual, he will play a full and important part in domestic activities, doing much to encourage and support those younger and also more senior to himself. In addition, he will help someone who has a rather awkward problem to deal with over the year and his wise counsel and considerate nature will be particularly valued. Those who know the Earth Rooster well have great faith in him and in 2001 he will do much to justify this. As well as playing a central role in family life, by suggesting activities others can be involved in, he will instigate some memorable occasions and find his home life highly rewarding. Those Earth Roosters who are keen socializers or who want to lead a more active social life will find the year serving them well, with an interesting range of social occasions to attend and the opportunity to add to their social circle. Some Earth Roosters will, however, because of their other commitments and interests, choose to have a quieter year socially and use their time in other but equally satisfying ways. Overall, the Snake year will be a positive one for the Earth Rooster with the aspects supporting him in much of what he does. His personal life will go particularly well and will bring him many happy and meaningful occasions.

FAMOUS ROOSTERS

Adamski, Francis Bacon, Dame Janet Baker, Dennis Bergkamp, Enid Blyton, Sir Dirk Bogarde, Barbara Taylor Bradford, Michael Caine, Enrico Caruso, Christopher Cazenove, Jean Chrétien, Eric Clapton, Joan Collins, Rita Coolidge, Daniel Day Lewis, Sacha Distel, the Duke of Edinburgh, Ernie Els, Gloria Estefan, Nick Faldo, Mohamed al Fayed, Bryan Ferry, Errol Flynn, Benjamin Franklin, Dawn French, Stephen Fry, Steffi Graf, Melanie Griffith, Richard Harris, Deborah Harry, Goldie Hawn, Katherine Hepburn, Michael Heseltine, Catherine Zeta Jones, Quincy

Jones, Diane Keaton, Dean Koontz, D. H. Lawrence, Martyn Lewis, David Livingstone, Ken Livingstone, Malcolm Lowry, Jayne Mansfield, Steve Martin, James Mason, W. Somerset Maugham, Paul Merton, Bette Midler, Alan Milburn, Van Morrison, Willie Nelson, Kim Novak, Yoko Ono, Dolly Parton, Michelle Pfeiffer, Priscilla Presley, Mary Quant, Nancy Reagan, Joan Rivers, Bobby Robson, Paul Scofield, Jenny Seagrove, Sir Harry Secombe, George Segal, Carly Simon, Britney Spears, Johann Strauss, Sir Peter Ustinov, Richard Wagner, Serena Williams, Neil Young.

10 FEBRUARY 1910 ∼ 29 JANUARY 1911   *Metal Dog*

28 JANUARY 1922 ∼ 15 FEBRUARY 1923   *Water Dog*

14 FEBRUARY 1934 ∼ 3 FEBRUARY 1935   *Wood Dog*

2 FEBRUARY 1946 ∼ 21 JANUARY 1947   *Fire Dog*

18 FEBRUARY 1958 ∼ 7 FEBRUARY 1959   *Earth Dog*

6 FEBRUARY 1970 ∼ 26 JANUARY 1971   *Metal Dog*

25 JANUARY 1982 ∼ 12 FEBRUARY 1983   *Water Dog*

10 FEBRUARY 1994 ∼ 30 JANUARY 1995   *Wood Dog*

THE
DOG

THE PERSONALITY OF THE DOG

We make a living by what we get, we make a life by what we give.

Sir Winston Churchill: a Dog

The Dog is born under the signs of loyalty and anxiety. He usually holds very firm views and beliefs and is the champion of good causes. He hates any sort of injustice or unfair treatment and will do all in his power to help those less fortunate than himself. He has a strong sense of fair play and will be honourable and open in all his dealings.

The Dog is very direct and straightforward. He is never one to skirt round issues and speaks frankly and to the point. He can also be stubborn, but he is more than prepared to listen to the views of others and will try to be as fair as possible in coming to his decisions. He will readily give advice where it is needed and will be the first to offer assistance when things go wrong.

The Dog instils confidence wherever he goes and there are many who admire him for his integrity and resolute manner. He is a very good judge of character and can often form an accurate impression of someone very shortly after meeting them. He is also very intuitive and can frequently sense how things are going to work out long in advance.

Despite his friendly and amiable manner, the Dog is not a big socializer. He dislikes having to attend large social functions or parties and much prefers a quiet meal with friends or a chat by the fire. He is an excellent conversationalist and is often a marvellous raconteur of amusing stories and anecdotes. He is also quick-witted and his mind is always alert.

The Dog can keep calm in a crisis and although he does have a temper, his outbursts tend to be short-lived. He is loyal and trustworthy, but if he ever feels badly let down or rejected by someone, he will rarely forgive or forget.

The Dog usually has very set interests. He prefers to specialize and become an expert in a chosen area rather than dabble in a variety of different activities. He usually does well in jobs where he feels that he is being of service to others and is often suited to careers in the social services, the medical and legal professions and teaching. The Dog does, however, need to feel motivated in his work. He has to have a sense of purpose and if ever this is lacking he can quite often drift through life without ever achieving very much. Once he has the motivation, however, very little can prevent him from securing his objective.

Another characteristic of the Dog is his tendency to worry and to view things rather pessimistically. Quite often his worries are totally unnecessary and are of his own making. Although it may be difficult, worrying is a habit which the Dog should try to overcome.

The Dog is not materialistic or particularly bothered about accumulating great wealth. As long as he has the necessary money to support his family and to spend on the occasional luxury, he is more than happy. However, when he does have any spare money he tends to be rather a spendthrift and does not always put his money to its best use. He is also not a very good speculator and would be advised to seek professional advice before entering into any major long-term investment.

The Dog will rarely be short of admirers, but he is not an easy person to live with. His moods are changeable and his standards high, but he will be loyal and protective to his partner and will do all in his power to provide a good and comfortable home. He can get on extremely well with those born under the signs of the Horse, Pig, Tiger and Monkey, and can also establish a sound and stable relationship with the Rat, Ox, Rabbit, Snake and another Dog, but will find the Dragon a bit too flamboyant for his liking. He will also find it difficult to understand the creative and imaginative Goat and is likely to be highly irritated by the candid Rooster.

The female Dog is renowned for her beauty. She has a warm and caring nature, although until she knows someone well she can be both secretive and very guarded. She is highly intelligent and despite her calm and tranquil appearance she can be extremely ambitious. She enjoys sport and other outdoor activities and has a happy knack of finding bargains in the most unlikely of places. She can also get rather impatient when things do not work out as she would like.

The Dog usually has a very good way with children and can be a loving and doting parent. He will rarely be happier than when he is helping someone or doing something that will benefit others. Providing he can cure himself of his tendency to worry, he will lead a very full and active life – and in that life he will make many friends and do a tremendous amount of good.

THE FIVE DIFFERENT TYPES OF DOG

In addition to the 12 signs of the Chinese zodiac, there are five elements and these have a strengthening or moderating influence on the sign. The effects of the five elements on the Dog are described below, together with the years in which the elements were exercising their influence. Therefore all Dogs born in 1910 and 1970 are Metal Dogs, those born in 1922 and 1982 are Water Dogs, and so on.

Metal Dog: 1910, 1970
The Metal Dog is bold, confident and forthright, and sets about everything he does in a resolute and determined manner. He has a great belief in his abilities and has no hesitation about speaking his mind or devoting himself to some just cause. He can be rather serious at times and can become anxious and irritable when things are not going according to plan. He tends to have very specific interests and it would certainly help him to broaden his outlook and become more involved in group activities. He is extremely loyal and faithful to his friends.

Water Dog: 1922, 1982
The Water Dog has a very direct and outgoing personality. He is an excellent communicator and has little trouble in persuading others to fall in with his plans. He does, however, have a somewhat carefree nature and is not as disciplined or as thorough as he should be in certain

matters. Neither does he keep as much control over his finances as he should, but he can be most generous to his family and friends and will make sure that they want for nothing. The Water Dog is usually very good with children and has a wide circle of friends.

Wood Dog: 1934, 1994

This Dog is a hard and conscientious worker and will usually make a favourable impression wherever he goes. He is less independent than some of the other types of Dog and prefers to work in a group rather than on his own. He is popular, has a good sense of humour and takes a very keen interest in the activities of the various members of his family. He is often attracted to the finer things in life and can get much pleasure from collecting stamps, coins, pictures or antiques. He also prefers to live in the country rather than the town.

Fire Dog: 1946

This Dog has a lively, outgoing personality and is able to establish friendships with remarkable ease. He is an honest and conscientious worker and likes to take an active part in all that is going on around him. He also likes to explore new ideas, and providing he can get the necessary support and advice, he can often succeed where others have failed. He does, however, have a tendency to be stubborn. Providing he can overcome this, the Fire Dog can often achieve considerable fame and fortune.

Earth Dog: 1958

The Earth Dog is very talented and astute. He is methodical and efficient and is capable of going far in his chosen profession. He tends to be rather quiet and reserved but has a very persuasive manner and usually secures his objectives without too much opposition. He is generous and kind and is always ready to lend a helping hand when it is needed. He is also held in very high esteem by his friends and colleagues and he is usually most dignified in his appearance.

PROSPECTS FOR THE DOG IN 2001

The Chinese New Year starts on 24 January 2001. Until then, the old year, the Year of the Dragon, is still making its presence felt.

The Year of the Dragon (5 February 2000 to 23 January 2001) will have been a difficult one for the Dog. Progress will not always have been as easy or as smooth as he would have liked and he will have had some misgivings over some of the events and changes that have taken place. However, 'every cloud has a silver lining' and many of the clouds that have descended upon the Dog are about to give way to sunshine.

Despite its awkward moments, the Dragon year will still have had some positive implications for the Dog. Not only will he have been able to draw on (and rediscover) some of his inner strengths and fortitude, but he will have also been able to add to his experience, learn from any mistakes or setbacks that might have occurred, and give thought to his present and future. Once the Dog has come up with some ideas about what he wants to do next, he will find himself getting back to his true form and will feel determined to make more of the next Chinese year.

However, in what remains of the Dragon year, the Dog does still need to proceed with care and avoid doing anything that would jeopardize his position or achievements. This includes remaining tactful and discreet in any awkward situations that may arise as well as giving of his best in his work, even though sometimes the situations in which he finds himself may not be as he would like. With the aspects about to turn in his favour, this is not a time for the Dog to 'rock the boat', no matter how tempted he might be!

The Dragon year is also one which calls for care in financial matters and in the closing stages of the year, the Dog must avoid taking unnecessary risks as well as keep a watchful eye over his level of spending.

In view of the challenging aspects that prevail, whenever the Dog does have any concerns or worries, he should not hesitate to seek the views and advice of those around him. He will not only benefit from any help others are able to give but will also be heartened by the obvious affection they have for him.

As the Dragon year draws to a close the Dog will sense that his fortunes are changing for the better. This will not only help lift his spirits but also allow him to enjoy the closing stages of the year more and immerse himself in the socializing and festivities that will take place towards the end of 2000.

THE DOG

The Year of the Snake starts on 24 January and will be a vastly improved one for the Dog. After the often demanding times of the Dragon year, the Dog will resolve to make this a better year for himself and will set about his activities with a greater determination. In addition to his own commitment, the aspects will be supportive, helping him to achieve some well-deserved success.

Many Dogs will have already given some thought to what they hope to accomplish over the next 12 months and any who have not really would find it helpful to do so. This is a time of growth and progress and by knowing the direction in which he is heading, the Dog will find himself setting about his activities in a more purposeful manner and achieving more as a result. The clearer his aims for the year, the better he will be able to reach them.

In the Dog's work this will be a particularly successful year and again his determined attitude will do much to aid his progress. After some of the pressures and difficulties of late, many Dogs will decide to take their career into their own hands and have a greater say in what they actually do. Some Dogs will feel that having achieved all they can in their present line of work, the time is now right for a switch to something new. These Dogs, as they start to review their options, would do well to contact professional bodies for information as well as speak to others currently in the line of work they are considering. They will not only be given helpful advice but also be much better prepared for any interview they are called to attend. By taking action and setting the wheels in motion, the Dog will find interesting possibilities will soon start to emerge and he may be set off on an interesting new course.

Those Dogs who start the year seeking work should also find out more about the type of positions they would like, as they too could find themselves being given useful leads and advised of possible openings. This really is a year for progress and the Dog should actively pursue the opportunities that arise or that he discovers or creates through his own efforts.

Some Dogs will be content in their current line of work but discouraged by their recent lack of progress. For these Dogs, the Snake year will again see an upturn in their fortunes and many will find that their loyalty and past service will now mark them out for promotion or more satisfying duties. When this happens, these Dogs will find that their enthusiasm and faith in themselves will be rekindled and they will set about their duties with far greater relish. As has been seen so often, once the Dog is inspired and motivated, there is almost no stopping him and this is what the Snake year will do – provide the Dog with the incentive and inspiration to give of his best and put his talents to good use.

Interesting work opportunities can occur at almost any time over the Snake year, but especially well aspected are the first quarter and the months from September to mid-November.

The improvement in the Dog's work prospects will also lead to an increase in his income and financial matters are fairly well aspected in 2001. With this improvement, many Dogs will decide to go ahead with some purchases they have been considering for some time, particularly items for the home. These will often mean a great deal to the Dog and bring him much satisfaction. In addition, the Dog should also try to add to his savings over the year and, if he is able, put a regular sum aside for a break later in the year.

The Dog will also get much pleasure from his personal interests and should ensure that he not only devotes time to these but also considers extending them in some way. This could be by learning more about a certain aspect or starting an ambitious project, one which would enable him to learn as he carried out the activity. In addition, there are many Dogs who give their time to helping others or serving the community in some way. For these Dogs, this will continue to be a particularly rewarding part of their life, with their activities being greatly valued by others.

The Dog's domestic life is also favourably aspected and he will play a full and appreciated part in family life. Over the year he will do much to encourage and support those around him, and others will often look to him for advice or help in some personal matter. The Dog will not only be glad to assist, but what he does will also often be of lasting value, particularly when the interests and education of younger relations are involved.

The Dog will also find that any interests and projects that he can carry out with those around him will lead to some meaningful moments. Not only will the activity itself often benefit from the pooling of talents and ideas – especially when related to home improvement projects – but this will also do much to maintain the closeness and understanding with others that the Dog so values.

As far as the Dog's social life is concerned, there will be many who will be content to keep this relatively low key, enjoying meeting up with existing friends but preferring to concentrate on their own activities rather than engage in a lot of socializing. However, for those Dogs who are keen on a more active social life, the Snake year will certainly provide opportunities for them to enjoy themselves and, if they wish, build up some new friendships. The Dog's level of social activity in 2001 is very much in his own hands, but whatever he chooses to do, he should always remember that he does have some loyal and trusting friends he can turn to should he have any matters which concern him.

In almost all respects this will be a positive year for the Dog and by putting his skills and experience to good use he can obtain some very pleasing results. In addition, his personal life and interests are favourably aspected, with both bringing him contentment.

As far as the different types of Dog are concerned, this will be an interesting year for the *Metal Dog*. Partly as a result of the events of last year and partly due to his own ideas, the Metal Dog will determine to make something of the Snake year. Rather than being such a victim of events, he will decide to set the agenda for the forthcoming year and take positive action to achieve what he wants. His sense of purpose will indeed lead to some impressive results. In his work significant developments are likely, with the Metal Dog taking deliberate steps to improve on his present position. Whether currently in work or not, he will actively look for ways in which to advance, including following up any interesting openings or promotion possibilities that arise. His determination and obvious desire to put his skills to more effective use will show through, with many Metal Dogs being given the chance to progress over the year.

Another feature of the year is that it will do much to restore the Metal Dog's faith in himself. Once inspired, he really will impress others and this too will help him advance. For work opportunities, the first quarter of the year and late summer will be especially promising times. This will also be a positive year for financial matters, although, with so many commitments to meet, the Metal Dog should still manage his money with care and make allowances for forthcoming expenses. If he is able, he should also try to make some savings for his long-term future. Although he is young, over the years savings made now could grow into a useful asset. The Metal Dog will also decide to spend money on his accommodation over the year, especially on new equipment and furnishings. With any large purchases he could find he is able to save a considerable amount by waiting for sales and other favourable buying opportunities rather than proceeding too hastily. Also, with travel well aspected, the Metal Dog should try to set some money aside for a holiday or break. The change of scene will not only do him good but he will also delight in some of the places he visits. The Metal Dog's personal life will bring him much pleasure, with his relations with others generally going well. He will play an active part in encouraging those around him and be particularly proud of the progress of a younger relation. He will also heartened by the support he is given in his own activities and should listen carefully to any advice that those close to him offer. They do speak with the Metal Dog's best interests at heart and could sometimes think of points which he might have overlooked. In this respect, the words of someone more senior will be most pertinent. With his various commitments, the Metal Dog may not always have as much time for social matters as perhaps he would like, but he will still enjoy the times he does meet up with friends as well as the parties and other social occasions he attends. Any Metal Dogs who may have had some recent personal problems or be feeling lonely should look on the Snake year as the start of a new chapter in their life. By going out more, meeting others and perhaps joining a local group, they can do much to bring about an improvement in their life and restore some meaning and happiness. Again, the Snake year is a time which will favour those prepared to take action to secure what they want. In so many respects, 2001 is a year which holds much potential for the Metal Dog and by deciding on his objectives and then working towards them, even he will be surprised at just what he is able to achieve. In addition, the year will bring him much personal contentment.

This will be a positive year for the *Water Dog* with pleasing developments in many areas of his life. His personal life is especially well aspected with the Snake year promising to be both a happy and memorable one. For those who are unattached, romance will beckon, with either an existing friendship or a new one developing in a significant way. There will indeed be many Water Dogs who decide to get engaged or married in 2001, such are the fine aspects that prevail. Also, for any Water Dog who may have had some recent sadness to bear and be starting the year in low spirits and perhaps feeling lonely, this is very much a time to concentrate on the present and, difficult though it sometimes might be, try to draw a line under the past and treat the Snake year as the start of a new chapter.

With a more positive outlook and a willingness to look forward, great change can take place and many will find that a new friendship will literally transform their life. The months of March and April and the summer are well aspected for meeting others and for significant personal developments. In addition to the happiness romance and new friendships will bring, the Water Dog will generally enjoy his social life, particularly with the many parties and other events he will attend. At some of these he will get to meet others and extend his social circle, something which those Water Dogs living in a new area will greatly appreciate. The Water Dog's family will also be important to him over the year and while there may be times when he may wish to be more independent in his actions, he will benefit from discussing his plans with family members, particularly with those more senior who are able to advise with the benefit of experience behind them. By listening to their words the Water Dog will gain a great deal and, in time, be grateful for their insights. Although the Water Dog's personal and romantic life will be prominent over the year, he will also get much satisfaction from his various interests and should set aside time to devote to these. In some cases, an interest will take on a significance of its own and, for some, lead to an additional source of income or provide the basis for a vocation. This is especially true for those Water Dogs who are more creatively inclined. Their communication and design skills will often develop in a positive manner. In addition to the benefits and pleasure the Water Dog's interests will bring, this is a good year for self-development, and any skills, training or qualifications he can obtain will often serve him well in the future. Water

Dogs who are currently studying for qualifications will find that by working diligently and steadily over the year, they can look forward to achieving some particularly pleasing results. This will also be an interesting year for work matters, with several positive developments taking place. For those Water Dogs seeking work, an opening could prove to be an ideal stepping-stone, and once in a position, they will be able to demonstrate their skills to good effect and mark themselves out for further progress. Similarly, those currently in work will also be able to build on their position, with many being offered the chance to take on other responsibilities and so further their experience. There will, though, be some Water Dogs who feel that what they are doing does not suit them or relate to their strengths or interests. These Water Dogs should seek to make a change and by pursuing positions more in line with what they want, many will succeed in making a change for the better. Although financial matters are not adversely aspected in 2001, the Water Dog does need to take care when dealing with money matters and if he takes on any new obligations, he must make sure he makes allowances for these. Over the year there could be many temptations for him to stretch his resources and while sometimes this may be unavoidable, the Water Dog really would be helped by managing his money carefully and keeping account of his spending. Overall, though, this will be a favourable year for the Water Dog, allowing him to make more effective use of his skills and talents as well as usefully extend his experience. Personally, too, this will be a year which will bring him much happiness, with new friendships and romance being of special importance.

This will be a satisfying year for the *Wood Dog*, although to get the best from its positive aspects, he should give some thought to what he would like to do over the next 12 months. This way he will find he is making more effective use of his time as well as obtaining better results. Also, as he will find, this will be a more settled year for him and will therefore give him a better chance to concentrate on his activities rather than be subject to too many distractions or delays. The activities the Wood Dog might consider for the year could relate to almost any aspect of his life, ranging from projects in his home and garden to developing personal interests, learning a new skill, travelling or fulfilling a long-held ambition. Whatever he chooses, this is a year for giving himself some objectives and then setting about achieving them. If not, in future years he could come to look back at this particular time and think, 'If only...' In planning his activities he would also find it helpful to speak to those around him and will often be given useful advice. One area which is likely to bring him especial pleasure is his personal interests and, if appropriate, he could consider setting himself a new project to tackle, one which could provide him with an interesting challenge. For those Wood Dogs who are creatively inclined, music, photography, art or craftwork could prove to be ideal activities, while any Wood Dogs who particularly enjoy writing could consider writing up some of their experiences or family history or something about one of their interests. In addition, some Wood Dogs may decide to spend some time over the year becoming more familiar with certain aspects of computing or the Internet, with some even designing their own website. Whatever he undertakes, the Wood Dog will find practical and creative pursuits a pleasurable and rewarding use of his time. The year is also favourably aspected for travel and the Wood Dog should not only follow up any invitations to visit friends or relations he has not seen for some time but also look into the possibility of visiting areas he has long wished to see. Again, talking to others can sometimes produce ways of bringing this about. Throughout the year the Wood Dog will value the support and encouragement he receives from his loved ones, as well as enjoy some family occasions that take place. These could include weddings within the family, the birth of grandchildren or the successes enjoyed by loved ones. In 2001, there will certainly be good reason for the Wood Dog to feel proud of those dear to him. August and September could be particularly special months for family activities. The Wood Dog's social life will also go well and he will enjoy meeting up to chat with friends as well as the various social events that he attends over the year. For any Wood Dog who may be feeling lonely or seeking new interests, a local society could be well worth joining. Not only would this allow these Wood Dogs to meet others of a similar age and interests, but it will often add a new dimension to their social life and the year. The Wood Dog will fare reasonably well in financial matters and by managing his money and setting funds aside for specific purposes, such as items for himself, his home or travel, he will be pleased with his general financial situation. He should, though, be wary of taking undue risks or of committing his money to schemes and ventures he may not fully understand. If in doubt, he should check. For those Wood Dogs born in 1994 this will be an interesting year, not only in extending and developing their interests but also in covering new material in their schoolwork. In these important formative years, the young Wood Dog really will respond positively to any encouragement he receives as well as additional assistance given. This is something those around him should bear in mind. In so many respects this will be a positive time for the Wood Dog and by deciding upon his objectives and then going after them, he can make this a rich and personally rewarding year.

Much will have happened in the *Fire Dog*'s life over recent years and the Snake year will at last give him the chance to take stock of all that has happened and build on his achievements as well as pursue activities more of his own choosing. In his work some particularly interesting developments are possible. Having already seen many changes taking place, the Fire Dog will now find himself well placed to make headway. This improvement in his position could either come about within his current company or organization or by him moving to a different one, but over the year the Fire Dog will certainly feel much more inspired by some of the opportunities that arise and the tasks given him. Similarly, those Fire Dogs seeking work could enjoy a stroke of good fortune over a year and be given a position which particularly interests them. Although this may sometimes represent a change in direction, it is one the Fire Dog will welcome and enjoy. Overall, 2001 will be a much more productive and fulfilling year for him and he should make the most of the favourable aspects that prevail. In addition, he will also have more chance to attend to activities he has been thinking about for a long time but not had the chance to do. These could include extending his interests or starting new ones, taking up a personal challenge or carrying out some other idea or project. By taking positive action to do the things he wants, the Fire Dog can make this a rewarding and personally satisfying time. This will also be a positive year for financial matters, with many Fire Dogs receiving an additional sum of money over the year. However, while this will be welcome, the Fire Dog should not be too hasty in spending any extra money, but consider carefully what he might like to do with it. By doing this he will find any purchases he does proceed with will often mean more than if he were to act too hastily. Also, the Fire Dog would do well to consider setting something aside for a break for later in the year as well as adding to his savings. With good financial management, he will generally be pleased with his situation. The Fire Dog always sets great store by his domestic life and he will delight in some of the family successes that the year will bring. These will not only include his own activities but also the progress of some of those dear to him. The Fire Dog will also do much to advise family members over the year and his considered views and judgement will be much appreciated. In addition to helping others, should he himself have any concerns, uncertainties or big decisions to make, he should seek the views of those around him. He will not only be reassured by the advice offered but will also find that a spirit of openness will do much to preserve the close relations he so values. The Fire Dog's social life will go well and he will not only enjoy meeting up with friends but also some of the often interesting social events that he attends. For those

Fire Dogs who are keen to make new friends, there will certainly be opportunities to do so, particularly in the early months of the year. Overall, this will be a positive year for the Fire Dog, but to get the most from the aspects that prevail, he needs to make the most of the opportunities the year will bring as well as aim to realize some of his plans. Positive and purposeful action really will bring some rewarding results.

Despite his best endeavours and keenness to make the most of himself and his skills, the *Earth Dog's* progress of late will not always have matched his expectations. Problems, difficulties and delays will have prevented him from doing all he would have liked and he may also have felt that some of his efforts have not always brought the response he thought was due. However, early in 2001 there will be a noticeable improvement in his fortunes. Periods of progress and growth often follow on from more challenging times and this will be the case in 2001. In the Snake year the Earth Dog will find himself in the right place and with the right experience to make considerable headway, with many of his former efforts and ideas now bearing fruit. Sometimes he will be offered new duties and responsibilities, or be successful in obtaining promotion or switching to a new job, but whatever he does the Earth Dog will generally find this a more fulfilling and successful year than of late. In 2001 he really can make good progress and, with determination and commitment, will obtain some impressive and heartening results. March, April and late summer will see some particularly interesting career developments. For those Earth Dogs seeking work, opportunities will sometimes arise in a surprising manner. Not only should these Earth Dogs remain alert for openings to pursue, but should also contact those in the line of work they want to enter. By taking action, building contacts and following advice given, they will often get the chance they have been waiting for. In their quest for a position they could also find it helpful to review their experience and skills and consider other ways in which they could use their talents. Some imaginative thinking could open up some interesting possibilities. For all Earth Dogs, 2001 is a year for moving forward and making the most of their strengths. With the positive aspects that prevail, the Earth Dog should also promote any ideas he has, and if he has a particular interest or skill he can promote, he should consider doing so. For the enterprising, the Snake year can bring some interesting surprises. All Earth Dogs will greatly value the time they spend on their various interests over the year, often finding these a good way in which to relax and unwind. If, at the moment, the Earth Dog does not have a particular hobby or interest he can turn to in his spare time, he should aim to take one up. He will find his life so much richer as a result. Also, if he is sedentary for much of the day and does not get much exercise, he should consider taking up some additional walking, cycling or swimming. He will feel much better for doing something that would help his well-being, although before starting he should seek medical advice about what would be the most appropriate activity for him. The Earth Dog will also find this a pleasing year for domestic matters. Not only will he do much to encourage and support those around him, but he will also delight in the progress of several family members. Over the year there could be cause for several memorable celebrations. However, while the Earth Dog will play such a central role in his home, he should not hesitate to avail himself of the help and advice others are often so willing to give. In 2001 he really can gain much from the input of those around him. Also, due to his own willing nature, he will sometimes find himself with a great many household chores to do. If he finds these mounting up, he should not hesitate to ask others for a helping hand rather than feel obliged to do so much on his own. However, while his domestic life may at times be busy, it will also bring him much joy and happiness. The Earth Dog's social life is also well aspected and whether he is content just to meet up with friends on an occasional basis or prefers to lead a more active social life, he can look forward to some fine social occasions. Overall, this is a positive year for the Earth Dog and its real value will come from the opportunities it gives him to take *active* steps to improve his life, whether professionally or personally. This really will be a rewarding and fulfilling year for him.

FAMOUS DOGS

André Agassi, King Albert II of Belgium, Jane Asher, Zoë Ball, Brigitte Bardot, Gary Barlow, Dr Christiaan Barnard, Candice Bergman, David Bowie, Michael Buerk, George W. Bush, Kate Bush, Max Bygraves, Naomi Campbell, Mariah Carey, King Carl Gustaf XVI of Sweden, José Carreras, Paul Cézanne, Cher, Sir Winston Churchill, Petula Clark, Bill Clinton, Leonard Cohen, Robin Cook, Jamie Lee Curtis, Charles Dance, Claude Debussy, Dame Judi Dench,

Frankie Dettori, Blake Edwards, Sally Field, Joseph Fiennes, Robert Frost, Ava Gardner, Judy Garland, George Gershwin, Barry Gibb, Lenny Henry, O. Henry, Victor Hugo, Barry Humphries, Holly Hunter, Michael Jackson, Al Jolson, Felicity Kendal, Sue Lawley, Maureen Lipman, Sophia Loren, Joanna Lumley, Shirley MacLaine, Madonna, Norman Mailer, Winnie Mandela, Barry Manilow, Rik Mayall, Golda Meir, Freddie Mercury, Liza Minnelli, David Niven, Gary Numan, Sydney Pollack, Elvis Presley, Paul Robeson, Linda Ronstadt, Gabriela Sabatini, Susan Sarandon, Jennifer Saunders, Claudia Schiffer, Dr Albert Schweitzer, Alan Shearer, Sylvester Stallone, Robert Louis Stevenson, Sharon Stone, Jack Straw, David Suchet, Donald Sutherland, Chris Tarrant, Mother Teresa, Donald Trump, Voltaire, Paul Weller, Prince William, Shelley Winters.

30 JANUARY 1911 ∿ 17 FEBRUARY 1912   *Metal Pig*

16 FEBRUARY 1923 ∿ 4 FEBRUARY 1924   *Water Pig*

4 FEBRUARY 1935 ∿ 23 JANUARY 1936   *Wood Pig*

22 JANUARY 1947 ∿ 9 FEBRUARY 1948   *Fire Pig*

8 FEBRUARY 1959 ∿ 27 JANUARY 1960   *Earth Pig*

27 JANUARY 1971 ∿ 14 FEBRUARY 1972   *Metal Pig*

13 FEBRUARY 1983 ∿ 1 FEBRUARY 1984   *Water Pig*

31 JANUARY 1995 ∿ 18 FEBRUARY 1996   *Wood Pig*

THE
PIG

THE PERSONALITY OF THE PIG

All life is an experiment. The more experiments you make, the better.

Ralph Waldo Emerson: a Pig

The Pig is born under the sign of honesty. He has a kind and understanding nature and is well known for his abilities as a peacemaker. He hates any sort of discord or unpleasantness and will do all in his power to sort out differences of opinion or bring opposing factions together.

He is also an excellent conversationalist and speaks truthfully and to the point. He dislikes any form of falsehood or hypocrisy and is a firm believer in justice and the maintenance of law and order. In spite of these beliefs, however, the Pig is reasonably tolerant and often prepared to forgive others for their wrongs. He rarely harbours grudges and is never vindictive.

The Pig is usually very popular. He enjoys other people's company and likes to be involved in joint or group activities. He will be a loyal member of any club or society and can be relied upon to lend a helping hand at functions. He is also an excellent fund-raiser for charities and often a great supporter of humanitarian causes.

The Pig is a hard and conscientious worker and is particularly respected for his reliability and integrity. In his early years he will try his hand at several different jobs, but he is usually happiest where he feels that he is being of service to others. He will unselfishly give up his time for the common good and is highly valued by his colleagues and employers.

The Pig has a good sense of humour and invariably has a smile, joke or whimsical remark at the ready. He loves to entertain and to please others, and there are many Pigs who have been attracted to careers in show business or who enjoy following the careers of famous stars and personalities.

There are, unfortunately, some who take advantage of the Pig's good nature and impose upon his generosity. The Pig has great difficulty in saying 'No' and, although he may dislike being firm, it would be in his own interests to say occasionally, 'Enough is enough.' The Pig can also be rather naïve and gullible; however, if at any stage in his life he feels that he has been badly let down, he will make sure that it will never happen again and will try to become self-reliant. There are many Pigs who have become entrepreneurs or forged a successful career on their own after some early disappointment in life. Although the Pig tends to spend his money quite freely, he is usually very astute in financial matters and there are many Pigs who have become wealthy.

Another characteristic of the Pig is his ability to recover from setbacks reasonably quickly. His faith and his strength of character keep him going. If he thinks that there is a job he can do or he has something that he wants to achieve, he will pursue it with a dogged determination. He can also be stubborn and, no matter how many may plead with him, once he has made his mind up he will rarely change his views.

Although the Pig may work hard, he also knows how to enjoy himself. He is a great pleasure-seeker and will quite happily spend his hard-earned money on a lavish holiday or an expensive meal – for the Pig is a connoisseur of good food and wine – or taking part in a variety of recreational activities. He also enjoys small social gatherings and, if he is in company he likes, can very easily become the life and soul of the party. He does, however, tend to become rather withdrawn at larger functions or among strangers.

The Pig is also a creature of comfort and his home will usually be fitted with all the latest in luxury appliances. Where possible, he will prefer to live in the country rather than the town and will opt to have a big garden, for the Pig is usually a keen and successful gardener.

The Pig is very popular with the opposite sex and will often have numerous romances before he settles down. Once settled, however, he will be loyal to his partner and he will find that he is especially well suited to those born under the signs of the Goat, Rabbit, Dog and Tiger, and also to another Pig. Due to his affable and easy-going nature he can also establish a satisfactory relationship with all the remaining signs of the Chinese zodiac, with the exception of the Snake. The Snake tends to be wily, secretive and very guarded, and this can be intensely irritating to the honest and open-hearted Pig.

The female Pig will devote all her energies to the needs of her children and her partner. She will try to ensure that they want for nothing and their pleasure is very much her pleasure. Her home will either be very clean and orderly or hopelessly untidy. Strangely, there seems to be no in between with Pigs – they either love housework or detest it! The female Pig does, however, have considerable talents as an organizer and this, combined with her friendly and open manner, enables her to secure many of her objectives.

She can also be a caring and conscientious parent and has very good taste in clothes.

The Pig is usually lucky in life and will rarely want for anything. Provided he does not let others take advantage of his good nature and is not afraid of asserting himself, he will go through life making friends, helping others and winning the admiration of many.

THE FIVE DIFFERENT TYPES OF PIG

In addition to the 12 signs of the Chinese zodiac, there are five elements and these have a strengthening or moderating influence on the sign. The effects of the five elements on the Pig are described below, together with the years in which the elements were exercising their influence. Therefore all Pigs born in 1911 and 1971 are Metal Pigs, those born in 1923 and 1983 are Water Pigs, and so on.

Metal Pig: 1911, 1971
The Metal Pig is more ambitious and determined than some of the other types of Pig. He is strong, energetic and likes to be involved in a wide variety of different activities. He is very open and forthright in his views, although he can be a little too trusting at times and has a tendency to accept things at face value. He has a good sense of humour and loves to attend parties and other social gatherings. He has a warm, outgoing nature and usually has a large circle of friends.

Water Pig: 1923, 1983

The Water Pig has a heart of gold. He is generous and loyal and tries to remain on good terms with everyone. He will do his utmost to help others, but sadly there are some who will take advantage of his kind nature and he should, in his own interests, be a little more discriminating and be prepared to stand firm against anything that he does not like. Although he prefers the quieter things in life, he has a wide range of interests. He particularly enjoys outdoor pursuits and attending parties and social occasions. He is a hard and conscientious worker and invariably does well in his chosen profession. He is also gifted in the art of communication.

Wood Pig: 1935, 1995

This Pig has a friendly, persuasive manner and is easily able to gain the confidence of others. He likes to be involved in all that is going on around him and can some-times take on more responsibility than he can properly handle. He is loyal to his family and friends and he also derives much pleasure from helping those less fortunate than himself. The Wood Pig is usually an optimist and leads a very full, enjoyable and satisfying life. He also has a good sense of humour.

Fire Pig: 1947

The Fire Pig is both energetic and adventurous and he sets about everything he does in a confident and resolute manner. He is very forthright in his views and does not mind taking risks in order to achieve his objectives. He can, however, get carried away by the excitement of the moment and ought to exercise more caution in some of the enterprises with which he gets involved. The Fire Pig is usually lucky in money matters and is well known for his generosity. He is also very caring towards the members of his family.

Earth Pig: 1959

This Pig has a kindly nature. He is sensible and realistic and will go to great lengths to please his employers and secure his aims and ambitions. He is an excellent organizer and is particularly astute in business and financial matters. He has a good sense of humour and a wide circle of friends. He also likes to lead an active social life, although he does sometimes have a tendency to eat and drink more than is good for him.

PROSPECTS FOR THE PIG IN 2001

The Chinese New Year starts on 24 January 2001. Until then, the old year, the Year of the Dragon, is still making its presence felt.

The Year of the Dragon (5 February 2000 to 23 January 2001) will have been a reasonable one for the Pig and while not everything may have gone as smoothly as he would have liked, there will still be much that will have brought him pleasure.

The closing stages of the Dragon year will be fairly active and in the remaining months the Pig should sort out his priorities, commitments and social engagements. If not, he could find his life becoming such a whirl of activity that the free time he so values has all but disappeared. To make the most of the last quarter of the year, the Pig needs to inject some order and planning into his life.

The Pig's domestic and social life will be especially busy, with a great deal to fit in and arrange. Again, advance planning will be of considerable help and should the Pig find himself with a lot to do in addition to all the usual household chores, he should ask for assistance rather than attempting too much single-handed. He should also resist the temptation of starting new tasks before others are finished and if he has matters which he has put to one side, such as unanswered correspondence, he could find that several concerted efforts will help deal with this and bring him reasonably up to date.

Busy though his personal life might be, the Pig can look forward to some splendid occasions with both family and friends as the year ends and will be much in demand. There will be parties, celebrations and other events to attend and, true to form, the Pig will greatly enjoy himself. He will also do much to help a close friend at this time or sort out a difference that has arisen and here his efforts will be much appreciated.

As far as the Pig's work is concerned, he may face some challenging moments during the latter part of the year and at such times he should try not to undermine his position by some hasty action or remarks. His work prospects are about to show a marked improvement and in what remains of 2000 he should tread carefully and do what he can to build on his experience and gain new skills. Those Pigs seeking work should take full advantage of any training or openings they are offered. What the Pig learns at this time can often bear fruit later.

Generally, if the Pig organizes his time and activities well, he will find the closing months of the Dragon year a rewarding, though active time.

The Year of the Snake starts on 24 January and it will be a mixed one for the Pig. He can look forward to some success, but there will also be areas of his life which could cause problems. By remaining aware of this, there is much the Pig can do to prevent difficulties from arising. However, this *is* a year for care.

One of the more favourably aspected areas of the Pig's life will concern his work and quite early in the Snake year he can look forward to some pleasing developments. He may be given more rewarding and interesting duties, successfully follow up promotion opportunities or transfer to another position. Work-wise, this is a year of advance, and by drawing on his skills and experience the Pig will both impress others and make good headway. He also possesses a keen and enterprising mind and if he has any ideas he wants to try out, he should do so. Many Pigs will find that what they propose over the year will produce a pleasing response and their plans could develop well. Similarly, if the Pig has a personal interest or skill he feels could be put to profitable use, he should try this out. His entrepreneurial skills and money-making abilities will be in fine form in the Snake year.

Those Pigs who are seeking work or who decide to switch to a different type of position will also enjoy some pleasing developments, some of which may arise in a surprising way. By making the most of the opportunities that occur, the Pig could find he is setting in motion a train of events that can have a positive bearing on his future. The first quarter of the year is particularly favourable for work matters, but interesting opportunities could occur at almost any time of the year, such are the positive aspects in this area.

The progress that the Pig makes will also result in an improvement in his finances and this will be something he will appreciate. As usual, the Pig will remain his astute self when dealing with money matters and if he is able, he would do well to make some carefully considered savings for the future. In time these could become a very useful asset.

With his fondness for the finer things in life, the Pig will also spend a fair amount on enjoying himself over the year as well as acquiring items for himself and his home. While many of these items will bring considerable pleasure, he should still take time to select them carefully rather than succumb to too much impulse buying. Without some control, he could find there will be occasions when his money could have been put to better use.

The Pig could also enjoy several strokes of luck during 2001 and if he sees any competition that interests him, he would do well to enter. He could find himself among the winners!

The more awkward aspects of the year concern the Pig's personal life and it is here that he must exercise care. Possible troubles could lurk in both his domestic and social life, and his masterful way of handling personal relations could be severely tested.

In his home life the Pig must remain keenly aware of the views and feelings of others. Fortunately his own perceptive nature will be of help here, but this is not a year in which he should consider proceeding with plans without adequate consultation. If differences do arise, the Pig should aim to resolve them as quickly and amicably as he can rather than letting them linger in the background or even escalate. At such times he could find it helpful to encourage a spirit of openness and seek discussion in order to resolve any difficult matter. Many Pigs will be able to deal quickly with any problems, or even prevent them from arising, but they do need to remain mindful that this can be a challenging year for personal matters.

Tricky though the year may sometimes be, there is still much in the Pig's home life that will bring him pleasure. This includes any interests and projects he can share as well as joint activities such as having friends round or going on a local outing or for a meal somewhere. By making a positive contribution to family life, the Pig will indeed play a valuable and appreciated role.

The challenging aspects, however, also extend to his social life and here too the Pig will need to remain careful. This includes not getting involved in any situations that could leave him open to censure or rebound on him in some way. He should also be wary of rumours or believing all he hears from dubious sources. If in doubt, he should check. Also, new friendships, especially of a romantic nature, need to be handled with care and the Pig must remain mindful of the views and feelings of any new friends he makes if the friendship is to endure.

More positively aspected are the Pig's own personal interests and he should make sure he devotes time to these, particularly as they can help him to unwind and provide a break from his usual preoccupations. In addition, the Pig should not ignore his own well-being and should make sure he gets sufficient exercise as well as eats a healthy and balanced diet. If not, he could find himself sometimes lacking his usual sparkle and energy. Pigs, do take note.

In many respects the Snake year will be an unusual one for the Pig. While his career and financial prospects are positive, his personal life will require a fair amount of care. The Pig's masterly way of handling personal matters will undoubtedly help, however, and provided he pays attention to the views and feelings of those around him, he can do much to prevent difficulties arising. This is a year for care, but it can also be one of considerable progress.

As far as the different types of Pig are concerned, this will be an important year for the *Metal Pig*. He will resolve to mark his thirtieth year by making something of it and his determination will indeed be rewarded in certain spheres of his life. In particular, the Metal Pig can look forward to some far-reaching developments in his career and for quite a few this year will represent a cross-roads in their working life. Although he may have made good progress of late, the ambitious Metal Pig will still be seeking greater fulfilment in what he does. As a result, many Metal Pigs will take decisive steps to move on, either by seeking promotion, swapping to another company or even switching careers. However, before taking any major action, the Metal Pig must give serious thought to the consequences of what he is considering as well as fully consult those around him. Although he may be ambitious, he must not be rash. Also, he must accept that not all his attempts to move on will work out as he envisaged and that though one door may remain surprisingly shut, another *will* open. In the Snake year it is important that the Metal Pig makes the most of what happens. Those Metal Pigs seeking work should continue to pursue the openings that the year brings but also aim to widen the scope of what they are looking for. This will not only increase the possibilities open to them but many will also find that by taking up a position with different duties they will discover new strengths which can, over time, develop in a really positive way. The Snake year will be a good one for financial matters, with many Metal Pigs enjoying an increase in their income. Indeed, their money-making skills will be in fine form and many could find that an enterprising idea they have or some freelance work they are able to carry out could lead to an additional source of revenue. Any Metal Pigs who may start the year with financial concerns would find it helpful to consider whether any of their skills could perhaps be put to profitable use. Again, the Snake year could be responsible for opening some very interesting doors. As with all Pigs, though, the Metal Pig's personal life is more awkwardly aspected and here he will need to exercise care. In particular, he should remain mindful of the views and interests of those around him and take care to consult others over any ideas he has or decisions he has to make. Indeed, it is failure to consult or bear in mind the views of others that could give rise to some tensions over the year and the Metal Pig must watch this. Also, with so much happening in his professional life, there is a chance that he could become preoccupied with his own activities at the expense of others. Again, if he senses this is happening or others point it out to him, the Metal Pig really should take steps to correct it before it starts to cause problems and resentment. Throughout 2001 he must make a special effort to balance his activities and make sure he gives adequate attention to those around him. If he can do this, then not only will he do much to prevent problems from arising but he can also help make this a meaningful year, with some rich and wonderful moments in his family and social life. In particular, the encouragement and instruction he is able to give to someone much younger will be of great value as well as bring a pleasing response. Also, if the Metal Pig can encourage more joint activities, he will find this will help maintain the rapport he so values. However, throughout the year, the Metal Pig's domestic life does call for positive input on his part. He also needs to exercise care in his social life, particularly if he finds himself in any situation in which he does not feel comfortable. This is a year in which he will need to be on his guard, avoid acting in any manner that could cause problems and remain mindful of the views and feelings of his friends. However, by remaining aware of the potential hazards of the Snake year, the Metal Pig can do a great deal to prevent difficulties from arising. In many ways, this will prove a significant year for him, with some interesting developments in his work which will, in time, lead him on to greater success. Provided he exercises care in his personal life, this too can provide him with many happy and meaningful occasions.

This will be an important year for the *Water Pig* with significant developments in many areas of his life. Both his personal and professional life will see much activity and, while care will be needed, he will be generally content with how events work out. As far as his personal life is concerned, this will be a busy year. Being so sociable, the Water Pig will find himself going out a lot, both meeting his many friends and making some new ones. He will generally enjoy the parties and social events he attends. However, while he may wish to be very much 'in' with his friends or group, the Water Pig should not let this lead him into situations he may feel uncomfortable with or to take any action he may later regret. Sometimes he will need to be discriminating and stand his ground rather than fall in too readily with others. Without such care, the Snake year could create some awkward problems for him. Water Pigs, take note. Those who are in a close relationship should also remain keenly aware of the views and feelings of their partner. To make assumptions or take decisions without adequate consultation could lead to differences and undermine the general rapport that has built up. Again, this is a year when it is essential that the Water Pig remains mindful of those important to him. For those Water Pigs who may be seeking new friends and perhaps romance, the year will bring many opportunities to meet others, but the Water Pig should let any new and potentially meaningful friendships develop naturally rather than be too hasty in entering into a major commitment. This way the relationship is more likely to be founded on a secure basis. For personal relationships, this will be an important year and one that can bring happiness, but equally, without care, it can also produce heartache. The Water Pig's family will be of great value to him over the year and he should not hesitate to raise any concerns he might have with them. As he will find, family members will be only too pleased to help, but the Water Pig does need to be forthcoming and ask. In particular, the advice of a more senior relation will prove especially timely. The Water Pig's personal interests could also prove important and he will enjoy the time he is able to devote to these, especially any that allow him to produce a finished product. For those Water Pigs who are creatively inclined, their work will not only bring satisfaction but could also earn considerable commendation from others. For some, this could even lead to the possibility of turning their hobby into a vocation. If tempted, these Water Pigs should contact those in a position to give expert guidance. By so doing, they could find themselves starting out on what will be an interesting and fulfilling personal challenge. There will also be travel opportunities for many Water Pigs and again these can lead to some interesting and memorable experiences. However, to make the most of any travelling that he does undertake, the Water Pig should make sure he reads up about his chosen destination beforehand and goes sensibly prepared. This will make his actual travelling easier and give added meaning to some of the places he visits. This will also be an important year for academic and work matters. Some Water Pigs will take exams which will have a considerable bearing on their future. Rather than leaving revision and project work to the last moment, these Water Pigs should aim to work consistently over the year. By being well prepared, they will obtain some pleasing results. For those Water Pigs in work or seeking work, the year will also contain important developments and by making the most of any opportunities they are offered as well as giving of their best, they will impress others and mark themselves out for future progress. This may only be the beginning of the Water Pig's working life, but the experience he can gain – which could be quite considerable – will serve him well in the future. As far as financial matters are concerned, the Water Pig will need to exercise care and although it may sometimes prove difficult, avoid stretching his resources too far. He should remember that money borrowed will have to be repaid, sometimes with high interest charges. As he will demonstrate in future years, he has considerable earning ability, but now is not the time to be too lavish in his spending or take undue risks. Although 2001 will contain its tricky moments, provided the Water Pig remains aware of these and takes care in his relations with others, he can do much to avoid some of the difficulties that might otherwise occur. In addition, the work experience he obtains, together with any qualifications he can gain, will do much to advance his longer term prospects. Given the Water Pig's abilities and rich personality, the future certainly hold much promise.

This will be a varied year for the *Wood Pig* and while it will contain its satisfying elements, there will be some potentially troublesome aspects. Fortunately, by being forewarned there is much that the Wood Pig can do to minimize or prevent some of the problems that the year might otherwise bring. One of the more pleasurable areas of the year will be how the Wood Pig spends his free time. His interests will continue to bring him much satisfaction and he should not only devote time to these but also develop them further, perhaps by setting himself an interesting project or challenge. In addition, if there is a skill that he has been wanting to learn or a subject that has been intriguing him, this would be an excellent time to find out more. Another well aspected area is travel and the Wood Pig should try to go away for a holiday or break at some time during the year, perhaps visiting somewhere he has long wanted to see. In addition, visits to areas in his locality could go well. Some Wood Pigs may decide to follow a certain theme over the year, visiting local museums or sites of interest that have a common link for instance, and this will often give added meaning to their trips out. Financial matters are also favourably aspected and many Wood Pigs can look forward to receiving an additional sum over the year, either as a gift, payment for work previously done, the fruition of an investment or, in some cases, even a competition win. However, while this will be welcome, the Wood Pig should reflect on how to put his money to best use rather than be in too much of a hurry to spend it. Indeed, time spent considering purchases as well as managing his money will lead to far better results than proceeding too hastily. As far as the Wood Pig's domestic life is concerned, he will take a fond and caring interest in the progress and activities of loved ones and will do much to offer support. Any interests and projects he can share can bring much pleasure. However, problems can also lurk and unless quickly dealt with could escalate and cast a shadow over the year. At the first sign of any differences of opinion the Wood Pig should try to sort the matter out in a way that is satisfactory to all concerned. Often, solutions to testing matters can be quickly found, but it will need the Wood Pig and those around him to take active steps to seek a solution rather than let any problem drift or get out of hand. A family member could also become worried over a certain matter and here the Wood Pig's understanding manner and sound judgement will be of great help. The Wood Pig is also one who values his social life and in 2001 his friends will prove important both in providing support and in sharing in the Wood Pig's various activities. He will also attend some interesting social events over the year and any Wood Pig in a society or group could find himself becoming more involved or even honoured for his contribution. In many respects, this will be a fulfilling year for the Wood Pig and provided he exercises care in his relations with others, his personal life can provide him with some rich and meaningful times. In addition his various interests will bring him much pleasure and he should aim to develop these. Generally, this is a year for the Wood Pig to enjoy but also be on his guard!

This will be a variable year for the *Fire Pig*, with some successes but also a few problems. However, by taking positive steps to deal with any difficulties as they arise, the Fire Pig can do much to lessen their effect on what can otherwise be a productive time. The most favourably aspected areas of the year concern the Fire Pig's work and personal interests and both will develop well. In work matters, quite a few Fire Pigs will have made good progress in recent years, successfully following up opportunities and putting their experience and skills to effective use. This pattern will continue in 2001 and for those keen on making greater progress, there will be some excellent opportunities, with February, March and May being especially favourable months. There will, though, also be some Fire Pigs who will feel that they have accomplished all they can in their present position and will decide to make a switch or even opt for early retirement. Whatever the Fire Pig decides, the Snake year can offer him some interesting opportunities and by considering his options and then following his ideas through, he can make this a positive and fulfilling time. Similarly, those Fire Pigs seeking work will be able to make the breakthrough they have been wanting for a long time. This could arise in a sometimes surprising manner, but by keeping faith with himself, the Fire Pig's patience will be rewarded and he will be offered something which will be an interesting challenge for him. This is also an excellent time for the Fire Pig to further his own personal skills and interests and if he has the chance to enrol on a course or undertake further study, he should take advantage of this. If there has been a subject that has been intriguing him, again this would be an excellent year in which to follow this up. Anything that the Fire Pig can do to add to his knowledge and skills will be both satisfying and often to his long-term benefit. As far as financial matters are concerned, this will be a generally positive year for the Fire Pig and by taking the time and care to manage his finances, he will be content with his position. He could, though, find it helpful to set aside certain amounts for known and forthcoming expenses rather than bear the brunt of these all at once. This particularly applies to transport and accommodation costs as well as any travelling and holidays. As with all Pigs, the difficulties of the year are most likely to arise in the Fire Pig's personal life and here he could find himself at variance with certain family members. This could occur through a difference in outlook, a misunderstanding or an error of judgement, but however it arises, the Fire Pig should take positive steps to try and sort the matter out. Discussion plus a willingness to reach an understanding will be of great help, while to do nothing or be too inflexible in attitude will only exacerbate the situation. Fire Pigs, take note and do handle relations with others carefully *and* thoughtfully. Provided the Fire Pig heeds these words, his domestic life can indeed be full and pleasant over the year. Any joint projects which help to enhance the décor and comfort of the home will be especially rewarding. The Fire Pig's social life in the Snake year will be fairly active and there will be a variety of events for him to attend. He will also enjoy keeping in regular contact with his many good friends and there will be chances to add to his social circle if he wishes to do so. Overall, 2001 will be a mixed year for the Fire Pig, bringing him greater fulfilment in his work and interests but also possible hazards in his personal life. However, if he can use his considerable skills to avert these or deal with any that do arise, then he will be generally content with how the year works out for him.

This is a year which holds considerable promise for the *Earth Pig* but, like all of his sign, he will need to proceed carefully and remain mindful of the views of others. In his work some particularly interesting developments are likely and as the year starts the Earth Pig would do well to reflect on his current situation and his next objectives. By giving some thought to these, he will find himself coming up with some interesting ideas and these in turn will inspire him to take action. Almost all Earth Pigs can make good headway in 2001, although how this is achieved is very much in their own hands. Some will decide to remain in their present line of work but build on their skills and experience, while others will decide to make a change and pursue a line of work that has been attracting them for some time. For these Earth Pigs, good possibilities await, but when embarking on any change, they should try to build up contacts and heed any advice given. The better informed and prepared they are, the better they will fare. As far as work matters are concerned, 2001 is very much a year for the Earth Pig to decide on his objectives and then take active steps to secure them. This also applies to those Earth Pigs who are seeking work. By remaining both active and persistent, they will often be successful in gaining a position which offers considerable potential for the future. While the whole Snake year will remain positive for work matters, the first quarter of the year and September and October could see particularly interesting developments. This is also a favourable year for financial matters, with almost all Earth Pigs enjoying an increase in income or receiving an additional sum of money during the year. While, thanks to his usual astute nature, the Earth Pig will put this to good use, he should consider adding to his longer term savings. In time, what he is able to put aside will build into a useful asset. The Earth Pig will also obtain considerable satisfaction from his personal interests over the year and should make sure he sets time aside for these as well as considers extending them in some way, perhaps by learning about a different aspect or starting a new project. In addition, travel and outdoor activities are well favoured and all Earth Pigs should try to have a holiday over the year. They will feel much better for any break they are able to take. Also, if the Earth Pig does not get much exercise during the day or relies a lot on convenience food, he could find it in his interests to take some additional exercise as well as follow a more balanced diet. He will feel a lot better for any extra attention he is able to pay to his well-being. The Earth Pig's domestic life will be busy over the year and while he will attend to all he has to do as best he can, there will be occasions when his patience runs thin or he finds himself becoming tetchy, either through pressure or general tiredness. If the Earth Pig feels he might be becoming short-tempered, he should not hesitate to ask for assistance rather than soldier on single-handed. At busy times he should prioritize what needs to be done and, if need be, temporarily postpone certain projects. In addition to asking for assistance, if he has any matters concerning or preoccupying him, he should seek the advice of those around him. They can be of great help, but the Earth Pig does need to ask. Despite its busy nature, his domestic life will still contain many happy and meaningful times and the Earth Pig will also be truly heartened by the success of a loved one. His social life, too, will bring some enjoyable occasions, especially over the summer months, although the Earth Pig does need to be wary of jumping to conclusions about the attitudes of friends. This is very much a year for treading carefully as far as personal relations are concerned. However, if the Earth Pig heeds this advice, then this can generally be a satisfying year for him, with what he achieves often having a significant bearing on his future success and prosperity.

FAMOUS PIGS

Russ Abbot, Bryan Adams, Woody Allen, Julie Andrews, Fred Astaire, Sir Richard Attenborough, Lucille Ball, Hector Berlioz, David Blunkett, Humphrey Bogart, James Cagney, Maria Callas, Dr George Carey, Richard Chamberlain, Hillary Rodham Clinton, Glenn Close, David Coultard, Sir Noël Coward, Oliver Cromwell, Billy Crystal, the Dalai Lama, Ted Danson, Richard Dreyfuss, Sheena Easton, Ben Elton, Ralph Waldo Emerson, David Essex, Henry Ford, Emmylou Harris, William Randolph Hearst, Ernest Hemingway, Henry VIII, Alfred Hitchcock, Elton John, Tommy Lee Jones, C. G. Jung, Boris Karloff, Charles Kennedy, Stephen King, Nastassja Kinski, Kevin Kline, David Letterman, Jerry Lee Lewis, Marcel Marceau, Marie Antoinette, Ricky Martin, Johnny Mathis, Meat Loaf, Dudley Moore, Patrick Moore, Wolfgang Amadeus Mozart, Camilla Parker Bowles, Michael Parkinson, Luciano Pavarotti, Iggy Pop, Prince Rainier of Monaco, Maurice Ravel, Ronald Reagan, Lee Remick, Ginger Rogers, Salman Rushdie, Baroness Sue Ryder of Warsaw, François Sagan, Pete Sampras, Arantxa Sanchez, Carlos Santana, Arnold Schwarzenegger, Steven Spielberg, Emma Thompson, Tracey Ullman, Suzanne Vega, Jules Verne, Jacques Villeneuve, Ann Widdecombe, Michael Winner, the Duchess of York.

APPENDIX

The relationship between the 12 animal signs – both on a personal level and business level – is an important aspect of Chinese horoscopes and in this appendix the compatibility between the signs is shown in the two tables that follow.

PERSONAL RELATIONSHIPS

KEY

1 Excellent. Great rapport.
2 A successful relationship. Many interests in common.
3 Mutual respect and understanding. A good relationship.
4 Fair. Needs care and some willingness to compromise in order for the relationship to work.
5 Awkward. Possible difficulties in communication with few interests in common.
6 A clash of personalities. Very difficult.

	Rat	Ox	Tiger	Rabbit	Dragon	Snake	Horse	Goat	Monkey	Rooster	Dog	Pig
Rat	1											
Ox	1	3										
Tiger	4	6	5									
Rabbit	5	2	3	2								
Dragon	1	5	4	3	2							
Snake	3	1	6	2	1	5						
Horse	6	5	1	5	3	4	2					
Goat	5	5	3	1	4	3	2	2				
Monkey	1	3	6	3	1	3	5	3	1			
Rooster	5	1	5	6	2	1	2	5	5	5		
Dog	3	4	1	2	6	3	1	5	3	5	2	
Pig	2	3	2	2	2	6	3	2	2	3	1	2

BUSINESS RELATIONSHIPS

KEY

1 Excellent. Marvellous understanding and rapport.
2 Very good. Complement each other well.
3 A good working relationship and understanding can be developed.
4 Fair, but compromise and a common objective are often needed to make this relationship work.
5 Awkward. Unlikely to work, either through lack of trust, understanding or the competitiveness of the signs.
6 Mistrust. Difficult. To be avoided.

	Rat	Ox	Tiger	Rabbit	Dragon	Snake	Horse	Goat	Monkey	Rooster	Dog	Pig
Rat	2											
Ox	1	3										
Tiger	3	6	5									
Rabbit	4	3	3	3								
Dragon	1	4	3	3	3							
Snake	3	2	6	4	1	5						
Horse	6	5	1	5	3	4	4					
Goat	5	5	3	1	4	3	3	2				
Monkey	2	3	4	5	1	5	4	4	3			
Rooster	5	1	5	5	2	1	2	5	5	6		
Dog	4	5	2	3	6	4	2	5	3	5	4	
Pig	3	3	3	2	3	5	4	2	3	4	3	1

YOUR ASCENDANT

The ascendant has a very strong influence on your personality and, together with the information already given about your sign and the effects of the element on your sign, it will help you gain even greater insight into your true personality according to Chinese horoscopes.

The hours of the day are named after the 12 animal signs and the sign governing the time you were born is your ascendant. To find your ascendant, look up the time of your birth on the table below, bearing in mind any local time differences in the place you were born.

11 p.m.	to	1 a.m.	The hours of the Rat
1 a.m.	to	3 a.m.	The hours of the Ox
3 a.m.	to	5 a.m.	The hours of the Tiger
5 a.m.	to	7 a.m.	The hours of the Rabbit
7 a.m.	to	9 a.m.	The hours of the Dragon
9 a.m.	to	11 a.m.	The hours of the Snake
11 a.m.	to	1 p.m.	The hours of the Horse
1 p.m.	to	3 p.m.	The hours of the Goat
3 p.m.	to	5 p.m.	The hours of the Monkey
5 p.m.	to	7 p.m.	The hours of the Rooster
7 p.m.	to	9 p.m.	The hours of the Dog
9 p.m.	to	11 p.m.	The hours of the Pig

RAT: The influence of the Rat as ascendant is likely to make the sign more outgoing, more sociable and careful with money. A particularly beneficial influence for those born under the sign of the Rabbit, Horse, Monkey and Pig.

OX: The Ox as ascendant has a restraining, cautionary and steadying influence which many signs will benefit from. This ascendant also promotes self-confidence and will-power and is an especially good ascendant for those born under the signs of the Tiger, Rabbit and Goat.

TIGER: This ascendant is a dynamic and stirring influence which makes the sign more outgoing, more action-orientated and more impulsive. A generally favourable ascendant for the Ox, Tiger, Snake and Horse.

RABBIT: The Rabbit as ascendant has a moderating influence, making the sign more reflective, serene and discreet. A particularly beneficial influence for the Rat, Dragon, Monkey and Rooster.

DRAGON: The Dragon as ascendant gives strength, determination and an added ambition to the sign. A favourable influence for those born under the signs of the Rabbit, Goat, Monkey and Dog.

SNAKE: The Snake as ascendant can make the sign more reflective, more intuitive and more self-reliant. A good influence for the Tiger, Goat and Pig.

HORSE: The influence of the Horse will make the sign more adventurous, more daring and, on some occasions, more fickle. Generally a beneficial influence for the Rabbit, Snake, Dog and Pig.

GOAT: This ascendant will make the sign more tolerant, easy-going and receptive. The Goat could also impart some creative and artistic qualities to the sign. An especially good influence for the Ox, Dragon, Snake and Rooster.

MONKEY: The Monkey as ascendant is likely to impart a delicious sense of humour and fun to the sign. He will make the sign more enterprising and outgoing – a particularly good influence for the Rat, Ox, Snake and Goat.

ROOSTER: The Rooster as ascendant helps to give the sign a lively, outgoing and very methodical manner. Its influence will increase efficiency and is good for the Ox, Tiger, Rabbit and Horse.

DOG: The Dog as ascendant makes the sign more reasonable and fair-minded as well as giving an added sense of loyalty. A very good ascendant for the Tiger, Dragon and Goat.

PIG: The influence of the Pig can make the sign more sociable, content and self-indulgent. It is also a caring influence and one which can make the sign want to help others. A good ascendant for the Dragon and Monkey.

HOW TO GET THE BEST
FROM YOUR CHINESE SIGN
AND THE YEAR

To supplement the earlier chapters on the personality and horoscope of the signs, I have included in this appendix a guide on how you can get the best out of your sign and the year.

Each of the 12 Chinese signs possesses its own unique strengths and by identifying them you can use them to your advantage. Similarly, by becoming aware of possible weaknesses you can do much to rectify them and in this respect I hope the following sections will be useful. Also included are some tips on how you can get the best from the Year of the Snake. The areas covered are general prospects, career prospects, finance and relations with others.

THE RAT

The Rat is blessed with many fine talents but his undoubted strength lies in his ability to get on with others. He is sociable, charming and a good judge of character. He also possesses a shrewd mind and is good at spotting opportunities.

However, to make the most of himself and his abilities, the Rat does need to impose some discipline upon himself. He should resist the temptation (sometimes very great!) of getting involved in too many activities all at the same time and decide upon his priorities and objectives. By concentrating his energies on specific matters he will fare much better as a result. Also, given his personable manner, he should seek out positions where he can use his personal relations skills to good effect. For a career, sales and marketing could prove ideal.

The Rat is also astute in dealing with finance but, while often thrifty, he can sometimes give way to moments of indulgence. Although he deserves to enjoy the money he has so carefully earned, it may sometimes be in his interests to exercise more restraint when tempted to satisfy too many extravagant whims!

The Rat's family and friends are also most important to him and while he is loyal and protective towards them, he does tend to keep his worries and concerns to himself. He would be helped if he were more willing to discuss any anxieties he has. Those around the Rat think highly of him and are prepared to do much to help him, but for them to do this he does need to be less secretive and guarded.

With his sharp mind, keen imagination and sociable manner, the Rat does, however, have much in his favour. First, though, he should decide what he wants to achieve and then concentrate upon his chosen objectives. When he has commitment, the Rat can be irrepressible and, given his considerable charm, he can often be irresistible as well! Provided he channels his energies wisely he can make much of his life.

Advice for the Rat's Year Ahead

GENERAL PROSPECTS
This year will test the Rat's resourcefulness and abilities more than usual. He will need to proceed carefully in much of what he does and remain mindful of those around him. His best gains will come from self-development, with the skills and experience he obtains now standing him in good stead for the future.

CAREER PROSPECTS
Although the year will present its challenges, by rising to these the Rat will both impress others and obtain much useful experience. Throughout the year he should keep faith with himself. He is, after all, a survivor and what he learns and accomplishes in the Snake year will be to his long-term good.

FINANCE
Throughout the year the Rat should make a careful note of all he spends and keep control over his purse strings. To succumb to too many temptations could leave his resources depleted. This is also a year to avoid unnecessary financial risks.

RELATIONS WITH OTHERS
The Rat's home life will often be busy and demanding. Throughout the year he should organize his activities well and not hesitate to draw on the assistance of others. If any differences of opinion arise, he should use his superb skills in handling personal relations to defuse them. This is a year for tact, discretion and remaining mindful of others.

THE OX

Strong-willed, determined and resolute, the Ox certainly has a mind of his own! He is also persistent and sets about achieving his objectives with dogged determination. In addition, he is reliable and tenacious and is often a source of inspiration to others. The Ox is a doer and an achiever and in life he often accomplishes a great deal. However, for him to really excel, he would do well to try and correct his weaknesses.

Being so resolute and having such a strong sense of purpose, the Ox can be inflexible and narrow-minded. He can be resistant to change and prefers to set about his activities in his own way rather than be too dependent on others. He should aim to be more outgoing and adventurous in his outlook. His dislike of change can sometimes be to his detriment and if he were prepared to be more adaptable he would find his progress would be easier.

The Ox would also be helped if he were to broaden his range of interests and become more relaxed in his approach. At times he can be so preoccupied with his own activities that he is not always as mindful of others as he should be and his demeanour can sometimes be studious and serious. There are times when he would benefit from a lighter touch.

However, the Ox is true to his word and loyal to his family and friends. He is admired and respected by others and his tremendous will-power usually enables him to achieve much in life.

Advice for the Ox's Year Ahead

GENERAL PROSPECTS

The Ox thrives in Snake years and in 2001 he will feel more inspired and motivated than for some considerable time. By deciding upon and working towards specific objectives he will obtain some very pleasing results.

CAREER PROSPECTS

A year of considerable opportunity. By making a special effort to improve on his present situation and pursuing the openings the year will bring, the Ox will make good headway as well as use his skills more effectively. What many Oxen achieve in 2001 will set them firmly on course for further success in later years.

FINANCE

A good year for financial matters and also to add to long-term savings.

RELATIONS WITH OTHERS

Family and friends will bring the Ox much pleasure and useful support over the year. He should, though, take time to consult them over new ideas, as much can be gained from their suggestions. Also, while so much will go well personally, the Ox should not jeopardize this by losing his temper too readily – or often! A fine year to make new friendships and excellent for romance.

THE TIGER

Lively, innovative and enterprising, the Tiger is one who enjoys an active lifestyle. He has a wide range of interests, an alert mind and a genuine liking of others. He likes to live life to the full. However, despite his enthusiastic and well-meaning ways, he does not always make the most of his considerable potential.

By being so versatile, the Tiger does have a tendency to jump from one activity to another or dissipate his energies by trying to do too much at any one time. To make the most of himself he should try to exercise a certain amount of self-discipline. Ideally, he should decide how best he can use his abilities, give himself some objectives and stick with these. If he can overcome his restless tendencies and persist in what he does, he will find he will accomplish much more.

Also, in spite of his sociable manner, the Tiger likes to retain a certain independence in his actions and while few begrudge him this, he would sometimes find life easier if he were more prepared to work in conjunction with others. His reliance upon his own judgement does sometimes mean that he excludes the views and advice of those around him, and this can be to his detriment. The Tiger may possess an independent spirit, but he must not let his independence go too far!

The Tiger does, however, have much in his favour. He is bold, original and quick-witted. If he can keep his restless nature in check he can enjoy considerable success. In addition, his engaging personality makes him one who is much admired and well liked.

Advice for the Tiger's Year Ahead

GENERAL PROSPECTS

Although some of its events may try the Tiger's patience, the Snake year can still be of considerable value. It will enable the Tiger to consolidate recent gains, acquire new skills and prepare himself for his longer term progress. Travel and personal interests will also bring him much pleasure.

CAREER PROSPECTS

By concentrating on areas he knows best and building on his expertise, the Tiger will greatly impress and find himself well placed when opportunities arise. He should also give thought to how he would like his career to develop and how he can bring this about. Ideas and plans formulated in the Snake year can be of great and lasting significance.

FINANCE

With many expenses to meet, there will be considerable demand on the Tiger's resources. This is a year which calls for careful financial management and the avoidance of risks.

RELATIONS WITH OTHERS

A busy year, with much happening domestically and socially. Relations with others can, for the most part, go well, but the Tiger does need to remain mindful of the views of others, take time to consult them and be more accommodating if differences of opinion do arise. Also, he should take care in potentially awkward or embarrassing situations, otherwise difficulties could result.

THE RABBIT

The Rabbit is certainly one who appreciates the finer things in life. With his good taste, companionable nature and wide range of interests, he knows how to live well – and usually does!

However, for all his finesse and style, the Rabbit does possess traits he would do well to watch. His desire for a settled lifestyle makes him err on the side of caution. He dislikes change and as a consequence can miss out on opportunities. Also, there are many Rabbits who will go to great lengths to avoid difficult and fraught situations, and again, while few may relish these, sometimes in life it is necessary to take risks or stand your ground just to get on. At times it would certainly be in the Rabbit's interests to be bolder and more assertive in going after whatever he desires.

The Rabbit also attaches great importance to his relations with others and while he has a happy knack of getting on with most, he can be sensitive to criticism. Difficult though it may be, he should really try to develop a thicker skin and recognize that criticism can provide valuable learning opportunities, as can some of the problems he strives so hard to avoid.

However, with his agreeable manner, keen intellect and shrewd judgement, the Rabbit does have much in his favour and invariably makes much of his life – and usually enjoys it too!

APPENDIX
Advice for the Rabbit's Year Ahead

GENERAL PROSPECTS
A positive year which will allow the Rabbit to advance his ideas and plans and make good progress as a result. Much satisfaction will come from developing skills and interests, with travel, too, being enjoyable.

CAREER PROSPECTS
Many Rabbits will look to this year as a time for making progress and will set about their activities with greater resolve. This persistence, together with the Rabbit's skills and personable nature, will lead to impressive results. A year of considerable opportunity and progress.

FINANCE
While an increase in income will be welcome, the year could prove expensive, with acquisitions for the home, repair bills and possibly moving costs. The Rabbit needs to remain his careful self and manage his resources well.

RELATIONS WITH OTHERS
A pleasant year with much useful support from others, although the Rabbit should be wary of gossip and scandal-mongering. For those seeking new friends or a more active social life, going out more and getting in contact with others will bring some happiness and sparkle back into life. Generally, this will be a year the Rabbit will enjoy.

THE DRAGON

Enthusiastic, enterprising and honourable, the Dragon possesses many admirable qualities and his life is often full and varied. He always gives of his best and even though not all his endeavours may meet with success, he is none the less resilient and hardy, and is much admired and respected.

However, for all his many qualities, the Dragon can be blunt and forthright and, through sheer strength of character, sometimes domineering. It would certainly be in his interests to listen more closely to others rather than be so self-reliant. Also, his enthusiasm can sometimes get the better of him and he can be impulsive. To make the most of his abilities, he should set himself priorities and set about his activities in a disciplined and systematic way. More tact and diplomacy might not come amiss either!

However, with his lively and outgoing manner, the Dragon is popular and well liked. With good fortune on his side (and the Dragon is often lucky), his life is almost certain to be eventful and fulfilling. He has many talents and if he uses them wisely he will enjoy much success.

Advice for the Dragon's Year Ahead

GENERAL PROSPECTS

By deciding upon his objectives and making good use of his time, the Dragon can look forward to satisfying results in most areas of his life. A constructive and enjoyable year.

CAREER PROSPECTS

By giving some thought to the way he wishes to progress and actively following up suitable opportunities, the Dragon can make excellent progress. The year will allow him to develop his skills and show his potential, and as a result he will greatly impress. His progress may be of considerable long-term value.

FINANCE

Although the Dragon will enjoy an improvement in income, this can prove a costly year with family and accommodation expenses to meet. The Dragon does need to keep a close watch over his finances.

RELATIONS WITH OTHERS

The Dragon will have much to occupy his time over the year but must make sure his commitments do not encroach too heavily on his family or social life. If not, his rapport with those close to him could suffer. In 2001 it is important he balances his activities and devotes time and attention to others. By doing so, his personal life can provide him with many happy and rewarding occasions.

THE SNAKE

The Snake is blessed with a keen intellect. He has wide interests, an enquiring mind and good judgement. He tends to be quiet and thoughtful and plans his activities with considerable care. With his fine abilities he often does well in life, but he does possess traits which can undermine his progress.

The Snake is often guarded in his actions and sometimes loses out to those who are more action-oriented and assertive. He can also be a loner and likes to retain a certain independence in his actions, and this too can hamper his progress. It would be in his interests to be more forthcoming and involve others more readily in his plans. The Snake has many talents and possesses a warm and rich personality, but there is a danger that this can remain concealed behind his often quiet and reserved manner. He would fare better by being more outgoing and showing others his true worth.

However, the Snake is very much his own master. He invariably knows what he wants in life and is often prepared to journey long and hard to achieve his objectives. He does, though, have it in his power to make that journey easier. Lose some of that reticence, Snake, be more open and assertive, and do not be afraid of the occasional risk!

Advice for the Snake's Year Ahead

GENERAL PROSPECTS
Superb. A year to go after goals, ideas and dreams.

CAREER PROSPECTS
A time of great progress. By making the most of his unique and special talents and pursuing opportunities, the Snake can make excellent headway. He should not allow himself to be fettered by past mistakes or failings, but give of his best and show everyone his true and incredible potential. This is a year for being positive, with enterprise and initiative being well rewarded.

FINANCE

A good year for financial matters. However, the Snake should aim to add to his longer term savings as well as set some money aside for a holiday and some personal treats over the year. He will deserve them!

RELATIONS WITH OTHERS

The Snake's domestic life will bring much happiness and he will benefit from the support of loved ones throughout the year. The prospects are also excellent for new friendships and romance. For the more reserved Snakes or those who may be lonely, this is a year to loosen up and go out more. By taking action these Snakes can put the sparkle back into their lives.

THE HORSE

Versatile, hard-working and sociable, the Horse makes his mark wherever he goes. He has an eloquent and engaging manner and makes friends with ease. He is quick-witted, has an alert mind and is certainly not averse to taking risks or experimenting with new ideas.

The Horse possesses a strong and likeable personality but he does also have his weaknesses. With his wide interests he does not always finish everything he starts and he would do well to be more persevering. He has it within him to achieve considerable success but when he has made his plans he should stick with them. To make the most of his talents he does need to overcome his restless tendencies.

The Horse loves company and values both his family and friends. However, there will have been many a time when he has lost his temper or spoken in haste and regretted his words. Throughout his life, the Horse needs to keep his temper in check and learn to be diplomatic in tense situations. If not, he could risk jeopardizing the respect and good relations so he values by a thoughtless remark or action.

However, the Horse has a multitude of talents and a lively and outgoing personality. If he can overcome his restless and volatile nature, he can lead a rich and highly fulfilling life.

Advice for the Horse's Year Ahead

GENERAL PROSPECTS

A challenging year. Throughout, the Horse should take careful note of all that is going on around him as well as be aware of the views of others. This is not a year in which he can be too independent in approach or attitude. However, what he does accomplish or sets in motion over the year can often bear fruit in the Horse's own year that follows.

CAREER PROSPECTS

Again, care is needed. In 2001 the Horse should adapt as well as he can to the situations in which he finds himself and take full advantage of any training opportunities that arise. Actual progress may be limited, but what he learns now will often be an important stepping-stone to future success.

FINANCE
With many temptations to spend, plus sometimes large family or accommodation expenses, the year calls for careful financial management and restraint. Not a time for taking risks.

RELATIONS WITH OTHERS
Throughout the year the Horse must remain mindful of the views of others and take the time to discuss his ideas and plans. He should also ensure that he plays a full part in family life rather than becoming too preoccupied with his own concerns. At all times he should avoid becoming involved in situations he may later come to regret. This is a year for care and forethought!

THE GOAT

The Goat has a warm, friendly and understanding manner and gets on well with most. He is generally easy-going, has a fond appreciation of the finer things in life and possesses a rich imagination. He is often artistic and enjoys the creative arts and outdoor activities.

However, despite his engaging manner, there lurks beneath his skin a sometimes tense and pessimistic nature. The Goat can be a worrier and without the support and encouragement of others can feel insecure and be hesitant in his actions.

To make the most of himself the Goat should aim to become more assertive and decisive as well as more at ease with himself. He has much in his favour, but he really does need to promote himself more and aim to be bolder in his actions. He would also be helped if he were to sort out his priorities and set about his activities in an organized and disciplined manner. There are some Goats who tend to be haphazard in the way they go about things and this can hamper their progress.

Although the Goat will always value the support of others, it would also be in his interests to become more independent in his actions and not be so reticent about striking out on his own. He does, after all, possess many talents, as well as a sincere and likeable personality, and by always giving of his best, he can make his life rich, rewarding and enjoyable.

Advice for the Goat's Year Ahead

GENERAL PROSPECTS

A significant upturn in the Goat's fortunes is indicated. To make the most of this he should decide on his objectives for the year and then actively pursue them. Initiative and enterprise will be well rewarded. Some of the shyer Goats should try to lose some of their reticence and become more assertive. The extra effort the Goat puts into the year really can produce fine results.

CAREER PROSPECTS

A year of great prospects, new chances and often fresh starts. This is a time for moving forward, for realizing potential and finding greater fulfilment. Throughout 2001 the Goat should make the most of his ideas and the opportunities that arise.

FINANCE

A positive year but, as always, there will be many temptations for the Goat to part with his money. More control over his purse strings would not go amiss. Also, he should aim to add to his savings.

RELATIONS WITH OTHERS

Many happy occasions are indicated with both family and friends. Some pleasing personal news as well as the successes of loved ones will add sparkle to the year. Socially, too, this will be an active year with excellent prospects of making new friends and starting a significant romance.

THE MONKEY

Lively, enterprising and innovative, the Monkey certainly knows how to impress. He has wide interests, a good sense of fun and relates well to others. He also possesses a shrewd mind and often has a happy knack of turning events to his advantage.

However, despite his versatility and considerable gifts, the Monkey does have his weaknesses. He often lacks persistence, can get distracted easily and also places tremendous reliance upon his own judgement. While his belief in himself is a commendable asset, it would certainly be in his interests to be more mindful of the views of others. Also, while he likes to keep tabs on all that is going on around him, he can be evasive and secretive with regard to his own feelings and activities, and again a more forthcoming attitude would be to his advantage.

The Monkey also possesses a most enterprising nature, although in his desire to succeed he can sometimes be tempted to cut corners or be crafty. He should recognize that such actions can rebound on him!

However, the Monkey is resourceful and his sheer strength of character will lead him to an interesting and varied life. If he can channel his considerable energies wisely and overcome his sometimes restless tendencies, his life can be crowned with success and achievement. Added to which, with his amiable personality, he will enjoy the friendship of many.

Advice for the Monkey's Year Ahead

GENERAL PROSPECTS
Resourceful and adaptable, the Monkey will enjoy making the most of the opportunities the year will bring as well as furthering his knowledge and skills. A fine year for personal development.

CAREER PROSPECTS
Many interesting opportunities will arise, allowing the Monkey to make good headway. Throughout the year he should make the most of the situations that prevail and his ability to adapt will serve him well. If he is able to add to his skills by training or retraining he could find this will considerably enhance his prospects as well as widen the scope of opportunities available to him.

FINANCE

A generally positive year. However, to avoid problems, the Monkey should manage his finances well, making sure he leaves himself sufficient to cover his commitments and forthcoming obligations. With care, this can be a favourable year, but it is not one for complacency or undue risks.

RELATIONS WITH OTHERS

A busy year both domestically and socially. Although the Monkey may like to keep tabs on everything and be involved in a great deal, he does need to be realistic about what he takes on. Also, it is important he pays close attention to the views of others. A good year for romance and building new friendships.

THE ROOSTER

With his considerable bearing and incisive and resolute manner, the Rooster makes an impressive figure. He has a sharp mind, keeps well informed on many matters and expresses himself clearly and convincingly. He is meticulous and efficient in his undertakings and commands much respect. He also has a genuine and caring interest in others.

The Rooster has much in his favour but there are some aspects of his character that can tell against him. He can be candid in his views and sometimes over-zealous in his actions, and without forethought he can say or do things he later regrets. His high standards also make him fussy – even pedantic – and he can get diverted onto relatively minor matters when, in truth, he could be occupying his time more profitably. This is something all Roosters would do well to watch. Also, while the Rooster is a great planner, he can sometimes be unrealistic in his expectations. In making plans – indeed, with most of his activities – he would do well to consult others rather than keep his thoughts to himself. By doing so, he will greatly benefit from their input.

The Rooster has considerable talents as well as commendable drive and commitment, but to make the most of himself he does need to channel his energies wisely and watch his candid and sometimes volatile nature. With care, however, he can make a success of his life, and with his wide interests and outgoing personality will enjoy the friendship and respect of many.

Advice for the Rooster's Year Ahead

GENERAL PROSPECTS
The more settled Snake year will give the Rooster greater chance to pursue his activities in his own way and as a result this will prove a satisfying and fulfilling time for him. A year when positive action and effort will be well rewarded.

CAREER PROSPECTS
In 2001 the Rooster will be able to use his skills and talents to good effect. By showing willing and taking up the opportunities that are offered he will not only make good progress but also improve his longer term prospects.

However, he must make sure that his important contribution is noted, even if this may mean blowing his own trumpet! This is not a year to undersell himself.

FINANCE
A positive year, although, as some Roosters are noted for their spendthrift tendencies, it would be in the Rooster's interests to keep watch over his purse strings.

RELATIONS WITH OTHERS
An active year both domestically and socially. In 2001 the Rooster will do much to help and advise others, with his sterling role and personable manner being greatly valued. However, he should make sure his domestic life is not all work and no play, and should encourage activities that all can enjoy. Socially, he will be in fine form and for those seeking new friends or romance, the year holds great prospects.

THE DOG

Loyal, dependable and with a good understanding of human nature, the Dog is well placed to win the respect and admiration of many. He is a no-nonsense sort of person and hates any sort of hypocrisy and falsehood. With the Dog you know where you stand and, given his direct manner, where he stands on any issue. He also has a strong humanitarian nature and often champions good and just causes.

The Dog has many fine attributes, although there are certain traits that can prevent him from either enjoying or making the most of his life. He is a great worrier and can get anxious over all manner of things. Although it may not always be easy, the Dog should try to rid himself of the 'worry habit'. Whenever he is tense or concerned, he should be prepared to speak to others rather than shoulder his worries all by himself. In some cases, they could even be of his own making! Also, the Dog has a tendency to look on the pessimistic side of things and he would certainly be helped if he were to look more optimistically on his undertakings. He does, after all, possess many skills and should justifiably have faith in his abilities. Another weakness is his tendency to be stubborn over certain issues. If he is not careful, this could at times undermine his position.

If the Dog can reduce the anxious and pessimistic side of his nature, then he will not only enjoy life more but also find he is achieving more. He possesses a truly admirable character and his loyalty, reliability and sincerity are appreciated by all he meets. In his life he will do much good and befriend many – and he owes it to himself to enjoy life too. Sometimes it might help him to recall the words of another Dog, Sir Winston Churchill: 'When I look back on all these worries I remember the story of the old man who said on his deathbed that he had had a lot of trouble in his life, most of which never happened.'

Advice for the Dog's Year Ahead

GENERAL PROSPECTS
A very positive year when the Dog should set his sights firmly on the present and future. This is a year for moving

ahead, for realizing plans and making headway. The Dog will also feel more inspired and motivated than he has been for some time and this too will help make the year all the more rewarding.

CAREER PROSPECTS

All Dogs should make every effort to improve on their position and seize the chances the year will bring. It is a year to be bold, enterprising and make the most of strengths, skills and ideas. For the determined, great progress awaits.

FINANCE

A favourable year. By managing their money and planning their purchases as well as adding to their savings, most Dogs will be pleased with their position by the year's end.

RELATIONS WITH OTHERS

A promising year with others offering valuable advice and support. The Dog will enjoy his domestic life as well as meeting up with friends. Personal interests and hobbies will also bring much pleasure and all Dogs should make sure they devote time to these.

THE PIG

Genial, sincere and trusting, the Pig gets on well with most. He has a kind and caring nature, a dislike of discord and often possesses a good sense of humour. In addition, he has a fondness for socializing and enjoying the good life!

YOUR CHINESE HOROSCOPE 2001

The Pig also possesses a shrewd mind, is particularly adept at dealing with business and financial matters, and has a robust and resilient nature. Although not all his plans in life may work out as he would like, he is tenacious and will often rise up and succeed after experiencing setbacks and difficulties. In his often active and varied life he can accomplish a great deal, although there are certain aspects of his character that can tell against him. If he can modify or keep these in check then his life will certainly be easier and possibly even more successful.

In his activities the Pig can sometimes overcommit himself and while he does not want to disappoint, he would certainly be helped if he were to set about his activities in an organized and systematic manner and give himself priorities at busy times. He should also not allow others to take advantage of his good nature and it would be in his interests if he were sometimes more discerning. There will have been times when he has been gullible and naïve; fortunately, though, the Pig quickly learns from his mistakes. He also possesses a stubborn streak and if new situations do not fit in with his line of thinking, he can be inflexible. Such an attitude may not always be to his advantage.

The Pig is a great pleasure-seeker and while he should enjoy the fruits of his labours, he can sometimes be self-indulgent and extravagant. This is again something he would do well to watch.

However, though the Pig may possess some faults, those who come into contact with him are invariably impressed by his integrity, amiable manner and intelligence. If he uses his talents wisely, his life can be crowned with considerable

334

APPENDIX

achievement and the good-hearted Pig will also be loved and respected by many.

Advice for the Pig's Year Ahead

GENERAL PROSPECTS

A year in which the Pig needs to keep on his mettle. While work and financial prospects are good, relations with others need to be handled with care. It is, though, a good year for furthering skills and interests.

CAREER PROSPECTS

There will be some interesting opportunities and excellent chances to progress. In 2001 the Pig should determine what he wants and then take action to get it. What he sets in motion can work out well and have positive consequences for the future. Work-wise, the Pig can do very well in the Year of the Snake.

FINANCE

A favourable year, with many Pigs enjoying an increase in income. Some may be able to supplement this through a hobby or skill. The Pig would do well to add to his savings over the year as well as take his time with any major purchases he is considering.

RELATIONS WITH OTHERS

In 2001 it is very important that the Pig remains mindful of the views and feelings of others as well as consults them over his plans and activities. To be too independent, obtuse or even stubborn could lead to differences of opinion and awkward moments. If the Pig bears this in mind, though, his personal life can provide him with some rich and pleasurable times.